DATE DUE

FEB - 5 1997	

BRODART   Cat. No. 23-221

This book is dedicated to
Maeve Blackman, age 4.

Planning Belfast

A case study of public policy and community action

TIM BLACKMAN

Chief Executive's Department
Newcastle upon Tyne City Council

Avebury

Aldershot · Brookfield USA · Hong Kong · Singapore · Sydney

Published by
Avebury
Academic Publishing Group
Gower House
Croft Road
Aldershot
Hants GU11 3HR
England

Gower Publishing Company
Old Post Road
Brookfield
Vermont 05036
USA

ISBN 1 85628 182 5

Printed and Bound in Great Britain by
Athenaeum Press Ltd., Newcastle upon Tyne.

Contents

Foreword   vii

1   Planning, property and politics   1

2   Planning inquiries in context   24

3   People and planning in Belfast   44

4   The Belfast Urban Area Plan 2001:
       mobilising the response   65

5   The outcome   93

6   Conclusion: new horizons for planning   116

Appendix 1
Participants at the Community Technical Aid
Conference on the Belfast Urban Area Plan   130

Appendix 2
CTA's objections to the Belfast Urban Area
Plan   134

Appendix 3
Paper for Second Meeting of CTA Advisory
Group   145

Appendix 4
Paper for Fourth Meeting of CTA Advisory
Group   163

Appendix 5
The Department of the Environment's response
to CTA's objections   187

Bibliography   222

Index   230

Foreword

I moved from Durham to Northern Ireland in 1982 and spent eight years teaching and researching in social policy at the University of Ulster. During that time I was closely involved with Community Technical Aid (CTA), an organisation established in the voluntary sector to provide architectural and planning assistance to community groups.

Much of my academic work was action research associated in one way or another with CTA. It was an exceptional learning experience and I was fortunate to have as colleagues and friends during this time people who were deeply involved in community work in Belfast. Particularly influenctial on my thinking were Rowan Davison, Derek Alcorn and Feilim O hAdhmaill.

This book is about CTA's biggest project to date, the Belfast Urban Area Plan 2001. I have used a case study of the project as a vehicle for analysing what I have come to see as key social issues in planning.

It is primarily an academic book. But I hope that community workers, urban policy makers, planners and those involved in urban politics will find it worth studying. It is not a book just about Belfast and is very much intended to be a contribution to agendas for change in any major city.

Writing the book has been a personal project. It was meant to be a collective effort with Community Technical Aid but circumstances prevented this. However, Una O'Boyle, Paddy Carroll and Irene Kennedy made invaluable contributions. In many ways this book is an acknowledgement of their outstanding commitment to community participation in planning. Mention should also be made in this respect of John Reid, the barrister who worked particularly closely with CTA during the Urban Area Plan project.

The Project would not have been possible without a substantial grant from the Department of the Environment for Northern Ireland to CTA. The research for the book was supported by the small grants scheme of the Economic and Social Research Council (R000221049) and the preparation for publication by the small grants scheme of the Nuffield Foundation. Roberta Woods gave invaluable support and assistance throughout and Dorothy McLoughlin wordprocessed the text for printing with impressive efficiency.

The responsibility for what follows is mine alone and none of the views expressed should be taken as necessarily reflecting those of CTA or any other parties connected with the project.

The book is not separated into descriptive and analytical parts. Analysis is presented throughout the text, and although it is more focused as the book progresses through accounts of planning and the Community Technical Aid project, the arguments stay deliberately wide ranging to encompass the many interconnected issues which a discussion of planning entails.

Chapter 1 introduces the book with a broad sweep through issues which reappear in subsequent chapters as more closely defined problems. The chapter's opening pages raise the question of societal choices and the pivotal role of planning in realising these choices. This leads to a discussion of the issue of property rights and the need for the public to share in these rights to realise community and environmental values in the development of cities. The first chapter concludes by introducing readers to the Belfast case study and to the dimensions of public participation and community action in planning which are especially relevant to it.

The book incorporates a sociolegal study of public inquiries in Chapter 2. This study is present partly because a focus on public inquiries brings to life many of the contradictions of the planning system. But the chapter also has the role of providing a context for the case study of the Belfast Urban Area Plan which is particularly concerned with the public inquiry into the Plan.

Chapter 3 is an account of planning in Belfast. It is written to show the similarities and differences in *social issues* between city and transport planning in the 1960s and 70s and the contemporary Belfast Urban Area Plan 2001. The focus of the chapter is a major public inquiry in 1977 into transportation plans for the city.

Chapter 4 begins in the mid 1980s and shows how community groups mobilised through the Community Technical Aid exercise to oppose the Plan, culminating with a public inquiry in 1987. The community groups made their cases after months of preparation and with the assistance of a small team of planners and barristers who were present throughout the proceedings. One of the arguments of the book is that these objections were an example of unity out of diversity, and presented the inquiry not only with an alternative view of the 'public interest' but with an alternative planning paradigm.   A year and a half later the Government made its decisions on these objections and the final Plan was adopted.

Chapter 6 concludes the book by considering the new horizons for planning opened up by a critical assessment of the Community Technical Aid project. While proposals are advanced for improving public participation in the planning process, this is qualified by the conclusion that a stronger voice for the public would in fact intensify the type of problems encountered by community groups at the Belfast inquiry.

Tim Blackman
Newcastle upon Tyne
January 1991

1 Planning, property and politics

Different views of what needs to be done

This book is about planning Belfast. But it is also a book about the ambiguities and contradictions of the British town and country planning system. In exploring these issues, it seeks to address some fundamental questions about democracy, participation and the public sphere. The concept of property is found to be at the heart of these questions. The present chapter begins the book with a discussion of these wider themes, while introducing the Belfast case study and sketching the political backcloth to it.

The city is a shared environment, its resources demanding shared management if they are to meet common needs. However, a city's human and physical resources are a basis for creating wealth as well as meeting needs. Part of this wealth becomes embodied in buildings and infrastructure to produce the urban space in which cities are experienced (Harvey, 1981; 1989). A constant and fundamental conflict exists between the exploitation of this space for further wealth creation and its use as personalised and collectivised environments (Gottdiener, 1986).

When people are invited to participate in urban planning, it seems that they are being invited to shape the qualities of urban life. But the production of space is dominated by the needs of wealth creation. It becomes a struggle to construct space in an alternative image based not on exploiting it to realise a financial return, but on using space as humanising settings for personal and social life. Such abstract use values make up the equally abstract concept of 'quality of life'.

1

Today, 'quality of life' has strong environmental connotations so that it implies improvements which are sustainable without damaging the environment or human beings. Policies based on this thinking have sought to conserve options and diversity, monitor and improve the quality of the environment, and conserve access to resources. To a large extent these reflect concerns about the future and that actions which the present generation may take to benefit itself should not be at the expense of future generations. But they also involve the problem of an equitable access to, and use of, the legacy of natural and cultural resources from the past. As Weiss (1989, pp. 5-6) writes in her discussion of intergenerational equity:

> Development and use of our natural and cultural resources raise three kinds of equity problems between generations: depletion of resources for future generations, degradation in quality of resources for future generations, and access to use and benefits of the resources received from past generations.

The traditional green belt around British towns and cities is an example of how assumptions underlying policies can become critically reassessed in the light of these positive concerns about how policy actually contributes to quality of life. The theory of the green belt is that a development stopline checks the physical sprawl of large built-up areas, prevents neighbouring towns from merging into one another and preserves the special character of town and countryside. Cullingworth (1988, pp. 182-184) writes that, 'The green belt ... formed a tangible focal point for what we now call the environmental lobby ...'. However, the policy has come to be questioned not only by developers looking for land profits, but because it may actually be inhibiting policies for a better quality of life in terms of failing to prevent a depletion and degradation of urban and rural resources, and failing to improve access to use and benefits of the countryside (Herington, 1990).

Green belts pose a threat to urban open space within the city because of a shortage of land to meet housing needs inside a tight development limit, while they have led to a general and uncoordinated growth of towns and villages in outer commuting areas just beyond them. House prices inflated by development land shortages cause difficulties for low income households seeking affordable urban housing. They have failed to promote rural development and to 'green' policy for the countryside. Yet although the green belt policy *may* have become outmoded and irrelevant to contemporary needs, none of these problems is likely to be solved without a strengthening of the planning system due to the fact that their solution is beyond individual action.

Because the city is a network of interdependent processes, individual self seeking actions are unlikely to achieve the objectives of the individuals concerned because these interdependencies will affect the outcome of actions. This is the so called 'prisoners' dilemma'. Without planning and shared management, disequilibria are likely to occur as when, for example, more and more individual decisions are taken to make journeys by car, followed by road building to cope with growing traffic, which then generates further car journeys in a spiral of congestion.

Societal choices are necessary to avoid the prisoners' dilemma, choices which have to be expressed and implemented through democratic institutions such as local government. Thus, disequilibria can be reduced by adopting explicit social and economic aims for planning which have been presented to the electorate, and managing the social and financial impacts of urban development on the basis of principles derived from these aims. On a large scale, this approach is exemplified in the Netherlands' National Environmental Policy Plan, *To Choose or to Lose* (Ministry of Housing, Physical Planning and Environment, 1989). For example, the land use planning policy of this plan is informed by the strategy of reducing harmful emissions from cars and trucks so that, 'the locations where people live, work, shop and spend their leisure time will be coordinated in such a way that the need to travel is minimal' (p. 195).

The establishment of popular social purposes for policies requires conditions and structures that maintain open and democratic public spheres. Otherwise, policy makers will be engaged in 'cultural imperialism or the dogmatic imposition of expertise' (Doyal and Gough, 1984, p. 22). No contemporary theories of the state establish any basis for such conditions and structures in capitalist societies, and two of the most influential theories, elite theory and neopluralism, 'overlap in arguing that liberal corporatist arrangements and technocratic government have displaced representative politics in determining such public policies as macro economic management, much delivery of welfare state services, or the direction of technological development' (Dunleavy and O'Leary, 1987, p. 324). Ham and Hill (1984, p. 44) comment, 'The central role played by elites - bureaucratic, business, trade union, intellectual, professional and so on - is apparent not just in the area of economic policy, but also in respect of welfare services and consumption policies. On issues of consumption a more pluralistic pattern of political activity exists with bureaucratic elites in a system which may be described as democratic elitism or biased pluralism'.

Decision making is also subject to often intense lobbying which can influence not just policy and implementation but the formulation of the problems policies seek to address. For example, in Britain the road and development lobbies have pressed their cases with government by appealing to 'needs' for *mobility* because growth in the form of more cars and trucks, major new roads or out of town shopping centres generates profits for the large companies that comprise these lobbies, but in an accounting system which

3

undervalues environmental and social costs. The democratic choice may not be the same. It may be *accessibility*, which is quite different. Accessibility is about good bus services, local supermarkets, doctors' surgeries within walking distance, and schools within walking or biking distance. Such options are often rejected as too costly, but this can largely be a result of a combination of fiscal discrimination in how taxes and subsidies are distributed, and failure to take into account social and environmental costs that eventually have to be met (Whitelegg, 1984).

Such contradictory interests explain many of the conflicts between state officials and citizens which are one of many sources of conflict in the policy process. Jessop (1982) considers these as conflicts in 'people officialdom' relations. 'Officialdom' is the agents of intervention in the state. This intervention is fundamentally about serving the conditions of existence of the economic system and its reproduction through social as well as economic policy (or if it is genuinely premised on alternative principles such as social care, is fundamentally affected by economic relations). 'The people' are the social objects of state intervention in *civil society*, which is a separate sphere of relations and practices within and between households, 'a set of social relations that lie between the economic structure and the state' (Urry, 1985, p. 10).

Public participation is in principle about people representing their views rather than being objects of state intervention, and has been strongly advocated by pluralists and many political scientists as a way of broadening democracy. Dunleavy and O'Leary (1987, pp. 312-313) define participation in a useful passage worth quoting in full:

> Participation procedures are special modes of representing citizens' views, supplementary to normal representative government mechanisms. They focus on a single, discrete area, unlike representative politics, which bundles up disparate issues into unconnected bundles, such as election manifestos or legislative programmes. Participation mechanisms often have a quasi-judicial or investigative form, with a neutral or unattached board, committee or inspector hearing both sides of an argument - unlike representative politics, where there is no role for a 'referee'. Participation mechanisms place a premium on relevant knowledge, analytic expertise, and the ability to establish *locus standi* in the case in question, again unlike representative politics, where a winning argument may be emotive, and decisive influence may simply be accorded to the most powerful or popular actors. Many public participation mechanisms are clearly designed to screen out 'ill-informed', 'irresponsible' or 'unrealistic' views, and to insulate public policy outcomes from destabilising or distorting political influences. Part of their

4

functions may also be education - to provide a forum where citizen knowledge can be extended by digging deeper into issues and generating a much larger volume of information than representative politics can usually achieve. Some countries have experimented with marrying public participation procedures to referenda, as in Austria and Sweden, where both countires voted on whether or not to continue with nuclear power programmes, following intensive scientific and political debates organized by the government. Neo-pluralists are interested in the possibilities of devising new, issue-specific forms of public participation to keep professional elites in line with public expectations.

As is discussed in the following chapter, planning inquiries do not have their origin in such neo-pluralist ideals for public participation, but have nevertheless become vehicles for participation.

The problem of disequilibria or imbalanced and uneven development is often a theme in development plan inquiries because of the interest of many members of the public in 'community needs'. Disequilibria have been a feature of the largely unplanned development of inner city waterfront zones by Urban Development Corporations during the 1980s, especially the problem of housing, new jobs and even existing vocational training schemes not matching local needs (House of Commons Environment Committee, 1988). The lack of any democratic or participatory role for local people in the corporations' decisions has been a major issue. Disequilibria have also, however, affected what have often been held to be the epitome of British planning - new towns - due to such problems as a lack of joint planning between state agencies (Mohan, 1984) and a lack of planning for labour market or sectoral adjustments to structural change in the world economy, which saw some of the new towns industrialise and deindustrialise within one or two decades (Blackman, 1987). But although possibly the epitome of British planning, new towns have not been models of democracy, and have often been marked by 'people-officialdom' conflicts (Blackman, 1987; Dickens, Duncan, Goodwin and Gray, 1985). It is noteworthy that Raymond Williams, whose analytical work is imbued with a radical conceptualisation of 'community', chooses the politics of new town planning as the backcloth to his exploration of the subordination of a community to the state and big business in his novel, *The Fight for Manod* (Williams, 1988). Williams' fictional civil servant, Robert Lane, explains the problem:

> If it ever gets built, and who knows about that, it will be one of the first human settlements, anywhere in the world, to have been conceived, from the beginning, in post-industrial terms and with a post-electronic technology ..... What the local people want is nothing so grand. They want

small local developments, improving but not altering the
kinds of place they've got used to. But then even for that
they need money, and to get the money, frankly, means
having to fit in with what other people want, which is
planned dispersal on a big enough scale to make the
investment economic. At the two extremes that's the basic
problem: two quite different views of what needs to be done.
(Williams, 1988, p.13)

Although new towns were planned, they in fact reflected the uneven
development of economies by channelling investment to selected
locations (Mohan, 1984). This feature of capital accumulation in
market economies generates inequalities in access to jobs, to
housing, to stable retail environments, to transport, to public
goods, and to durable, non-polluted environments. The victims of
these processes become very much objects of state intervention as
social security claimants, state housing tenants and social work
clients, rather than empowered citizens. Their rights to vote or
participate are largely useless against an economic marginalization.
The situation has given rise to fears about an 'underclass' which
lives with cumulative disadvantages in areas put into decline and
made uneconomic by the migration of capital and population.
Business decisions that their areas are obsolescent are a condition
for creating economic demand, new development and profits
elsewhere (Reade, 1987, pp. 200-201).

The boundaries of personal interests

Tackling these disequilibria focuses policy on questions of stability,
equity and state intervention which, as central elements of the
political philosophy of socialism, has placed the issue of planning
and shared management firmly in the political arena. Planning,
critics of such an approach argue, harms the dynamic of wealth
creation and interferes with free enterprise, personal liberty and
choice.

These anti-collectivist criticisms have also been applied to the
principle of 'public goods', often cited with the 'prisoners' dilemma'
as justification for planning. These are goods and services which
are needed by everyone and cannot be left to market forces because
of the danger of 'market failure'. In Britain, examples include the
police, education and health provision.

Formerly regarded as public goods, the nationalised water and
electricity industries in Britain are being privatised, but the new
enterprises will be subject to regulations designed to guard against
'market failure'. The logic of the market place, however, will
replace that of the public interest, and this is seen most clearly in
the contradiction between an electricity industry governed by the
market logic of maximising sales of the product, and the public
interest in measures to reduce energy consumption to tackle global

warming.

Pollution from a power station or congestion in a city are examples of negative 'externalities' - costs experienced by others as a by-product of the use of property. Externalities can also be positive, such as proximity to a fire station and thus enhanced fire protection. The inability of the market mechanism to allocate resources efficiently when externalities are present has been one of the most common arguments for planning (Harvey, 1973, pp. 57-60). The need for planning, however, derives from a deeper problem with property rights:

> Externalities exist because property rights are defined on too small a scale for the consequences of the use of property to be felt by those who determine that use. They consist of costs or benefits that are not taken into account by narrowly self-interested decision-makers since some of the effects of using the property are borne by or benefit others. The extent and distribution of such external effects depends on the distribution of property rights. Externalities are the theoretical basis for the standard distinction between private and social costs and benefits. (Devine, 1988, pp. 14-15)

Claims for private individuals' property rights are the major constraint on planning, and have been used to attack the principle of planning generally (Hayek, 1944; 1960). However, instead of treating such rights as conditional on the popular franchise, the most extreme advocates treat private individuals' property rights as something basic and separate from politics; a non political sphere to be defended against unjustifiable invasions by the state (Nozick, 1974). These special claims are not sustainable as anything other than an ideology - a political philosophy about legal and economic arrangements which is profoundly anti-democratic (Harrison, 1987). Shared management is a necessary condition for democracy, so that social priorities determined through the democratic political process can be put into practice (Devine, 1988).

Far from reflecting human nature, as is often claimed, the liberal free market argument against planning conflicts with people's 'extended interests' by appealing solely to 'self interest'. Extended interests are especially a feature of the culture of strongly labourist areas such as Tyneside in North East England. Drawing on a study of this area, Byrne (1989, p.159) explains extended interests in the following terms:

> Historical analysis has to take account of more than the immediately material or the longer-term real material interest. People's interests are also constituted in terms of their cultures and the survival of those cultures may form part of their material interests. We also have to look carefully at the boundaries of personal interests. Contrary to the

individualistic psychology of economic 'man', people take account of others when they construct a sense of what matters to them.

Thus, Byrne notes that in an area that is relatively ethnically homogeneous - with a high degree of residential stability - the bonds of family, friends and community, reinforced by common experiences of schooling and work - or lack of it - create extended interests within and across generations which form the basis for trade unionism and socialism, and for collective solutions to problems of unemployment, deskilling and poverty. Underlying this political culture is a sense of belonging which involves much more than just legal property (Williams, 1983).

Recently, awareness of extended interests both within and especially between generations has been aroused on a wider scale than local cultures by evidence that harmful changes to the world's climate are occuring as a result of the pursuit of immediate and longer-term material interests through growing energy consumption and pollution. Fairness to future generations has become a political issue as societies look to develop means of meeting present needs without damaging the ability of future generations to meet their needs (Weiss, 1989). A different conception of property is also involved here through the notion of stewardship.

Until recognition of the greenhouse effect and ozone depletion changed public attitudes, the disadvantages of an economic system based on exploitation of the natural environment, rather than sustainability, were generally hidden from the standpoint of the individual - they were not reflected in money terms and only became prominent with major accidents and catastrophes. The market did not assign a value to the environment and, in microeconomic accounting terms, it made sense for industry to minimise private costs by using all available 'costless' social and natural conditions (Beckenbach, 1989). Because it is ultimately experienced as social costs, the exploitation of nature is also an exploitation of society as pollution, environmental destruction, damage to health and destruction of capital incur costs of supervision, planning, repair and prevention. It is very difficult to 'monetize' these costs because of incomplete information and difficulty in assigning costs to damages and attributing damages to producers and consumers. Taking account of social costs is a question of nonmonetary evaluation; of setting standards for the quality of life, evaluating social costs and benefits, formulating trade-offs and establishing priorities. Such planning is not possible if there is a separation of legal, political and economic spheres, the foundation of anti-collectivist philosophies.

Property: the limits to state intervention

The ideological separation of legal, political and economic spheres

8

is particularly important to the concept of property. In Britain, legislation - particularly town and country planning legislation - has in effect defined private property as a 'bundle of rights'. Although the owner has an especially large share of this bundle of property rights, the public also have a share in the form of, for example, land use planning and development control, whereby the state guides and licenses land use 'in the public interest' (Harrison, 1987).

Planning controls are exercised by the state because land use requires coordination with other uses and the control of externalities such as traffic generation which are borne by - or benefit - people other than those who determine the use of a particular piece of property. In other words, there is recognition that the property rights of one person cannot be allowed to restrict the rights of others to freedom from pollution or access to the countryside, for example.

In Britain, decisions by planning authorities about whether or not to grant planning permission to a developer are often based on an assessment of the affect of the proposed land use on 'amenity', which has been principally interpreted in terms of visual intrusion and traffic generation. As Cullingworth (1988, p. 196) notes:

> It is a term widely used in planning refusals and appeals; indeed the phrase 'injurious to the interests of amenity' has become part of the stock-in-trade jargon of the planning world.

The concept of amenity illustrates a problem inherent in the British planning system: nowhere in the legislation does a definition of the term appear, and there is enormous scope for disagreement about judgements based on the concept. The difficulty is one which relates to the general problem of the limits to state intervention in property. Two interesting issues arise from this intervention which concern how big a share of the bundle of property rights the state is to have.

First, what are the limits to this intervention, given that a coordinating function and the mangement of externalities entail social and economic costs and benefits as well as environmental ones? Should intervention be confined to a separate sphere, such as the form and layout of buildings, or should it extend to social and economic spheres, to who buildings are for, and how and for what purpose they are produced? Permission to build in rural areas, for instance, can open up opportunities to realise substantial development profits, while the price of the new housing may be out of the reach of people in housing need. Refusing planning permission in a rural area, however, can condemn local communities to a process of depopulation and geriatrification. Decisions based on assessments of amenity will have significant social and economic effects.

Second, is state intervention on behalf of other private owners or is it to pursue policies based on the 'public interest', 'community' or 'welfare' which embody collective principles based on a different political philosophy to private ownership?

Most debate on these issues in planning circles is very conservative because of the influence, noted above, of the liberal idea that private individuals' property rights have a special status or moral claim which should only be reduced when there is an overriding justification to do so, and this has mainly been in consideration of the requirements of other property owners. As McAuslan (1980) analyses in detail, even though planners and administrators may espouse an ideology of public interest which they claim governs their practice, the courts have espoused an ideology of private property in interpreting legislation and making case law. McAuslan shows how the ideology of public participation has been victim of ideologies of private property *and* public interest, both of which are rights claims. However, as Harrison (1987, p. 47) puts it: 'Some community rights can be deduced logically from rights of participation implicit in local electoral representation: consequently they have more status than mere moral rights *claims*'. Thus:

> There is no reason ... why more positive managerial planning could not be legitimated through the notion of shared community property rights. We have only to reconsider questions about controlling occupancy of second homes in Wales to see the idea's relevance: local people are advancing property rights claims that go well beyond powers over the appearance of buildings or land-use allocations. (Harrison, 1987, p. 48)

Planning: obscuring or clarifying political choices?

Town and country planning has frequently been criticised for presenting political issues about the distribution of resources such as housing and employment as technical problems requiring coordination and solutions based on physical standards such as density requirements (Reade, 1987). Whilst planning to many lay people appears to involve the exercise of power, as Harrison (1987, p. 50) comments: '... some aspects of professional power and administrative discretion arise precisely *because* of the desire of governments, lawyers and businessmen to confine planning to "technical" rather than socio-political questions'.

The real power in the built environment is, as Ambrose (1986) analyses, the development industry and the dynamic of capital accumulation through investment development, speculative housebuilding and contracting. Ambrose (1986, p. 269) concludes:

> Ideally all planners should have a good working knowledge of the way an entrepreneur's mind assesses opportunities in

each of these fields, which financial interests are involved, how schemes are promoted and roughly what rate of profit is to be expected. The planner can then make a reasonable assessment of the commercial value of the development consent the entrepreneur is seeking, which at present often amounts to a licence to print money, and can enter into a realistic debate about the distribution of future benefits and profits. For example, it might make sense to ensure that a proportion of the development profits is fed back to the authority granting the consent and earmarked to cover the cost of rehousing those currently living on the site.

Planning decisions bestow benefits, but they also impose costs which, as in the case of displacement and rehousing, are often paid for socially by the public sector, while the benefits accrue to the private sector. The deregulation of planning and containment of public expenditure which have occurred during the last ten years have meant that often social costs are not met, with social polarisation occurring as a consequence. In a revealing study, Rees (1988) shows how the closure of a Tesco store in a district of Swansea in 1984 led to a marked polarisation between low income carless households that had no choice but to continue shopping in the district centre, despite a marked reduction of shopping opportunities, and car owning households that were able to shop in the new Tesco superstore in Swansea's Enterprise Zone. Closure of the old Tesco store had been necessary to safeguard investment in a new superstore built in the Enterprise Zone, but this polarised shopping patterns in a markedly regressive way because the new store was inaccessible without a car, whilst closure of the old store precipitated the decline of an accessible shopping area. Indeed, Rees shows that even most car-owning shoppers would have preferred to patronise the district centre rather than the Enterprise Zone store given the choice denied by the closure. Whilst she recognises that planning can have a role in steering large stores to established district centres, she notes that possible subsequent closure of such monopolistic stores may inflict an even greater blow on district centres than locating elsewhere in the first place. Frequent and convenient public transport might be a better solution.
Ambrose (1986) suggests that the shifts in wealth brought about by land development and the exercise (or absence) of planning controls may be as significant as those caused by taxation, yet they are rarely treated as social policy issues in the same way as the impact of taxes on the distribution of income. Instead, planning is largely concerned with standards. As Harrison (1987, p. 45) comments:

Standards partly represent a response to pressures to portray planning as neutral and technical, rather than as

11

inherently partly political (and redistributive in its outcomes). Fears that local planning authorities might discriminate between developers on welfare grounds, or introduce obviously political criteria into decision-making, have encouraged restricted views as to the proper scope of planning powers.

This point is not only relevant to welfare considerations. Byrne (1989) raises the question of whether planning powers should be used to prevent the preempting of riverside sites that could support reindustrialisation on Tyneside. Sites acquired by the Tyne & Wear Development Corporation have been developed for 'non productive' housing and leisure uses. Short term profits have attracted investment denied to maritime industry. As he puts it:

> The Tyne & Wear Development Corporation is not about employment, although employment glosses are sometimes offered. No long-term employment plan would convert shipyards into housing estates when perfectly suitable housing sites which could be developed without subsidy to the private sector are readily available within 2 miles. It is rather a kind of ideological device with money which represents the future as non-industrial. (Byrne, 1989, p. 133)

The public's share of private property rights embodied in the system of planning by elected authorities invites claims by the public to be consulted, to participate in the process and to influence outcomes. This has been recognised in town and country planning for many years, and at various stages in the planning process the public have a right to inspect draft plans placed 'on deposit' in planning offices and public libraries, to object to planning proposals and to have those objections heard at a public inquiry. This is most well developed in local plan making for district council areas which, unlike county structure plans, as non strategic plans do not have to be approved by the Secretary of State for the Environment. Cullingworth (1988, p. 86) gives a very clear account of the public process of making local land use plans in Britain:

> (T)he local authority is required to give 'adequate publicity' to its proposals *before* they are included in a local plan, and to give 'adequate opportunity' for the making of representations on its proposals. In these and similar ways public participation is actually written into the legislation ... (T)he normal statutory procedure applies for the deposit of plans, the making of objections and the holding of an inquiry or hearing by an independent inspector and the publication of the inspector's report. The important difference from the

traditional procedure is that the inspector reports to the local authority, not to the secretary of state. This follows, of course, from the principle that the local plan is a local authority, not a central authority, matter. It is clear that public participation is more than a desirable adjunct to the system: it is an essential feature of it. If public participation fails, so will the system.

However, criticism of planning has focused on its tokenism towards public participation as much as the lack of consideration given to redistributive, welfare and economic consequences (McAuslan, 1980). The lay experience of planning has frequently been one of a top-down process which fails to build upwards from local concerns and opinions, whilst making a token gesture to hear such concerns through consultation periods and public inquiries. The need for a strategic perspective is often cited by planners and inquiry inspectors responding to community groups' arguments that plan making is occurring at a scale beyond their neighbourhoods, when it is their communities which will be most directly affected. In other words, despite the planners' claim that they are planning in the public interest, actual people seem to present a plurality of different needs and views at often very local levels with which a development plan for a whole city cannot cope. This was indeed the Belfast experience, and this forms the major case study at the centre of this book.

The inability of planning to cope with its redistributive consequences and with community concepts is a major problem in view of the relatively extensive opportunities that exist for the public to comment on land use proposals and development plans. Public comment is rarely inhibited by planners', or indeed the courts', narrow definitions of planning powers. The implication of this is that effectively people, through the state, are often seeking a larger share of the private owner's bundle of property rights than the law is prepared to grant. People comment on all the aspects and implications of a land use, which can be very wide ranging across social, economic and cultural matters. Major frustration can occur when, invited to comment on proposed land uses, people find their comments treated as irrelevant to how 'their' neighbourhood or city is to develop. These issues raise fundamental questions about public policy in relation to private property, which are explored in this book through a case study of urban planning in Belfast.

The case study: Belfast

Why use a case study from Northern Ireland to undertake such an exercise? The reason is that far from being a unique society with problems not found elsewhere - and thus with experiences of no relevance beyond its borders - this region of Europe presents a complex concentration of issues which are universal, and which are

13

found to varying degrees in all societies. These are issues of civil and minority rights, nationalism and ethnicity, economic inequality and discrimination, which have tested, and found wanting, the institutions of 'modernity': the political bureaucracies and economic power centres of industrialised countries.

Under the leadership of the Unionist prime minister Terence O'Neill, it was thought that by starting to modernise Northern Ireland's political and economic policies the problems of Catholic resentment towards a Protestant dominated Unionist state could be resolved. Some modernisation occurred during the 1960s. Under O'Neill, the Irish Congress of Trade Unions was officially recognised for the first time, ambitious physical and economic plans were adopted, and the historic act of inviting the Irish Republic's prime minister to Stormont for talks about economic cooperation took place. But this was not sufficient to prevent a political crisis and violent confrontations which forced the United Kingdom parliament to prorogue the Northern Ireland legislature in 1972 and end fifty years of continuous Protestant Unionist rule of the province (Bew, Gibbon and Patterson, 1979).

Since 1972, with one brief intermission, Northern Ireland has been ruled by civil servants responsible to British ministers under a system known as Direct Rule. In effect, this is an extreme centralisation of state power to deal with a local political crisis by attempting to depoliticise, and dedemocratise, local administration and the processes of policy formulation and implementation. The aim is to govern in a way that is perceived as fair, and this puts a gloss on the reality that what is going on is an imposition of the ideology and political strategy of whatever government is in power in London on potentially disruptive groups of individuals.

During the period of Thatcher governments in the UK, such removal of local administration out of the local political arena into agencies effectively unaccountable to elected representatives became more common, not just in Northern Ireland. Such a description applies, for example, to Urban Development Corporations, Enterprise Zones and Inner City Partnerships. In general, the bureaucratisation of policy making and the professionalisation of knowledge detach those who make decisions from those who experience their consequences; in the case of these agencies, more than this problem is involved: a type of colonization is under way which is using both seduction and repression. The glittering developments of waterfront regeneration which are the typical products of Britain's Urban Development Corporations are the seductive side of market dependency and its 'colonization of a growing volume of needs' (Bauman, 1987, p. 166). However, those who through poverty cannot buy their way into the lifestyles and life projects offered by the market's 'revalorization' of these areas find the substitution of repression for seduction, policing for public relations, authority for advertising, and norm imposition for needs creation. Bauman's (1987) description of 'postmodern' society is

14

exemplified in Belfast planning, as the following analysis of its new urban plan brings out very clearly:

> Expressions and images can readily change the terms of the planning debate. Back in the late sixties in Belfast what had been customarily described as 'neat little terraces' in a city of villages very quickly became 'slums' in urgent need of demolition. The old way of life was to change. It was presented as inadequate to the modern age. Rather, new bright houses in the growth centres or radically different housing forms in situ could provide all the amenities that were lacking in the inner city. The image was important. It displayed clean, modern materials, geometric forms and open spaces and it represented the possibility of an improved way of life. The current Belfast Urban Area Plan is even more image laden than previous initiatives. However, a different set of priorities now exist. They demand a new language and new visual metaphors. No longer are the working class communities the direct target of the planners since there is no need to repattern the geography of working class Belfast. Rather, the problems of the most impoverished neighbourhoods have been side stepped in favour of an urban regeneration programme geared to the personal disposable incomes of those in work and to capitalizing resources such as the River Lagan and the green fields on the urban fringe. (Mooney and Gaffikin, 1987, pp. 66-68)

Urban management in Belfast has necessitated separating the spheres of officialdom on the one hand and ordinary people on the other to a far greater degree than is normal even in centralised political democracies such as Britain and the Republic of Ireland. Under the system of Direct Rule from London which followed the collapse of Northern Ireland's own regional government in the early 1970s, the state bureaucracy is only accountable to a cabinet minister elected in Britain; there is no downwards accountability to a local electorate. The absence of local government in housing, planning, social services, education and other public services means that access to information is also curtailed because the civil servants are bound by Britain's Official Secrets Act. This separation of spheres has a spatial component: the space of officialdom is an abstract one of territorial administration which is at a larger scale than the everyday human scale of 'social space' at which people go about and experience day to day life. Thus, conflict between state and civil society often finds expression in conflict about the spatial scale at which urban issues are investigated and acted upon.

Public participation: its meaning and limits in planning

Land use planning is the one area of public policy in Northern

15

Ireland and Great Britain in which public consultation is a relatively highly developed part of the decision making process. This is particularly significant in Northern Ireland because of the suspension of local democracy. Here, the Department of the Environment - the planning authority - is under the political control of the UK government in London. During the 1980s the Department's policies derived largely from the political strategies of Thatcher administrations. These were adapted when opportune in order to relieve the political and military crisis, such as the delayed running down of the public sector housebuilding programme in deprived areas compared with Great Britain. As already noted, there is a strong parallel between state policy in Northern Ireland and the special programmes and direct central government interventions in Britain's inner cities (see Duncan and Goodwin, 1988). Economic crisis has long dogged many areas of the UK space economy, but Northern Ireland and the inner cities have attracted high profile initiatives because the state responds not to economic crisis as such, but to when serious political repercussions arise from such crisis, not least as urban riots (Jessop, 1983, p. 235). In such a context, public participation is often seen as cooperating with and legitimising state measures which address the symptoms but not the causes of urban deprivation, and is contrasted with protest and radical political mobilisation. This position is also associated with a rejection of social democracy as merely the political shell of an undemocratic economic system based on inequality.

Marx identified the French Revolution and the birth of 'the citizen' as marking the accomplishment of a separation of politics and the state from 'civil society' or everyday life. Although democratic elections may link these two spheres, states that claim legitimacy or authority on the basis of election by a majority of individual citizens are under constant pressure from real class or social conflicts in society which cannot be resolved by the deprived using a vote (see Duncan and Goodwin, 1982). In Jessop's (1985) analysis, the division between a majority of comfortably off citizens and a minority of deprived and oppressed people has been actively exploited by a Thatcherite two nations strategy which has seen a widening income and wealth gap between these two 'nations'.

Thatcherism's political success was largely a result of a commitment to 'strong government' (Jessop et al, 1988). One casualty has been local government, the autonomy of which has been greatly curtailed, mainly but by no means only by controlling local spending. The process has brought local administration in Great Britain closer to the system in Northern Ireland than at any time since Direct Rule was introduced in 1972, and indeed in Scotland and Northern England the situation in the early 1990s is one of de facto direct rule from Westminster. However in Northern Ireland the legitimacy of such a degree of centralised power, based outside the region, is far more under question; indeed, it sets the political agenda. The region has a system of elected local councils, but responsible for only minor services. Voting behaviour reflects positions on the constitutional link with Britain, and hardly ever concerns these local services. Councils are consulted about planning matters, and Belfast City Council has a town planning committee. During the making of the Belfast Urban Area Plan, however, wider political events surrounding Unionist protest against the Anglo Irish Agreement signed in 1985 meant no council in the Belfast Urban Area made any significant input before or at the public inquiry.

Yet this did not mean that local people had the same attitude to the Plan. Just as studies in Britain show how many people who express concern in opinion polls about high unemployment or underfunding of the health service vote Tory in general elections, in Northern Ireland the concerns and actions of people in civil society are not obviously reflected in what they do at the ballot box. An apparent desire for strong government at one level is not reflected in an attitude that government knows best when it comes to planning and the development of neighbourhoods and cities at another. Yet, as will become clear in later chapters, local participation cannot get far before coming up against 'the established parameters of government policy' (Northern Ireland Planning Appeals Commission, 1989, p. 11).

Is participation, then, only possible in planning when politics is avoided? The Skeffington Committee, chaired by the then Joint Parliamentary Secretary to the Minister of Housing and Local Government, proposed in its 1969 report 'community forums' which would 'provide local organisations with the opportunity to discuss collectively planning and other issues of importance to the area' (quoted in Cullingworth, 1988, p. 376). As Cullingworth (1988, p. 376) remarks, 'The Skeffington Report noted that it was feared that a community forum might become the centre of political opposition, but the only comment made was: "we hope that that would not happen; it seems unlikely that it would, as most local groups are not party political in their membership" '. This view seems to treat neighbourhoods as largely politics free zones, and to assume that:

> ... at a local, face-to-face level people can live without difference, or that differences can be easily resolved. This is founded on the belief that there is a private realm, where economic inequalities cease to exist or matter, beyond and opposed to the public and political world. (Boys, 1989, p. 49)

Whilst 'community' in this sense is a regressive ideology, it also has a radical usage most notably in the work of Raymond Williams. Williams (1983) argued that local forms of human and human environment relationships are more 'real' in the sense of lived experience than the imagined communities of nation states or, indeed, the local state (see Cockburn, 1977). States, he claims,

17

have grown from quite different roots as ruling class projects, and seek to achieve effective power over local social relations.

This feeling that the state is something alien and 'from quite different roots' is acute for both communities in Northern Ireland today. Thus, local participation in a process such as the public inquiry into a strategic development plan raises issues both of according a statutory process legitimacy when this cannot exist and achieving some change in policy that improves the conditions or prospects of local communities. This is the same, albeit more intense, contradiction which has faced local pressure groups in Britain, and is reflected very well in the title to Wendy Le-Las' (1987) guide for objectors at inquiries, *Playing the Public Inquiry Game*.

The town and country planning system has a degree of openness to public participation and social activism which, despite defects, is unique in public policy. Yet it is fundamentally a system by which the state decides 'the public interest' in land use decisions. This public interest, which is considered more fully in chapter 2, is not easily identified, and actually reflects a complex balance of power between landed interests, industry and finance, and labour and consumers ('citizens'). In participating in how the public interest is arrived at, rarely do the public manage to climb beyond the first few rungs of Arnstein's (1969) famous ladder of citizen participation (see Figure 1).

Arnstein's analysis tends to relate to public officials as managers or gatekeepers of urban resources such as housing and employment. This 'urban managerialism' thesis was promoted in Pahl's (1975) work, *Whose City?*, but was revised in the face of many studies showing that public officials do not have extensive control over resources of which they can be dispossessed by organised citizen action (Saunders, 1986). Power over the wealth creating resources of people, capital, technology and space lies elsewhere, in the economic system, and places pressures and limits on what can be achieved by state action.

The content of policies can also be shaped in particular conditions by demands and aspirations coming up from below, although this often has a more marked effect on the style in which policies are administered rather than their actual content. For example, the 'packaging' of special inner city measures such as partnership projects in areas where there have been problems of disorder, and sometimes urban riots, contrasts with the large cut backs in government grant to the mainstream services of urban local authorities during the 1980s. In Belfast, Gaffikin and Morrissey (1990) calculated the value of cuts in social security benefits since 1980 and found that this roughly equalled the 'extra' funds allocated for tackling the inner city's social problems through the high profile 'Making Belfast Work' initiative. A plethora of community based projects had accompanied a growing gap between the incomes of the poorest and those of middle and upper income earners.

18

Figure 1.1   Arnstein's ladder of citizen participation

Rung on the ladder	Meaning of participation
Citizen power	Direct control
Delegated power	Negotiation with public officials from position of power
Partnership	Power sharing by agreement
Placation	Advice is sought from citizens who are organised to press their case
Consultation	Unorganised citizens are consulted
Informing	One way flow of information from the state
Therapy	Local measures which label citizens as social problems
Manipulation	Cynical public relations exercises

It is clear that planners work within this wider policy environment, but does this mean that their relationship to the people they plan for is governed by this environment? Does the fact that economic and social policies are implicated in growing inequality mean that planners cannot respond positively to cases made in public participation exercises for a redistribution of land uses and means of transport in favour of deprived communities? This book's case study is about community groups participating in the Belfast Urban Area Plan, but this introductory analysis tends to suggest that their decision to 'play the public inquiry game' would achieve very little. Indeed, as we shall see, many of the groups thought this would be the case, but nevertheless invested time and effort in making informed objections to the plan.

The existence of the public inquiry procedure is central to understanding this apparent contradiction. Hutton (1986) argues that lay beliefs in democracy and justice can be reinforced by the sense of fairness created by inquiry inspectors despite the powerful legal forces often opposing lay objectors to proposals from big developers. As a result, he argues that objectors often participate in their own defeat, rather being 'crushed' by the state. However, in the case of the Belfast inquiry there was little likelihood that community groups would expect justice, and every likelihood that they would be immune to an artificial atmosphere of fairness if it was manifested in the inquiry hall.

The explanation for their participation is largely in terms of a strategy worked out in advance of putting officialdom under examination - of exploiting an opportunity in an undemocratic city of calling the state to account. If actual gains were won, all the better, but the main principle behind participation was to establish that the plan as proposed did not reflect the needs and concerns of community groups in Belfast.

Community action

At the heart of Northern Ireland's political/military crisis is the existence within a single region of two communities, Unionist and Nationalist, with conflicting national identities, British and Irish, and different religions, Protestant and Catholic. A history of discrimination and inequality has made it impossible to sustain peaceful democratic government within this part of Ireland. But despite a lack of political progress, civil society has been a sphere of progressive community action.

Community groups have delivered services and undertaken campaigns which have been largely concerned with the defence and social development of localities. This has often reflected social division and territoriality, but at times it has created a basis for common interest and collective action, as when Loyalist and Republican action groups united in their opposition to the Belfast Urban Motorway (see chapter 3). State intervention has occurred to investigate, channel and depoliticise this activity, such as the Community Relations Commission set up by government in the early 1970s, and more recently the policy of terminating grants to groups with any committee members believed to have paramilitary connections (Political Vetting of Community Work Working Group, 1990). The state has also, together with charitable trusts, supported the growth of a large sector of grant aided voluntary organisations.

There have been attempts by community activists to build on appeals to community and class to construct new non sectarian political movements, but overall voluntary and community groups are strongly service orientated with fairly specific constituencies and interests (Woods, 1989).

Urban renewal, however, has been a particular stimulus to 'community action' as opposed to community service. In Kraushaar's (1981) words, 'extreme local disruptions, such as large scale urban redevelopment schemes ... encourage a collective response' (p. 113). Kraushaar discusses the ways in which the state has in turn responded to community campaigns against its strategies of displacement and redevelopment in the inner cities during the 1960s-70s. By coopting organisations with origins in protest against its

20

policies, the state offsets spontaneous and disruptive actions, increases information about its external environment, gains legitimacy for its activities, and promotes self help solutions to social conflict and fiscal strain. Parson's (1981) study of urban renewal in Belfast shows how this was done there during the 1970s by introducing British legislation which directed the efforts of community activists into setting up and running local housing associations.

Two factors combined in the early 1980s to stimulate a new response in the community to the lack of control people had over what was happening to their neighbourhoods. Firstly, the poor and often deteriorating quality of the environment in the estates of mass public sector housing built in Belfast in the '60 and '70s was sparking off organised action by tenants. Increasingly these campaigns sought to use technical evidence in their attempts to press for better housing conditions. Secondly, the renewal of redevelopment areas declared in the 1970s was nearing completion, and Northern Ireland's public housing authority, the Housing Executive, decided to review the condition of the remaining inner city housing stock, leading to the declaration of a number of smaller redevelopment areas in the *Belfast Housing Renewal Strategy* (Northern Ireland Housing Executive, 1983). Community groups in the areas affected formed to oppose the plans, and began to look for technical evidence to support claims that their homes should not be demolished.

Responding to these events, a small group of community workers and academics promoted the idea of a planning aid centre which could support community groups with technical assistance that would be under their control. The proposal was taken to a conference of community groups held in Derry in May 1983. A steering committee was formed to raise funds and establish the centre. A £30,000 seeding grant from the Joseph Rowntree Memorial Trust meant that the project got off the ground quickly.

Evidence was submitted to an inquiry into the *Belfast Housing Renewal Strategy* being conducted at the time by the Environment Committee of the Northern Ireland Assembly. This Assembly was a short lived attempt at 'rolling devolution' for Northern Ireland and, whilst having no legislative powers, its comments on policy were being taken seriously by the British government in an attempt to establish credibility for the initiative. Although boycotted by the Nationalist Social Democratic and Liberal Party (SDLP) because no all Irish initiative accompanied establishment of the Assembly, the participating Unionist and Alliance Parties were highly critical of the Housing Executive's proposals. The former had particular concerns about the protestant neighbourhoods where redevelopment was proposed and where population losses were feared, whilst the latter had a liberal commitment to public participation. The Environment Committee's report strongly recommended government grant aid for a planning aid centre run as a voluntary organisation (Northern

Ireland Assembly, 1983).

The centre was established in 1984 as Community Technical Aid (CTA), run by a committee largely elected from member community groups. Building rather than planning problems came to monopolise CTA's early work, but from 1986 this changed with the government's decision to make a strategic land use plan for the whole Belfast area in response to mounting development and traffic pressures - the Belfast Urban Area Plan (BUAP) 2001. The background to this decision is the subject of chapter 3. CTA responded to the opportunity to involve community groups in the strategy of land use planning in Belfast by making a successful case for special government grant aid to support the employment of planners to work directly with community groups in the city. The final chapter discusses this decision in detail, and although obviously one entailing the motives Kraushaar (1981) identifies when the state is faced by potentially disruptive mobilisation in the community, it was seen as an astounding decision by some commentators. The *Irish Times* environment correspondent, Frank McDonald, ended his endorsement of the whole planning exercise by writing:

> Most startling of all, the Department of the Environment in Belfast, which is the planning authority for Northern Ireland, has just agreed to finance a coalition of community and conservation groups to the tune of £50,000 (sterling) so that they can put together a coherent case *against the Department's own plan.* (*Irish Times*, 11.12.87, p. 15)

The result of CTA's work was a *common* response from community groups to the plan, presented and defended at a six week public inquiry during the summer of 1988. The present book shows how a collective response arose from both the constitution of interests which fed into this common front, mainly interests constituted around community concepts and the city as a shared space, and the statutory planning process to which all parties decided to relate, a factor which encouraged common identity, cooperation and organisation.

Conclusion

This introduction has considered the case for planning and shared management, and has shown how central to this is the concept of property as a 'bundle of rights' in which the public as well as the property owner share. However, various ambiguities in the planning system as it exists today have been noted, principally whether state intervention is on behalf of other private owners or it to pursue policies based on the 'public interest', 'community' or 'welfare' which embody collective principles based on a different political philosophy to private ownership. Public participation in planning highlights these ambiguities. The book's case study of Belfast is an empirical investigation of them.

The public inquiry, 'the most common public listening and debating device in British public administration' (McAuslan, 1980, p. 45), forms the subject of the next chapter. The public inquiry into the Belfast Urban Area Plan was at the centre of the participation process, and the chapter explores in depth the sociolegal dimensions of this instrument, and how far it can test the planning system. Chapter 3 then explains the origins of the Belfast Urban Area Plan 2001 in an analytical account of the development of planning policy for the city and its region, which has been a story of 'modernisation' and 'post modern' restructuring. chapter 4 describes the plan, the mobilisation of community groups which followed announcement of its proposals, and the cases constructed by the groups during the consultation period. The chapter highlights the conflicts between the different perspectives of the community groups and the planning authority, and considers whether they amounted to different planning 'paradigms'. Chapter 5 is an account of the public inquiry and analyses what impact the community groups' cases made on the plan. The final chapter returns to the themes of chapter 1 to discuss the future for democratic planning in Belfast and elsewhere.

2 Planning inquiries in context

Managing conflict

This chapter considers the instrument of government which is at the heart of this book's case study: the public inquiry. In chapter 2, the public inquiry was introduced as a participation procedure, a special mode for representing citizens' views 'supplementary to normal representative government mechanisms' (Dunleavy and O'Leary, 1987, p. 312). It was noted that it is a quasijudicial instrument. Indeed, the public inquiry in urban planning is an interesting example of the exercise of state power because it appears to embody basic justifications of state intervention: adjudication, mediation, representation, and checks and balances.

As a stage in the planning process, the inquiry is inevitably about managing conflict. Urban planning brings about a physical basis of conflict because it alters the physical environment and in doing so creates winners and losers (Ball, 1983, pp. 193-242). Changes in the physical environment bring about changes in the distribution of 'real income', as Harvey (1973) applies the term. This real income is the net effect of external costs and benefits brought about by planning and urban development, such as the windfall land profit that may follow planning permission or the completion of a new access road, and the costs that may be suffered from pollution or the closure of local public facilities such as a school or hospital.

Reference was made in chapter 1 to Ambrose's (1986) argument that planning controls may have the same significance in relation to the redistribution of wealth through land development as taxation has in relation to the distribution of income. However planning controls are rarely treated as social policy issues. Social policy studies have neglected town and country planning in recent years, despite the post-war establishment of the planning system as part of the welfare state.

There has not been the same neglect in urban sociology, where urban planning has been the subject of many studies. The literature is generally highly critical. Marxist work has criticised city and regional planning for being technocratic and denying the existence of class conflict over land use (Lefebvre 1968, 1977; Ambrose 1976; Castells 1978). Non marxist research has also concentrated on the mystification of interests. Dennis (1970, 1972) and Davies (1972) interpreted professional planning rationalities as evangelistic ideologies at odds with everyday life in working class communities, while Flynn (1981) interpreted planners' role as one of broker and consensus seeker. To varying degrees these analyses regarded state power as oppressive. This position was developed by Saunders (1980) in his argument for expanding the ability of people to control their own lives by reducing as far as possible state power in the sphere of consumption. Frankel (1987) identifies the problems with this argument; the state cannot be regarded to be innately oppressive.

As well as creating a physical basis for conflict, which has received considerable attention in urban sociology, urban planning creates the administrative frameworks through which conflicts are fought out. This sociolegal dimension is a much less common subject in the literature. The rubric of the planning system and its ideological discourse mediate between people and officialdom in conflicts over land use, and this establishes limits to action and debate. Conflict arises from the competing claims made on land in particular places, such as those made by developers seeking profit, public bodies seeking to meet needs, home owners seeking to safeguard their amenity, or conservation groups seeking to protect the countryside.

The planning inquiry is a means of managing such conflict, and once channelled into an inquiry conflict is highly regulated in a way that defines arguments and evidence as legitimate or illegitimate, relevant or irrelevant. This is achieved by the different parties classifying, framing and examining knowledge and information in what amounts to a *public inquiry discourse*. This discourse is supposed to enable an independent inspector to identify 'the public interest'. This is a deeply problematic task because increasingly inquiries have become contests between competing versions of this 'interest'.

The purpose of this chapter is to use a sociolegal study of public inquiries to draw out the underlying tension between social values and a technical planning system by showing the ways in which the system has suppressed social questions. Together with chapter 1, it completes the policy backcloth to the Belfast case study presented in subsequent chapters.

The public inquiry: rules of the game

The British planning system is essentially a system for licensing the use of land. An applicant refused permission by the local planning authority to develop or change the use of land may have an appeal to the Secretary of State heard by a planning inspector. The draft plans upon which decisions to licence land uses are based, and the applications themselves, may be examined in a public inquiry if the government considers such a procedure is called for before a final decision is made.

Today, the basic legitimation for public inquiries is that they are fair; as Wraith and Lamb write, their purpose is 'to give relief to anyone who may consider himself aggrieved and on the other hand to assist a Minister to come to the best possible administrative decision' (quoted in Purdue, Young and Rowan-Robinson, 1989, p. 522). Inquiry procedures in England are governed by delegated legislation and judge made rules of the common law and administrative guidelines contained in circulars issued by the Department of the Environment. However, inquiry inspectors always have some discretion in how the proceedings are conducted. In Northern Ireland there are no written adminstrative guidelines, although English practice is followed by convention.

Public inquiries are used in planning to hear representations, usually objections, made about planning applications and draft development plans (in England, the 1968 Town and Country Planning Act replaced public inquiries with an 'examination in public' for county structure plans, and this procedure has some important differences compared with conventional public inquries; these are discussed later in the chapter). The Secretary of State for the Environment has a degree of discretion about when to apply the public inquiry procedure (see Purdue *et al*, 1989, pp. 523-524). Major planning inquiries entail a decision by the Secretary of State, while more minor issues are decided by the inspectorate. Major planning inquiries, such as the Belfast Urban Area Plan inquiry, will often last many weeks. They are few in number compared with appeals against refusals of planning permission, although it is often argued they should be more common (Le-Las, 1987). They can be avoided by the Secretary of State not 'calling in' major planning applications, leaving the decisions to the local planning authority. Governments have been reluctant to use this call-in power. They can also be avoided by the use of parliamentary bills to promote either developers' or public sector schemes.

Planning inquiries are quasijudicial in that they are adversarial and the procedures are quite formal. The inspector, however, has an investigatory role and there are no judicial rules of evidence and procedure. The basic aim is to allow all parties to put their case and to answer all significant points made against them. The inspector is appointed by the Secretary of State, together with any technical assessors; they are named and all parties must be informed of the matter on which a particular technical assessor is advising the inspector.

Before the inquiry, information is exchanged, the principal issues identified and a timetable organised. Parties who have made representations to the local planning authority within a specified time period following the advertisement of the planning application or draft plan are entitled to appear, together with those with an interest in the land affected. In practice, the inspector will normally grant permission to appear to anyone who so requests. Participants may appear in their own right or represented by someone else, usually counsel or a solicitor.

While in the past the procedure in England was that only the local planning authority was required to serve a 'statement of case' before the inquiry started, since 1988 an applicant for planning permission has been required to serve such a statement, and other parties may also be required to do so. This statement has to contain full details of the case which a person proposes to make at the inquiry, and a list of any documents to be used as supporting evidence. Written material may be accepted by the inspector during the inquiry provided it is disclosed to participants.

At the inquiry, it is normal practice for the applicant or authority responsible for a draft plan to present their case first and to have the final say. The inspector decides the order in which other people are heard. Other parties may call evidence but are not *entitled* to cross examine the applicant or planning authority unless permitted by the inspector to do so. Entitlement to cross examine witnesses is limited to the applicant, the planning authority and those with an interest in land which is affected by proposals. But it is very unusual for any party to be refused a request to cross examine a witness unless this is considered by the inspector to be irrelevant or repetitious.

Irrelevant cross examination includes the merits of government policies, which are beyond the scope of a public inquiry. This can often cause public frustration when these policies are central to the issue, not least in the case of BUAP inquiry. The inquiry can, however, consider whether government policy should be applied in a particular case or in a particular locality. This remains a contentious area.

During the 1970s a number of major road inquiries, including the inquiry into the Belfast Urban Motorway discussed in chapter 3, were disrupted by protests about the inadequacies of public inquiry procedures to support fair debate which included the merits of government policy. In major inquiries objectors may address all matters relevant to whether national policy should be departed from in their locality (see Purdue *et al*, 1989, pp 560-561). However, the Town and Country Planning Association, among others, has argued strongly that the adversarial, and therefore often confrontational, nature of public inquiry conduct is not conducive to finding the best solution to a major planning issue (Armstrong,

1985). Even where a more investigative approach is adopted, as happened at the Sizewell B nuclear reactor inquiry, inquiry procedure comes under strain:

> ... the institution of the inquiry can combine an adverarial with an inquisitorial/investigatory approach. At Sizewell B Sir Frank Layfield QC the inspector appointed his own counsel, commissioned research, invited independent witnesses and caused the appointment of technical assessors. However, this approach undoubtedly helped to increase the length and expense of the inquiry which ran for 336 working days ... and which cost the CEGB (Central Electricity Generating Board) at least £15 million. The Sizewell B inquiry was a very special inquiry but the increasing length of major inquiries is of concern to both developers (whose projects are dealyed and to objectors (who cannot afford fully to take part). The underlying problem is that an institution set up to deal with local site-specific problems is being asked to cope with major investigations of policy. (Purdue *et al*, 1989, pp. 561-562)

This problem was acknowleged in the late 1960s with legislation for a new institution, the Planning Inquiry Commission, but this has never been used. Instead, public inquiry procedure has been revised in an attempt to tackle some of the problems posed by major inquiries. In 1988 a new set of Secretary of State rules were introduced for inquiries in England and Wales (SI 1988, No. 944 (Inquiries Procedure) Rules 1988 and SI 1988, No. 945 Appeals (Determination by Inspectors) (Inquiries Procedure) Rules 1988; see also Department of the Environment Circular 10/88). Of relevance to major inquiries are:

1.   The provision for a pre inquiry meeting, which when held has the following consequences:

> i.   The local planning authority and an applicant for planning permission must serve on each other and the Secretary of State an outline statement of case not later than eight weeks from announcement of an inquiry;
> ii.   Other people who have informed the Secretary of State they wish to appear at the inquiry may be required to produce an outline statement of case within four weeks.
> iii.   The Secretary of State must issue a statement of what he/she believes to be the relevant issues, and this effectively defines the expected scope of the inquiry.

2.   DoE Circular 10/88 contains a non statutory Code of Practice for major public inquiries. Inquiry participants will be categorised as a basis for organising the inquiry, informal meetings are

suggested as a way of getting agreement on technical matters, and the inspector may draw up for circulation a statement of generally agreed facts and matters still in dispute. An investigatory role for the inspector is recognised, such as calling his/her own expert witnesses.

Public inquiries raise awkward questions about the objectivity of participants, and there are no strict rules of evidence as in court. A rather unrealistic distinction is made between 'experts' and 'advocates'. This is expressed in a comment by David Widdicombe QC sitting as a deputy judge in *Multi Media Productions Ltd v Secretary of State for the Environment*:

> while there is no rule against someone combining the role of advocate and expert witness at an inquiry, it is generally speaking an undesirable practice. That is why local planning authorities are not represented at inquiries by planning officers. An expert witness should be trying to give his time and unbiased professional opinion to assist the inspector. An advocate is trying to argue the best case he can for his client. Someone who combines these conflicting roles must not be surprised if an inspector or a court approaches his evidence with a degree of caution. (quoted in Purdue *et al*, 1989, pp. 541-542)

Yet, in *Wholesale Mail Order Supplies Ltd v Secretary of State for the Environment*, Lord Widgery CJ stated, 'it is a complete misconception to take the view that matters of professional opinion, in planning in particular, require the sort of factual support in evidence which is required in proving the existence of a criminal case' (quoted in Purdue *et al*, pp. 548-549). Conflict between professional opinion and public opinion, with often no means of demonstrating factually the merits of one against the other, is a fundamental problem for public inquiries, and a cause of objectors sometimes calling for local referenda (which have no status in planning law).

Most inquiries are decided by the inspector, but in the case of major inquiries the inspector makes a report with conclusions and recommendations to the Secretary of State, who makes the decision. In the latter case, reasons must be stated for any disagreement with the inspector.

The Secretary of State and, where the case has been transferred to them, inspectors have the power to order payment of costs incurred by parties to the inquiry. This is very unusual in planning inquiries. It normally occurs when one party has acted unreasonably, e.g. no evidence is produced to substantiate a refusal of planning permission, in which case the appellant's costs will be awarded against the local planning authority. Unreasonableness in these circumstances would also include refusal solely based on local opposition to the planning application. It is

29

exceptional for third parties to be awarded costs, in favour or against.

The public inquiry: instrument of control or participation?

The classification and framing of public inquiry knowledge and information are a common cause of feelings of 'unfairness' among many lay participants at public inquiries. Rodger (1985) discusses how agendas are set by public bodies and developers fielding expert witnesses who insist on talking only to their specific briefs. Cross examination can be deployed against witnesses by counsel at inquiries to bias the discourse. Stocks (1989) observes, in a passage about objections to out of town shopping centres at the 1987-88 Greater Manchester shopping inquiry, that withholding or cutting short cross examination appears to be used as a device to lessen the significance of objectors' points. He writes:

> ... witnesses who may have valuable experience to offer make less impact on the proceedings (thought not perhaps to the Inspector) if they are deprived of the opportunity to defend and amplify their evidence in cross examination. In the Greater Manchester Inquiry, the Bishop of Manchester and academic witnesses flown in from the USA, all offering evidence against out of town centres, found their arguments muffled by an apparent conspiracy among counsel to withhold or cut short cross examination. (p. 68)

As Purdue *et al* (1989) comment, 'Whilst the adversarial process has advantages in terms of the thorough testing of evidence, the inquiry is in effect a confrontation between parties who are likely to be more concerned with defending their position than with determining where the public interest lies' (p. 561). Similarly, Purdue *et al* observe, '... inequality between the parties in matters of access to information, expertise and funding may result in an unequal contribution to the inquiry. This will not only be seen as being unfair but may be inefficient if the inspector is not provided with the best available evidence upon which to advise the Minister' (p. 561). Both of these observations are echoes of the underlying Weberian concept of bureaucracy: a legal/administrative system with rules legitimised as fair, impartial and rational (Albrow, 1970). Indeed, the reason for the inception in 1909 of the British Housing and Planning Inspectorate was in the first place to recommend where the balance between public interest and private property should lie, with the public interest defined by the state or 'officialdom' (McAuslan, 1980).

Planning inquiries originated during the second half of the nineteenth century to enable land use conflicts to be resolved without recourse to private bills, which were overburdening parliament. Industrial capitalists were coming into conflict with landowners opposing plans for new utilities across their land, which proliferated as Britain industrialised. The new entrepreneurs argued that these schemes would benefit the community as well as their own pockets, and promoted private bills to override the legal protections private property enjoyed. Faced with so many bills, parliament delegated many of its powers to ministers or to local government with a right of appeal to ministers. Inspectors were employed to hear objections in the locality and to report to the minister. Nowadays most decisions are delegated to inspectors.

Inquiries are an intervention in the 'bundle of rights' which comprises private property. This inevitably meant that they were run along similar lines to courts. But this legalism has not meant that in ideology public inquiries reflect the judiciary's concern with property rights; they in fact reflect the ideology of bureaucratic rationality theorised by Weber (1946, 1949). Inquiry inspectors have evoked the public interest against either private property or public opinion. However, unlike courts of law, the opinions of non expert witnesses are admissible evidence, 'rights of audience' extend to all participants, and almost always all parties pay their own costs.

Public participation in planning inquiries is a relatively recent phenomenon. It stems, essentially by default, from the original necessary participation of property owners in establishing the balance between private and public interests. Indeed planning appeals, whereby the developer appeals to the Secretary of State against a local authority's refusal of planning permission, are more common than public inquiries and exclude third parties (those without any direct property interest). It was the Franks report (1957) on administrative tribunals and inquiries that unwittingly initiated an opportunity for the public as 'third parties' to participate in public inquiries examining proposals for the use or development of land. McAuslan (1980, p. 6) writes that the Franks committee

> ... were concerned to redress the balance between the ideology of public interest, which was considered to have become too dominant , and that of private property. But a call for openness, fairness and impartiality (the Committee's formulation of the attributes of good administration) cannot be confined to openness, fairness and impartiality for the land owner but not for the rest of society so that changes in law and practice which came about as a result of the Franks Report have provided, unwittingly, for this was not their purpose, some of the legal and administrative underpinnings for the growth of participation since then.

The increase in third party participation which occurred after the Franks report overloaded the system. The most notable case was the Greater London Development Plan, approved in 1976, which generated 28,000 objections that took two and a half years to hear. McAuslan (1980) comments that given the implications of the plan this number of objections was surprisingly low! Yet it caused a review of inquiry procedure. The result was the introduction of the Examination in Public (EIP) of draft county structure plans. The EIP retains third party participation but removes the public right of participation; the Secretary of State invites only parties deemed to be 'relevant'.

Recently, the private bill procedure has enjoyed a renaissance as an alternative to facing a public inquiry. A private bill leads to a private act which benefits a particular interest such as a company or local authority. Parliament is petitioned for an enactment, while objectors petition against it. The biggest group of private bills are for development projects. Like planning applications, private bills are publicised to bring them to the notice of those capable of being affected. British Rail has been at the forefront of this return to the private bill route to promote urban development. As well as the Heathrow Express rail line proposal in London and other BR projects, recent schemes promoted by private bills have included the River Tees and Cardiff Bay barrages, 'supertram' systems in Manchester, Sheffield and Southampton, and a clutch of urban waterfront developments. The procedure avoids public inquiries and the environmental impact assessments now required of many big projects by European Community Directive 85/337. Its recent prominence reflects the scale of UK land use restructuring during the past decade, also manifest in the more than doubling of developers' planning appeals between 1983 and 1988. But so many bills have been introduced that events have turned full circle back to the nineteenth century situation of private bills overburdening parliament (*The Guardian*, 17 November 1989). As a result, BR has urged bills to be promoted by the government, which would ensure a less risky passage through parliament (*The Financial Times*, 12 January 1990).

Whilst the promotion of urban development by private bills has been criticised for not permitting consideration of the full impact of major proposals, it does offer bodies such as protest groups direct access to the parliamentary decision making process rather than just to officials as with public inquiries. Munt (1989), a planning/transport researcher with the Docklands Forum in London, comments that this has distinct advantages for public participation:

> New rail proposals are unusual in that they are secured through private parliamentary Bills. While of late this procedure has come under heavy criticism, unlike planning and compulsory purchase order inquiries, it does offer local organisations *direct access to the parliamentary decision-making process*. Anyone is entitled to petition a Bill *if they are able to prove that their interests will be affected by it* ... while at the same time avoiding the costly implications of

engaging counsel. (p. 243) (emphasis added)

The relative success of petitioning in this example appears to have had a lot to do with the 'common front' between local authorities and community organizations with *locus standi*. For petitioners to have *locus standi* they must have or represent interests that are directly affected, in contrast to public inquiries where it is convention that anyone can participate and have their say. The same claims to rationality, fairness and impartiality which mark public inquiry ideology are also present in this parliamentary procedure. However, objectors' arguments are not reported at length as in public inquiry reports, and only brief reasons are given for decisions on petitions, although parliamentary committees make an immediate decision (in contrast to the delay of many months which can follow inquiries). Members of parliament with any local or other interest in the bill may not sit on the committees, which are equally balanced between the two principal political parties. As with inquiries, the ideology is one of an apolitical and superordinate public interest.

Especially given the UK's highly centralised state, there are obvious limits to how much time MPs can spend examining arguments for and against big development schemes compared with professional public inquiry inspectors. And while private bills may offer people direct access to parliamentary decision making, the procedure is not democratic. The bills have to pass through both houses of parliament and if a bill fails in the unelected House of Lords it cannot pass into law.

Even so, the undemocratic private bill procedure is viewed by some as a better, if imperfect, instrument by which the citizen can have his or her say. Yet despite Munt's comments about avoiding the cost of hiring counsel, the problem of accessing specialist help to support cases is common both to petitioning private bills and public inquiries. Indeed, this has often become such an issue that the principle of the importance in themselves of the views of lay people has been lost amid arguments about technical back up and access to advocates and experts. Public inquiries are, however, run rather like courts of law, and in an adversarial situation with cross examination the inability of many lay people and community groups to employ specialist advocates, usually barristers, is a particular bone of contention. One of the most thorough critical studies in this respect is Armstrong's (1985) analysis of the Sizewell inquiry.

Milne (1989), though, sees the opportunity to cross examine to be a positive feature of inquiries from the layperson's perspective. He writes that the long running inquiry into the Hinkley C nuclear power station in Somerset was the subject of a fact finding visit by a Soviet delegation from the Ministry of Nuclear Energy, investigating the possible role of public hearings in managing growing domestic unease about nuclear power. In reporting the visit and arguing in favour of public inquiries, he commented that the opportunity for the public to interrogate officials particularly impressed the Soviet party, and concluded:

> ... the British public inquiry has its critics. Many perceive it as a tremendous waste of time and energy, an exercise in window dressing for projects which will inevitably go ahead. Such a view is understandable. But it is not the whole story. Those who dismiss the procedure as either quaint British custom or a monument to boredom are missing the point. Public inquiries provide a unique opportunity for the public, whether individually or as part of a concerned group, to air their views and question their 'betters'. In person. Directly. (p. 60)

Despite these opportunities, which many lay people find too intimidating to use, inquiries serve only to report facts, opinions and recommendations to ministers, who make the final decision or delegate to civil servants. This arrangement is based on the idea that land use is controlled at the local level by special interests, and that only an independent authority at a higher level can regulate the use of land in the public interest and stand apart from special interests. In the 1980s, the government was often accused of using public inquiries and planning appeals to impose on localities policies about which there had been no public consultation. Successive decisions displayed coherent government positions, and this happened in the absence of any strategic planning statements made after opportunities for public comment on the strategies. Inevitably the situation has been seen as part of the general extension of the exercise of central power outside public scrutiny which has been a feature of Thatcherism (Hansard, 1989a, pp. 76-117).

An exception is public inquiries into local land use plans where the inspector reports to the district council which drafted the plan. But such plans are far from the principle of policy statements made by autonomous district councils constrained by participative local electorates. They have to be prepared within the strategic policy framework of county structure plans, which have to be approved by the Secretary of State at central government level. The government is now proposing to drop the need for this approval, but is narrowing the scope of county planning down to an essentially coordinating rather than policy making role (Secretary of State for the Environment, 1989). This weakening of strategic development planning seems set to cause protracted local public inquiries and legal disputes in the absence of any clear strategic guidance as to the 'public interest' (Gwilliam, 1989). If this happens, the involvement of the courts is likely to see a strengthening of the ideology of private property and a weakening of ideologies of either public interest or public participation.

If the accusation has not been that big public inquiries have been used to make policy through the back door, then it has often been that they are pointless processes because government policy is already established and will inevitably determine the outcome of the hearings. This, for example, was the reason why Greenpeace boycotted the inquiry into a pressurised water nuclear reactor at Sizewell; in their view prior government announcements and commitments made the decision a *fait accompli*. Nevertheless, inquiry inspectors have often interpreted their brief liberally to permit debate on the wider public interest. This contrasts with the private bill procedure where if a bill has passed the second reading stage it is not possible to petition on the policy involved.

The public interest in practice

Given that 'public interest' is an ideological concept, how is it employed by inquiry inspectors? Ideas that planning decisions should be determined on the basis of either local referenda or the market have been firmly rejected, so that what is left is often largely professional opinion about what is right in the circumstances. Two examples from inquiry reports by Northern Ireland's Planning Appeals Commission - a body similar to the English Planning Inspectorate but independent of the Department of the Environment (NI) - illustrate this (Planning Appeals Commission 1989; 1989a). The first (1989a, p. 37) relates to a planning application for new private flats in an old quarter of a seaside town:

> One of the arguments put forward by many of the objectors was that planning decisions should reflect the views of local people and given the strong opposition in the neighbourhood this proposal should be rejected ... However, this concept of planning by referendum does not entirely commend itself since the motivation of objectors is an important consideration and the crucial test of the acceptability of a planning application is whether or not the proposed development would do harm to interests of acknowledged importance.

Thus, decisions are made with reference to 'interests of acknowledged importance'. The public's views are of relevance only if they are founded upon valid 'planning reasons'. This is not, however, a question of simply consulting the appropriate planning policy guidance note. Questions of amenity or the weight to be attached to different factors entail subjective decisions. In the United Kingdom the resolution of such issues is achieved through decisions being taken by an authority external to the people directly affected and legitimised as fair because they are based on professional opinion. So far, this approach seems to have largely remained insulated from the challenges against such professional closure by community architecture and planning aid (Blackman

1987). The motives of people who are directly affected by a proposed development are regarded as suspect, while the motives of speculative developers are regarded as valid and are generally not open to examination. In the above example, what particularly angered objectors was the behaviour of a speculative developer who stated at the inquiry that he acquired the site to build apartments because it 'suited his pocket'. This motive was not of course questioned by the inspector; yet self interest on the part of the objectors was at least implied as the reason why a referendum was not acceptable.

In fact, an underlying social issue was at the heart of the dispute; one which Mellor (1989) conceptualises very well as a perceived 'invasion' of family housing neighbourhoods by 'afamilial' apartments whose occupants' prime identifications may be non local. In terms of financial motive, neighbouring objectors would actually have gained by converting their houses to apartments and selling up. Although clearly if a need is demonstrated development has to go somewhere, in a case like this where there was no strategic statement made at an appropriate decision making scale, the inspector could only apply his professional judgement to the site specific case. Professional opinion did not extend to sensitivities about ties to place and community.

The same 'objectivity' is evident in the second example (PAC, 1989, pp. 128-129). Here neither the market nor a 'special case' argument were accepted by the commissioners as bases for making a decision. The case relates to an objection at the BUAP inquiry which argued for an additional housing zoning in Belfast's green belt. The commissioners commented:

> ... we would acknowledge the popularity of Drumbeg as a location in which to live and it is certain that such homes as might be built would find a ready market. However, given its location at a sensitive point where the Lagan Valley Regional Park merges with open countryside, we are persuaded that a demand or market led approach is inappropriate and that the wider public interest is best served by a policy of constraint ... The detailed submission of Ostick and Williams relies heavily on creating a development which would provide, in large part, specifically for the requirements of the active elderly and the benefits which would accrue from non-institutional provision for this increasing sector of the population ... (But) one must question, on grounds of equality or fairness, whether the active elderly should in a sense be privileged in that homes for their occupation should be permitted in locations where homes for other sectors of the population would be refused.

The second point, that planning cannot favour one particular social group, reflects successive governments' conception of planning that, ' ... the purpose of the planning system is to regulate the development and use of land in the public interest. It is not to protect the private interests of one person against the activities of another' (Hansard 1989b, p. 583). This view was used to justify the government's rejection of a recommendation by the House of Commons Environment Committee in 1986 that funding should be available to support the participation of third parties at big public inquiries. The government decided that such funding would be inappropriate because objectors were concerned with defending their own interests and not with arguing for alternative public interests (House of Commons, 1986). As noted above, the adversarial process and cross examination structure public inquiry discourse on the assumption that sectional interests will be defending their positions. This does not facilitate open debate about alternative conceptions of the public interest.

How is the public interest defined when the situation is perceived as one of many sectional and often conflicting interests, and a supply of land that is fixed in space? In fact, the public interest is actually a combination of government policy and the ethos of ministerial rhetoric, as we shall see below. Sometimes it is framed more directly; despite claims that inquiry inspectors are not briefed by the government, Home (1985) reports objectors revealing such a briefing at the 1982 Coin Street inquiry in London by exercising their right to see all material before the inspector.

The antinomies of public interest ideology

The situation in planning inquiries where decisions are justified with reference to the public interest, as defined by officialdom, contrasts with public local inquiries into compulsory purchase orders, held under housing legislation. Since 1981 the people directly affected by these orders frequently have a deciding say. If house owners declare at the inquiry that they are willing to improve unfit dwellings the Department of the Environment is unlikely to confirm orders made by local authorities to remove such dwellings from the housing stock (Department of the Environment, 1981a). At the time, the Institution of Environmental Health Officers (1981, pp 9-10) commented that, 'This policy is regrettable as it inhibits the ability of a local authority to deal with substandard houses ... There have already been a number of unfortunate examples where orders have not been confirmed despite recognition that the properties were unfit'. Thus, in 1976 (when wholesale clearance was already being abandoned in British housing policy) an inspector could justify the demolition of unfit pre 1919 housing stock by stating that, ... achievement of the Council's proposals far outweight the personal difficulties and considerations raised by the objectors (Department of the Environment). In 1980 a new Housing Act introduced a new grants system intended to promote retention of as much of the pre 1919 private housing stock as possible. By

1981 housing of a similar age, type, condition and location was reprieved from the council bulldozer by an inspector who cited 'a strong local wish that the houses should be improved' (Department of the Environment, 1981b).

These statements reflect an ideological process whereby what were previously classed as slums become potential ideal family dwellings, a process which has been clearly associated with the availability of public funds for council housebuilding (Moore, 1987). Furthermore, what now appears to be a contradiction between the treatment of local views in relation to conceptions of the 'public interest' at planning inquiries and CPO inquiries is not actually so. It reflects a consistent government policy to expand the market in property (or recommodify) by both protecting owner occupied housing from its replacement by council housing and denying the subordination of private property rights to collective values, other than to the necessary authority of public bodies.

Wraith and Lamb (1971) take the view that public inquiry inspectors ensure consistency across the country in the application of policy by numerous local authorities. However, much is made of the political independence of inspectors, who do not regard themselves as agents of central government but as officials who, at their discretion, identify the public interest to advise government ministers. Their position is indicated in a statement by commissioners at the recent Belfast Urban Area Plan inquiry. In response to objectors' claims that the Plan was basically imposing Thatcherism on Belfast, the commissioners stated:

> It seems understandable to us that whatever political and economic theories can be discerned in the Plan, these would reflect Government thinking of the day, and while such matters are outside the remit of the Commission, we are satisfied that such is the inherent flexibility of the Belfast Urban Area Plan that whatever the outcome of the Inquiry, the essential strategic framework will not inhibit the inevitable changes in public attitudes which will take place as Belfast approaches the third millennium. (Planning Appeals Commission, 1989, pp. 12-13)

Not only is the content of the framework largely dismissed in this statement, but the framework itself is presented as apolitical, rational and impartial. The inspectors' decision about what is fair and rational is then communicated to the minister; and the real political world is reentered. Under Thatcher administrations during the 1980s public power concentrated in the hands of ministers. During the 1970s the recommendations of the Northern Ireland Planning Appeals Commission were overturned in only one very minor case by a minister. It seemed to be convention that ministers should accept the Commission's judgement. But in 1983 a recommendation that a planning application for 500 houses in

Belfast's green belt at Cairnshill should not receive permission was overturned by a ministerial decision (Singleton, 1983). The decision followed an announcement in 1982 that the minister was inviting development proposals for a number of green belt sites. The Cairnshill application followed, and a public inquiry was held. The Commission took the view that *need* for further housing beyond the development limit had not been established. An attempt to quosh the minister's decision to contradict the recommendation of the commissioners failed in the High Court. The judgement stated that:

> It must always be remembered that a planning decision is a decision on a policy, which involves consideration of what is the best action to take, therefore a person or body, while acting on good faith, could reach a different decision on the same facts from another person or body. The applicant could not succeed therefore on the ground of unreasonableness. (*Bulletin of Northern Ireland Law*, 1986, p. 89)

In other words, we are dealing with rhetoric; whatever is claimed from the 'facts' is contestable, a situation which is the life blood of public inquiries and many other institutions! (Rydin and Myerson, 1989). In adjudicating between competing claims the judiciary accepts that of the highest authority, in this case the minister, and such interpretations then become an ethos. Critics of the minister's assessment of the 'facts' argued that he was asserting *demand* for housing over the *need* for a green belt. This was denied, but the ethos of the decision was that there should be no distinction between demand and need. In 1985 the Commission itself upheld an appeal on this ground. A private developer had been refused permission for a housing development in a small village because a planning statement for the area referred to the undesirability of speculative development and required evidence of need. An application by the public housing authority, however, was 'receiving consideration'. The Commission argued that the planning statement:

> ... lay uneasily with the Ministerial statement of August 1981 which sought to encourage the private house builder. Moreover, permission should relate to the land and not to the applicant and a refusal of permission to a private developer followed by a grant of permission to a public authority would be improper. (*Bulletin of Northern Ireland Law* 1985, p. 96)

The tension between social values and planning

An interesting attempt to employ planning as a vehicle of collective decision making about the future of a city was the process undertaken by Sheffield City Council to examine its City Centre

Plan (Alty and Darke, 1987). The council encouraged the presentation of collective views on the plan, and serviced twelve advisory groups to represent different interests, with socially disadvantaged sections of the population strongly represented. Instead of an open public inquiry format, each advisory group presented its views at an informal meeting with a small panel of councillors, and at a final Saturday morning meeting of all the groups councillors made their response, followed by a short debate.

Alty and Darke (1987, p. 12) comment that any scepticism about the point of participating in the plan was overcome by being able to put cases directly to key councillors. But even this process seemed too formal for some groups, such as the unemployed and young people, and they suggest a need for community development which echoes aspects of the Skeffington Report (1969) on public participation in planning. Their observation that some councillors and officers in Sheffield questioned the representativeness of the advisory groups also reflects the tension between 'community forums' and local councils which Skeffington acknowledged (but did not address satisfactorily).

Sheffield attempted to use the City Centre Plan as a participative vehicle of bottom up planning that would inform activities across the council's programmes. However, while this might be an improvement in the methods and techniques of participation, the planning system itself is far from capable of accommodating public views. What it can accommodate is tightly constrained by convention, legislation, government guidance and planning case law. Many community groups have embarked on participation exercises in planning with the objective of winning, for example, social facilities or even jobs, only to find that planning's negative controls are not matched by positive planning instruments or the money to use such instruments. This is of course the fundamental weakness of British planning, especially since the demise of both the taxation of increases in land values and large public investment programmes (Reade, 1987).

Public participation is often about social strategies - policies of positive discrimination or community development for example - yet it is debatable how far social strategies could defend subsequent local planning decisions. There is very little statutory guidance on the goals of the planning system. Schedule 1 of the Town and Country Planning (Structure and Local Plans) Regulations suggests a very wide range of topics from employment to social services to which plans should 'relate'. Plans are implemented through the negative powers of development control, under which the vast majority of built development and changes in the use of land and buildings require planning permission. But development control decisions must also have regard to other 'material considerations' as well as the development plan for an area (Section 29, Town and Country Planning Act 1971). Loughlin (1980) cites a judgement by Lord Denning in *Esdell Caravan Parks Ltd v Hemel Hempstead RDC* as the most significant court case in the confused legal area of the scope of town planning. This indicated that planning considerations could include the capacity of the sewerage system, the capacity of schools, traffic, shopping difficulties, amenity considerations and the effect of a development on the social balance of a community. Being able to control land use would on this basis seem to confer considerable, albeit negative, social planning powers on local authorities. Loughlin (1980, p. 176) concludes:

> The LPA (local planning authority), therefore, is not directly concerned with private cost-benefit analysis but instead weighs the social costs of development against any social benefits which may arise from that development in reaching its decision. These social costs and benefits are assessed in terms of housing, employment, education, etc.

We are considering here situations where local authorities are deciding whether or not to licence land uses according to wider social factors, rather than promoting land uses themselves for social purposes, such as schools and parks. These situations are likely to become critical with the effects of the uniform business rate on local authorities. For example, Leopold (1989) suggests that the massive King's Cross Railway Lands development in London may leave the local council out of pocket rather than, as would have been the case under the old rating system, boosting its local tax revenue. This new scenario is likely to intensify the question of Section 52 planning agreements whereby local authorities 'trade' planning permission for contributions to physical or social infrastructure by the developer, already prominent due to a decade of major cutbacks in local government capital spending. These scenarios intensify the need for planners to analyse the redistributive effects of new plans and planning applications, and to ensure that negotiations with developers have a strong financial and social content.

The courts, however, have used the ground of unreasonableness to limit how far town planning can become social planning. This has been achieved by establishing as unreasonable a local authority using the *regulatory* power of development control to achieve an *ulterior object* not related to the development in question. An example is imposing a condition on the grant of planning permission to a private developer for housing to secure access for applicants on the authority's housing waiting list, when the housing acts offer the appropriate means for seeking this object (Loughlin 1980). In other words, positive goals require the exercise of positive powers. Similarly, in Northern Ireland the Planning Appeals Commission upheld an appeal by an applicant seeking a change of use to bed sitting accommodation because the planning service's main ground, that the intensity of use did not comply with housing legislation, was not a planning consideration (*Bulletin of Northern Ireland Law* 1983, p. 128). But even given existing planning legislation some leeway is available in the light of legal judgements which indicate that what is material in any given case depends on the circumstances. This appears to have been exploited in the case of attempts to manage the social and economic consequences of the proliferation of private residential and nursing homes in seaside towns (Phillips *et al*, 1987).

The achievevent of social goals through the planning system has frequently been frustrated by the argument that planning control relates solely to the use of land and not to tbe occupants or owners. For example, reference was made above to the Northern Ireland Planning Appeals Commission's view that development control decisions should not distinguish between private and public developers seeking the same land use, albeit different tenures. Ambiguity is introduced into this area by the common rural planning policy which restricts the occupancy of new houses granted planning permission in the countryside to people who can demonstrate a need to live there, such as farmers. At the recent Belfast Urban Area Plan inquiry the planning service defended the green belt in one location by referring to 'considerable development pressure unrelated to the needs of the local community', a statement never applied to urban neighbourhoods. The rationale for such policies seems to have been to protect rural amenity and character as a public good rather than to ensure that development meets local needs. Recently, however, the government has justified relaxing rural planning controls in order to encourage planning permissions in country areas for 'affordable housing', pointing out, though, that this does not constitute a fundamental shift in planning policy! (Howard, 1989).

It is clear that there are great limits to the achievement of social purposes through what is the UK's only comprehensive planning machinery, the town and country planning system, without clear statements of such purposes in legislation. At present, government ethos is that planning should address 'land issues' and not social and economic objectives. Indeed, a developer who appeals a refusal of planning permission on account of 'non land use matters' is likely to have costs awarded against him or her for unreasonable behaviour.

As Ambrose (1976) argues, the profit motive is the driving force behind the development and use of land. It is extremely difficult to resist this logic. There have been examples of 'people's plans' which attempt to do this. In London the Association of Waterloo Groups presented such a plan at the 88 day Coin Street inquiry in 1982. It countered a developer's large commercial scheme with proposals to tackle the '... continuing struggle to keep family life and local ties together against a background of the gradual withdrawal of the necessary shops, chemists, doctors and schools' (quoted in Home, 1985, p. 78). Such arguments have proven weak against both the ideology of wealth creation and claims that locations attractive to capital have 'metropolitan significance' beyond local

42

needs. Clearly, though, the openness of planning processes to social activism can be a problem for urban management, and it is salutary to note that following Coin Street another South Bank development at Hay's Wharf was approved by a government special development order, denying any right to object or a public inquiry.

Even in day to day development control the question of a return on investment is appearing as a planning consideration. A Planning Appeals Commission consideration in 1988 held an appeal against a refusal of permission for a change of use from a dwelling to offices in a conservation area because the alternative, flats, was not a 'realistic economic use' (*Bulletin of Northern Ireland Law* 1988, p. 155). Yet still the ideology of public interest reigns over public inquiries and the operation of the planning system in general. The use of land, without which no social or economic activity is possible, is governed by some of the strongest powers of licensing available to the state, but when the ideological veil is removed we find a system that is an adjunct to the market. While markets may be indispensable, what is of concern is that, to quote the Department of the Environment (NI) on the BUAP, it is not the purpose of planning 'to deal with the social, economic and other aspects involved' (1989, p. 2). To deal with these aspects would threaten the ideology of public interest and consensus which pervades planning (Flynn, 1981).

Whilst marxist work in urban sociology has emphasised the crucial structural relations in the economy which generate inequality in the city, the urban location and allocation processes which have formed a focus for much non marxist and weberian work are of considerable intrinsic importance because these are areas of social action in civil society (see Byrne 1989). One such location/allocation process is the planning system. This chapter has considered how the planning inquiry, while open to social activism, falls far short of being an open, democratic means of resolving inevitable conflicts about land use. The problem lies partly in procedure, but more fundamentally in the legal underpinnings of the planning system which confine and redefine the basic political problems and conflicts which public participation brings into this arena. As a result, the scope of planning often does not extend to match public expectations about it as a means of deciding on the location and allocation of urban resources. The next three chapters turn to an examination of these issues as they worked out in planning Belfast.

3 People and planning in Belfast

The strategic planning of Belfast began in the 1960s, when the regional strategy of the Matthew Plan demanded the displacement of thousands of families in inner city redevelopment areas to new growth centres located within a thirty mile zone around the city (Matthew Report, 1963; Wiener, 1980). Much of the land released by this wholesale clearance of old working class housing areas was to be transformed into commercial property and roads.

Until the 1960s, Belfast Corporation was opposed to the redevelopment of inner city properties. This opposition reflected the class base of the ruling Unionist Party, with landlord and business interests resistant to expenditure from local property taxation. However, the escalating potential value and yields from inner urban land cleared of working class housing changed the basis of their economic calculations. A growing section of the Unionist Party was prepared to sell out to external capital. Wiener (1980, p. 43) observes that:

> These differences of interest reflected a split within the Orange system between those who stood to gain by the entry of new capital and those who stood to lose. It was in the former's interests to make an alliance with central government forces pushing for reform and it was this which explains why the two major planning teams for Belfast, Travers Morgan and Building Design Partnership came to be jointly appointed by both Belfast Corporation and the Ministry of Development.

44

The modernisers accepted that a precondition for attracting new industrial capital to Northern Ireland was investment in infrastructure and housing to assemble pools of labour in 'growth centres', most notably the new town of Craigavon (Blackman, 1987). But the appointment of the planning consultant Sir Robert Matthew, who had worked on a new town solution to Glasgow's urban growth problems, was also a move by the Stormont Government to defuse pressure from Belfast Corporation for the inclusion of large tracts of land within extended city boundaries to cope with housing land shortages (Oliver, 1978). Both political and economic ends would be served by adopting the Matthew Plan's strategy of containing Belfast within a development stopline and decentralising growth to new centres within the Protestant heartland of the Belfast region.

The appointment in 1965 of Travers Morgan & Partners (NI) to produce a transportation plan for Belfast marked the beginning of plans for Belfast's modernisation. The consultants developed major road proposals made back in 1946 by the Planning Commission, a body established to plan for post war reconstruction, but rejected at the time by the ruling Unionist Party. Travers Morgan proposed an elevated inner motorway ring, two ground level ring roads and the upgrading of three existing radial routes to dual carriageways. The system would link the city to the Matthew Plan's growth centres in the Belfast region.

After the Second World War, policy discrimination in favour of road vehicles saw the decline of public transport services in Northern Ireland. During the 1960s there were cuts in services and steep fare rises. Post war redevelopment dispersed local populations, but the provision of employment, shops, leisure and community facilities was centralised. Travers Morgan noted these trends and projected a trebling of the number of cars in the Belfast area between 1966 and 1983. Inner urban houses had to be cleared to make way for roads, their occupants rehoused in the growth centres or in blocks of flats and maisonettes in the city. The people bearing the brunt of the road schemes were those least likely to benefit from them as only a minority of inner city working class households owned cars (Wiener, 1980).

To complement the transportation plan, Building Design Partnership was appointed to make a development plan for Belfast. Their proposals were adopted by the Belfast County Borough Council in 1969. But in 1972 - with Direct Rule introduced and legislation to bring planning into line with British practice - the Ministry of Development decided to hold a public inquiry into the plans. By this time much of the land for what became known as the Belfast Urban Motorway had been cleared. The inquiry, however, was considered necessary to hear the number of objections about the social and environmental costs of the motorway.

The inquiry inspector's report concluded that the cases of people affected by the roads did not outweigh 'the benefit of the community at large'. It recommended that land and funds should not be diverted from motorway building to housing construction and the improvement and subsidy of public transport (Rutherford Report, 1973).

Building was in fact delayed by threats from paramilitaries, but the affected areas remained blighted. In 1973 an ad hoc group of people associated with the Queen's University of Belfast formed the Belfast Urban Study Group which put together a researched case against the motorway and for a commitment to public transport.

The early 1970s were a time of growing grassroots mobilisation around civil rights and community action in Belfast. Matthew had advised of the need 'to give the community a bigger say in the physical shaping of the country' (Oliver, 1978, p. 84), but the grassroots demands for reform by civil rights activists precipitated a crisis that forced the British Government to remove decision making from the sectarianism of local politics. Beginning with public sector housing in 1969, local administration by elected councils was taken over by direct control from the centre - initially by Stormont and then under Direct Rule by Westminster. The violence and breakdown of state legitimacy in many areas encouraged the formation of hundreds of community groups which aspired to control what happened in their neighbourhoods, just as state power was delocalised.

Popular opposition to the motorway grew, this time bringing in a few Protestant groups that had initially supported the plans, as well as the Belfast Urban Study Group, the Republican Clubs and the Alliance Party. Unionist politicians, despite the fracturing of the Unionist bloc caused by the rise of the Vanguard and Democratic Unionist Parties at the time, were not against the motorway initially, although they voiced reservations. At the first full meeting of the new Belfast City Council at the end of 1973, however, the Unionists split in the face of the amount of working class protest, and a motion was carried asking Stormont to think again.

The Council, along with all of Northern Ireland's new post 1972 local councils, no longer had planning powers. Despite this, the Ministry adopted a strategy of personal persuasion, promises and delaying tactics to win the City Council round to the plans. Sandy Row and Hamill Street, where opposition was particularly strong, won locally significant changes. In July 1974 the Council voted in favour of a compromise finally proposed by the Ministry:

> the first leg of the motorway should go ahead (as well as a river crossing that no one objected to) while phases 2 and 3 would be postponed until the affects of phase 1 could be seen; some adjustments would be made to the line of roads, particularly as regards Sandy Row and full consideration would be given to how environmental factors could best be mitigated. (Wiener, 1980, p. 68)

By this time economic forces beyond the local situation in Belfast had radically changed the scenario. The UK's deteriorating economic position and the impact of oil price rises meant that the British Government could not afford both to build the motorway in Belfast and renew the housing stock. The latter was now seen as particularly important in relieving a major cause of civil unrest. A review of the whole transportation plan was announced. Meanwhile, community groups engaged the Northern Ireland Housing Executive in a series of struggles over redevelopment, displacement and plans for flats and maisonettes. These programmes too were wound down in the face of militant opposition and economic pressures which saw UK housing policy as a whole shift to the rehabilitation of older housing rather than its replacement. These major structural changes marked the end of a period of large scale modernisation (Blackman, 1987).

Travers Morgan were appointed to review their original strategy. The new factors which the review had to address were reduced central government spending compared with the growth of expenditure during the 1960s, inner city population decline, fewer jobs than had been forecast, much lower levels of car ownership than had been projected in the 1960s, and less travel by bus than had been expected. The consultants identified six possible strategies which were presented as interim findings in May 1975 to the City Council and other interested bodies, inviting comment within six weeks. Belfast City Council supported two of the strategies. In the event the Department selected three for further consideration by the consultants, one based on extensive road building, one on scaled down road building and improvements to public transport, and one on a mixed approach.

These alternatives were presented for public comment in the booklet, *Transport for Belfast: What are your Views?* Seven thousand copies were distributed to councillors, community groups and the general public. An exhibition was mounted from September 1976 until May 1977. The booklet and the exhibition were the subject of press releases in September. By setting out three alternative options the booklet presented definite choices for public consultation, but the text was essentially shallow with little detail.

All three proposals involved building roads. For the Department of the Environment the main issue was how transport spending should be shared between road building and bus services. Travers Morgan proposed that fares could be raised by 40-45 per cent in real terms over ten years in order to support operating costs entirely from this revenue, or raised by 20-25 per cent, or more extensively subsidised to keep fares in line with inflation (BDP and Travers Morgan & Partners, 1976). The first strategy would mean that 65.7 per cent of the transport budget would be spent on highways and 6.2 per cent on bus services, the second that 49 per cent would be spent on highways and 29.5 per cent on buses, and the third that 36 per cent would be spent on highways and 52.4 per cent on buses. All three strategies involved broadly similar spending on the rail system and management and environmental measures. The main means of restraining car commuting was to control parking.

The consultants carried out a cost benefit analysis of the strategies. They concluded that the benefits gained by bus users from either the second or third strategies were more than outweighed by the costs to private and commercial traffic. Thus the first strategy ranked top on economic merit in their calculations.

In 1972 planning in Northern Ireland had been broadly brought into line with Britain through the Planning (Northern Ireland) Order of that year. This implemented the rights to consultation, comment and objection contained in the British legislation. However, given that central government was the planning authority in Northern Ireland, it was necessary to establish a separate independent body, the Planning Appeals Commission, to conduct appeals and public inquiries. It was this body which held the public inquiry into the transport strategies of Travers Morgan.

The 1977 Belfast transportation inquiry: protest and planning

Only a very small minority of the public participated in the 1977 inquiry into the transportation strategies. The Department of the Environment stated at the inquiry that the public exhibition on the transportation review had been poorly attended, with no more than 200 people visiting it during its eight months, and most of these calling during the first few days. From October to December 1976 Belfast City Council had sought views on the strategies, inserting press advertisements inviting submissions. But among certain sections of the community the strategies sparked off considerable reaction. In an interview for this book conducted in August 1988, a senior planner reported that at the time the level of awareness about the plans among community groups was high, and that 'dozens and dozens' of meetings were attended with local redevelopment associations. Interviews with community workers active at the time suggest a low initial level of awareness, which was heightened by the disruptions which occurred at the public inquiry and the media coverage.

The consultants had published their report in December 1976. In April the following year a one day conference of community groups agreed the setting up of the Community Groups Action Committee on Transport (CGACT) to oppose road building. The CGACT had among its members professional community workers and a solicitor from Belfast Law Centre. An important background to this mobilisation was the disruption by protestors of a number of major road inquiries in Britain. A focus of the Belfast protest was the 'Westlink' motorway section which would cut a swathe through West Belfast. The Roads Service was seen to wield considerable power, able to blight areas for years by drawing road protection lines, and distorting planning with a roads mentality which marginalised housing, recreation and other needs.

This roads ideology conflicted with the inner city anti poverty initiatives being pursued by the British Government at the time, encapsulated in Belfast by the 1976 report, *Belfast Areas of Special Social Need* (Project Team, 1976). It was some of the areas targeted for extra social spending by this report which were threatened by the Department of the Environment's road plans. The road plans also threatened areas where recent government grants had helped rehabilitate the housing stock, notably the Hamill Street neighbourhood (which was in fact reprieved from its planned fate as a central distributor box).

Community groups were invited to send representatives to meetings and members of the CGACT visited committees of community groups likely to be affected by the strategies. But the CGACT was divided about how it should respond to the public inquiry. One section felt they should participate in it and accept the 'rules of the game', feeding local action about the planning proposals into the public inquiry. Another wanted to boycott it and organise protests against what they claimed was a sham. The former opinion seemed to prevail, with the argument that the April conference had elected the committee to organise community groups' submissions to the inquiry, and that the inquiry would provide a platform for local groups. The committee invited John Tyme, a well known British campaigner against road strategies, to join them in formulating opposition tactics, but Tyme's strategy was to criticise the whole inquiry process and call for a thoroughgoing consultation exercise.

The inquiry opened on 31 May 1977. The inspector was C M Lavery, QC, aided by two assessors. The community organisations which made objections at the inquiry were:

Hamill Street Residents' Association
Lower Falls Residents' Association
Lower Ormeau Road Community Association
Community Groups Action Committee on Transport (CGACT)
Bone and Ballybone Redevelopment Association
St Matthew's Tenants' Association
Turf Lodge Advice Centre
Churches Central Committee for Community Work
Save the Shankill Campaign
Greater West Belfast Community Association
Sandy Row Redevelopment Association
Tyndale Tenants' Association
North Belfast Community Resource Centre
North and West Belfast Federation of Tenants' Associations
Dundonald Community Committee
Whiterock Housing Action Group

49

On day 1 of the inquiry the Law Centre's solicitor, Francis Keenan, acting on behalf of the CGACT, set out their opposition to all three strategies and called for a fourth strategy to be drawn up in consultation with local communities and an adjournment of the inquiry. Opposed by the Department of the Environment, the adjournment was initially refused by the inspector. The decision was met with uproar in the hall and the inspector had to suspend the inquiry. Subsequent events are recorded in the inspector's report:

> After this I presided over two private meetings with representatives of the Department of the Environment and representatives of certain persons interested in the Inquiry ... As a result of these meetings I decided that the Inquiry should proceed on Wednesday 8 June at 11 am, with the hearing of the Department of the Environment's opening statement and evidence. After this part of the Inquiry was completed it was proposed that the Inquiry should adjourn for a minimum period of three months. This was subject to the hearing of other persons before the adjournment as they so wished. The Department of the Environment undertook not to engage in certain road schemes which might prejudice the outcome of the Inquiry until the Inquiry had reported. Mr. Kennan expressed himself satisfied with these arrangements. The demands made by other representatives that the Inquiry should appoint and finance what they called 'independent consultants who would genuinely consult public opinion' were not accepted. (Lavery Report, 1978, p. 5)

The inquiry resumed on the morning of 8 June. It emerged that Keenan, who had accepted to inspector's proposal, had had his instructions withdrawn by the CGACT and would now represent the Greater West Belfast Community Association, which was more involved in addressing local impacts of road proposals than the strategic issues. Disruption again forced another suspension. An attempt was made to resume the inquiry in the afternoon, including requiring those present in the hall to sign an undertaking that they would observe directions given by the inspector. But further unrest forced him to move the proceedings to a private room and relay the Department of the Environment's statement to the main hall. The protestors walked out.

The CGACT withdrew from the inquiry at this point, and organised a picket outside. The disruption stopped and the inquiry continued quietly on with the Department of the Environment presenting its case unchallenged by the CGACT. The action committee had wanted an immediate adjournment for at least six months to allow for public consultation and an independent firm of consultants to carry out the consultation exercise. They were refused an independent review and any financial assistance by the

Department of the Environment.

On day twenty four of the inquiry the Inspector heard renewed applications for an adjournment. Despite the DoE's objections, this was given for two months. The CGACT used the adjournment to administer a small scale questionnaire to gather information about conditions and needs in the inner city. The results were presented at the first day of the resumed inquiry in September 1977. Little credence was given to this evidence by the Department or the inspector because many of the interviewers were members of the action committee, the people interviewed would not have been informed commentators on transportation planning, and no attempt was made by the CGACT to translate the findings into a transport policy.

In contrast, a submission based on official statistics on social deprivation in the inner city won a favourable response from the inspector. This submission competently related these social data to planning policy. In his report, the inspector recommended that policy had to take full cognisance of these social needs, stating that, 'I certainly will give them the fullest weight in making my recommendations'. (p. 154). This appears in his reasoning as follows:

> I have been told that the people of Belfast need houses and not roads. The truth of the matter is that they need both ... One must be careful ... in attempting to ameliorate the lot of the less well off people in the short term, to avoid damaging their long term interests. It is in their long term interests, as I have pointed out, that the city should prosper ... It is in the inner city, however, that land is at its greatest premium and this area is more sensitive to environmental damage. Believing as I do that the forecasts for car ownership are too high and applying the criteria that I have set out earlier I consider that the proposals for this area can be scaled down significantly ... (Lavery Report, 1978, pp. 161, 163, 176).

A considerable amount of evidence was presented to the inquiry by Keenan on behalf of the Greater West Belfast Community Association, making a case for an integrated public transport system, restraining the use of private road vehicles, and more thorough consultation. Their strategy was rejected as excessively expensive and unrealistic by the Department and the inspector.

The lessons of 1977

Lavery in his report on the transport inquiry recommended a strategy which he considered was a compromise, 'an equitable and sensible balance which will produce a workable transportation system'. This was accepted by the Department, although the inspector's proposal for a Transport Review Authority to provide a vehicle for public consultation and participation was rejected on the basis that regular reviews could be conducted by existing bodies. In fact, regular reviews were not carried out, and the first review was that commissioned in 1986 for the Belfast Urban Area Plan (BUAP) 2001.

Lavery recommended to the Minister the proposed rail link between Belfast's two rail termini. This was not built by the time of the 1988 public inquiry into the BUAP 2001. Improvements he recommended to rail and bus services were, according to the General Consumer Council, carried out 'by only a fraction of what was envisaged' (Transecon International, 1986). His recommendation that a central bus station be constructed was accepted, but it was not built by the time of the BUAP 2001. The introduction of concessionary fares was the only public transport recommendation that was fully implemented. The argument for eliminating black taxi competition with the buses was accepted but not implemented. Also accepted but not implemented was the recommendation for a study of bus priority measures in traffic management. The recommendation that privately owned car parks should be brought into public ownership was not acted on, undermining the related recommendation that car parking charges be used to discourage the car commuter.

Of the recommended highway measures several road schemes *had been completed* by the time of the BUAP 2001. The lack of activity with regard to public transport reflected the new political climate after the election of a Conservative Government in 1979. The period from 1979 saw an even lower level of investment in public transport than had been envisaged in 1977, resulting, de facto, in a private road vehicle based emphasis rather than the balanced emphasis recommended by Lavery following the 1977 inquiry. Only part of the budget envisaged by Lavery for public transport was spent, leading the General Consumer Council to conclude that the mobility gap between those with access to private cars and those without had widened by 1986 (Transecon International, 1986).

Planning in Belfast had proved a piecemeal and uncertain process in the face of macro and micro factors impinging on it. The macro factors were the pressures exerted by wider economic and political changes: deindustrialisation and the undermining of growth centre strategy, and the election of the Thatcher Government in Britain. The micro factors were the pressures exerted by community action and the resistance to urban renewal in many inner city neighbourhoods.

Whilst there was a significant input to the 1977 inquiry from community groups, they did not have access to professional planners. The inspector only had regard to reasoned planning argument, and rejected the many calls made at the inquiry for more thorough consultation. He set out his argument as follows:

An attempt to consult people directly and to let people decide directly in the way that I understand was being urged has grave risks of being totally undemocratic. This type of exercise gives great advantage to the articulate and energetic irrespective of how representative they are. I have always entertained grave doubts as to how representative the Action Committee were of the working class people in the city. There is considerable apathy on issues like transport planning unless persons are immediately and directly affected. Where there is general apathy it is extremely easy for a number of active organised people to proclaim themselves as the authentic voice of the people and by shouting louder than anyone else to impose their views upon the community. (Lavery Report, 1978, p. 152)

This is a very clear example of an inspector's self perception as guardian of the 'public interest'. As we shall see later in the book, no such doubt was cast over the cases made by community groups at the BUAP 2001 inquiry, where the public interest was seen to be served by community action about the Plan. But the situation was very different in that the Department of the Environment had funded Community Technical Aid to guide this action and play by the rules of the game. On the one hand, the motivation for this funding could be interpreted as one of incorporation and heading off the sort of disruption seen at the 1977 inquiry. On the other hand, it could be interpreted as an attempt to accord legitimacy to the community groups and their interests in the planning process. It is possible to speculate about this on the basis of knowledge about the views of civil servants who had influence over the decision at the time, but this would be no more than speculation. In chapter 5 we will consider the effectiveness of CTA's role in terms of the actual influence on the content of the final plan.

There is little doubt that the experience of the 1977 inquiry and other planning campaigns during that decade influenced subsequent developments at community level. A number of interviews for this book of people involved with community groups active about planning in the 1970s were conducted during 1988 to gain a picture of what happened (1). One of the community workers involved in the 1977 inquiry stated:

> Communities have a negative power - to block things, stop things - but what they lacked was the positive power to bring forward alternatives and to conceive and draw these alternatives, to get them on paper to argue them. This was what was missing in 1977 and left an impression on many and, in fact, was part of the reason why Community Technical Aid was set up. It was no longer enough to say no. You've actually got to get into the process and fight the

professionals at their own game with similar levels of professional expertise.

Many community groups perceived the Department of the Environment at the 1977 inquiry as arrogant and unaccountable, and confrontation was inevitable. This put the inspector, Michael Lavery QC, under considerable pressure and one interviewee stated that, 'A comment heard at the time was that Lavery was the only one in the bar library who could have pulled the inquiry off successfully for the DoE.'

The imbalance of resources which the decision to fund CTA for the 1988 inquiry was meant to address was felt very keenly by the community group side at the 1977 inquiry. It was reported that, '... in the 1977 inquiry there was no public telephone or toilet, no photocopier, typing, etc., yet the Department of the Environment had a room of typists, photocopiers, etc.' It was commented that the atmosphere was very formal and very adversarial 'if community groups were there, though at other times it could be quite relaxed.' In general, this respondent summed up the community groups' impact on the inquiry as follows:

> Hamill Street was highlighted by Lavery (the inspector) and the DoE as a working class area where community action could be successful. This community altered the shape of the inner distributor box - it did change road plans and road lines but in a sense it was a foil to show up the rest of the community groups, almost tactical. Those groups who employed a solicitor did get a more positive response from the inspector. These groups, unlike CGACT, did accept the ground rules of the inquiry - ' playing the game', e.g. dressing up in a suit ... Hamill Street got their views across. They employed a solicitor. But the broad thrust of the community groups' case was totally lost. Their response was poor, uncoordinated and lacked expertise. The 'fourth strategy' was never presented.

Against this view that the community groups could have had a greater impact are the conclusions of more radical activists. This is a not untypical quote, which looks back to the community organising of the 1970s:

> Government departments treated people with contempt. Planning and consultation were exercises in political expediency, a complete and utter waste of money ... Really the civil servants know they are powerless. Power is concentrated elsewhere, controlled by a small number of people.

54

Yet, although the little that was achieved following the 1977 inquiry seems to justify the above view, the willingness of community groups to get involved in the BUAP 2001 inquiry suggests a continuing source of action in the community even when it is clear that the odds are stacked against. One academic commentator stated in an interview in 1988 that the 1977 inquiry had been in

> ... different political times, not just in the state of the Irish war or the Irish struggle or the Irish conflict, but also in terms of people's perception of the state, the welfare state. People nowadays really know they're up against it and I think they've learned they have to use and organise around whatever resources can be found, and they're few and far between, so if somebody's presenting some organisational framework around which you can present issues, discover what issues are, then that's a good thing. That wasn't around then.

He added about the 1977 inquiry that:

> It was antagonistic. There was a feeling from the start that the dice were loaded. People didn't expect much out of it. Nobody had much belief in the inquiry that it would yield benefits for the working class. They were quite right to feel that, but that doesn't mean they should have approached it the way they did. Really what was being argued about was the lack of resources available for community groups to represent a case. The attempt to get resources having failed, they moved into the inquiry to protest that they hadn't had the resources to present a case. The public inquiry should have been disrupted until the community groups did get the resources they needed. It was sticking on that, rather than saying look we're clearly not going to get the resources therefore what the hell can we cobble together.

While clearly taking the view that there were not the resources to enable community groups to present their cases, this commentator was sceptical whether any strategic interest could be built from the community groups' arguments:

> One wonders would there have been any coherence of views had there been any resources available, or whether instinctively people were just trying to defend their traditional areas, localities, from the builders ...

Indeed, much of the strength of the CGACT at the 1977 inquiry was due to the Hamill Street residents. Moving beyond this localism raises issues for community organising as well as planning advocacy, and indeed in some people's minds planning advocacy is a distraction if it can only work within the 'official' view of what is possible, as the above commentator stated:

> You can buy in any solicitor, professional help, etc., but that's not necessary. Many people would argue that those resources already exist among communities and they should be encouraged to exist. I suppose the difficulty is that if you are in a position of heavy conflict and the other side has legal heavyweights then you're not going to be in an advantageous position. People do need resources - organisational ability, to be able to convene groups, canvassing skills - they need to be aware of alternatives and options ... It's not, I would have thought, a lack of knowledge of technical questions per se, but it's a question of vision, of knowing what could be different or how it could be different when you're stuck in the bloody ghetto.

It is the question of vision - of the planning ideology - which is fundamentally at issue. The next sections of this chapter will consider some aspects of how this ideology is formed. It will begin with the regional framework; important not only because in 1977 the modernising ideology of this framework as contained in the Matthew Plan was considerably toned down (thus we also see the scaling down of the road proposals for Belfast), but also because a regional framework was much less in evidence in 1988 than it was when BDP and Travers Morgan worked on their plans. In 1988, in place of modernising whole regions and cities with new infrastructure and housing there was an emphasis on city image and only very modest urban change despite worse social and economic problems than in the 1960s-70s. In place of Minister of Development Brian Faulkner's statement in the foreword to the 1969 Belfast Urban Area Plan that the plan '... underlines the existence of major problems calling for urgent action - particularly those relating to renewal and change ...' is Environment Minister Richard Needham's statement in the 1987 BUAP that, 'The balance between old and new, conservation and development is an inescapable aspect of the planning of a great and living city'. And while Brian Falkner begins his foreword by referring to the Matthew Plan's regional strategy, there is no mention of regional strategy in Richard Needham's introduction.

The regional context

In December 1975 the Government announced that it was to adopt a new strategy for future regional planning in Northern Ireland. The *Regional Physical Development Strategy 1975-1995* (RPDS), adopted in 1977, revised the Matthew Plan of the early 1960s. It was based on the concept of concentrating population in Belfast and 23 'district towns'. The district towns were selected on the basis of their positions as the main centres of Northern Ireland's district council areas. Although not strictly a statutory plan, it is an official statement of strategy for the physical development of Northern Ireland as a whole until 1995. It thus provides the framework into which the Belfast Urban Area Plan and other development plans should fit.

The RPDS confirms Belfast as a regional capital. The city's declining population, the RPDS argues, can be turned to advantage to reduce high residential densities and improve standards of open space and community facilities. The stopline was no longer a means of deconcentrating growth but a boundary to limit urban sprawl and to protect the natural setting of the city (para. 3.08). The one exception would be Catholic West Belfast where the combination of political segregation and population growth in this sector meant that there was a shortage of land for housing within the stopline and a need to develop beyond it.

The RPDS envisaged a decline in the population of the Belfast urban area from 560,000 in 1975 to around 520,000 in 1995. In fact, the population had fallen to 495,000 by the time the BUAP 2001 was in preparation. The strategy stated, 'given rather better environmental standards than those presently existing, the area within the Belfast stopline can comfortably accommodate a population of around 520,000'. The BUAP 2001, however, proposed to zone greenfield sites for housing, pressed for by speculative builders, beyond this stopline to accommodate its 'target' population of 520,000.

The only public consultation carried out before the RPDS was adopted was a prior discussion paper setting out six alternative 'strategic options'. The paper strongly advocated the strategy that was eventually adopted - a middle position between a diffused pattern of physical development across Northern Ireland and the linear accretive growth of Belfast. This was the district towns strategy (Department of Local Government, Planning and Housing, 1975). The RPDS states:

> Planning and development of the environment is not simply a matter for Government. Its success depends upon the consent of those whom it affects... Because of the extent of community interest therefore the Government in setting out to review its Regional Strategy sought to obtain as wide a cross-section of public opinion as possible. (Department of the Environment (NI), 1976, para. 1.06)

Comments on the discussion paper were received from district councils, the Northern Ireland Economic Council, the Northern Ireland Committee of the Irish Congress of Trade Unions, chambers of commerce, the Sports Council, academics and the general public. In the foreword to the RPDS Roy Carter, then Parliamentary Under Secretary of State, wrote:

Of special importance will be the role to be played by District Councils whose local knowledge of the needs and potentials of their areas will be of particular value in guiding future physical development.

The RPDS presents the following brief analysis of the comments received on the discussion paper:

A significant body of opinion favoured a more rigorous implementation of the growth and key centre strategy on the grounds that it would be more effective in economic terms, but the overwhelming weight of opinion - including that of most District Councils who submitted comments - supported the District Towns Strategy.

References to the new district councils' role in influencing planning strategy (over which they had no control) was much more prominent than in the case of the BUAP 2001. The new councils, bereft of major powers, were being encouraged as forums for 'responsible' local politics, but largely became forums for the expression of Unionist or Nationalist ideologies.

Overall, the RPDS abandoned the Matthew growth centre strategy, sought a rationalisation of population distribution and public and private investment in district towns, and recognised the inner city problem in Belfast. It was thus a strategy of retrenchment, while prioritising the 'regeneration' (rather than renewal) of inner urban Belfast. The strategy reflected how '... policy was now directed towards containing problems in the older urban areas and selectively revalorising parts of these areas with "investment potential" on which public spending was targetted' (Blackman, 1987, p. 59).

As well as having a regional context, planning in Belfast also had a European context. In 1979 the Belfast urban area was designated an Integrated Operations Zone (IOZ) by the European Community. IOZ designation was designed to encourage the coordination of all available local, national and European funds for economic regeneration where there were acute social and economic difficulties. The aim was to achieve greater effectiveness than separate, uncoordinated programmes. The BUA was selected as one of only two IOZs in the EC in view of its special problems.

In 1981 public expenditure proposals were published which it was claimed 'exemplified an integrated approach to the city's development' (Department of the Environment (NI), (1981). Expenditure on interrelated projects totalled £486 million. This was focused on tackling urban deprivation, especially improving housing conditions in inner city areas through new public sector provision. A Belfast Coordinating Committee (BCC), chaired by the Environment Minister, was set up. Through the Urban Programme Working Group it would oversee implementation of the IO programme, monitor and evaluate progress, and identify new opportunities as they arose. Belfast City Council endorsed the 1981 document and participated in the BCC, although there was no consultation with the public.

In 1985 a second document was published, updating and continuing the process, and in particular seeking 'to identify measures and projects which will contribute to the economic regeneration of the urban area and the alleviation of social deprivation' (Department of the Environment (NI), 1985).

The Government was under pressure from Europe as well as at home to take positive steps which targeted social deprivation and involved community and voluntary organisations. Midway through 1988 the Northern Ireland Environment Minister announced the 'Making Belfast Work' initiative, which would fund projects '... to increase economic activity, reinforce local enterprise, improve the quality of the environment and equip the people of the disadvantaged areas to compete successfully for available employment' (Northern Ireland Information Service press release, 30 January 1989).

The whole draft BUAP 2001, however, emphasised the private sector's role and indeed the willingness of private capital to invest is presented as a determinant of whether the plan will be realised:

> The speed with which the development opportunities can be exploited or further economic growth can take place will... be affected by the wider national and international economic climate prevailing during the Plan period as well as by the response of the business community to the development framework provided by this Plan. (Department of the Environment (NI), 1987)

This is very different to the confident assertions of the 1969 Plan, whose authors clearly felt they could plan for a better way of life:

> To prepare the Belfast Urban Area Plan it has been necessary to visualise new ways of life of people living in or around the area. It may sound presumptious for anyone to visualise ways of life for others, but without a clear idea of the way of life it is foolish to try to produce a plan. (Building Design Partnership, 1969, p. 6)

This is an absolutely fundamental change in planning ideology. In the 1960s it was thought possible to change whole ways of life according to a social purpose. In the 1980s the planners related not to a vision of a new way of life but to the market, to what was necessary to establish business confidence.

59

Belfast remains a working class city. The BUAP, however, is largely about a post industrial future for a city that had its raison d'etre as a major industrial centre. In September 1988 a Northern Ireland Information Service press release celebrated 5 years of investment in the city by major retailing and office developers, quoting the Environment Minister as saying:

> ... the Belfast of the 1980s is a place of bustling streets, busy shops, smart new restaurants and ever increasing activity in the commercial sector.

In October another release quoted the Minister as stating at a lunch with British retailers:

> The Belfast branch of Boots tops the company league table on turnover; Littlewoods branch is third, BHS is fifth and the Belfast Marks and Spencer, out of 260 branches, is tenth overall and second on food turnover' ... Mr Needham said a great deal more new development was in the pipeline for Belfast, including the massive Laganside development, a £250 million investment in riverside housing, leisure and office space.

Many working class communities felt these developments were no basis for the reconstruction of their areas. The Government's emphasis on private housebuilding also appeared to be about policy following purchasing power rather than compensating for market inequalities. Indeed, the lobby from housebuilders for attractive greenfield sites around Belfast was one of the main pressures on the Department of the Environment to produce a new plan for Belfast, and to do it quickly (Northern Ireland Assembly, 1985).

The draft BUAP published for public consultation in November 1987 was a colourful 120 page document full of designer photographs of the city. Its central features were policies for a strong commercial city centre, land releases for housing in some green belt locations, and a waterside regeneration concept for 'Laganside', the Belfast riverside.

In making the Plan, the Department of the Environment related it to the image building strategies of British ministers. In this respect, the jewel in the crown was the Laganside proposals. However, the Government was committed to Laganside regardless of the outcome of the BUAP inquiry. The existence of this commitment had considerable significance beyond the local impact because its symbolism set the ideological tone of the BUAP, and because there was to be no public debate about whether it was a good thing or not. In his foreword to consultants' 'concept plan' for Laganside, the Environment Minister wrote:

This study of Laganside was commissioned by my Department as a contribution to the Belfast Urban Area Plan. It describes the potential which exists to transform completely the environmental quality of a vital part of the City, and by this means to help transform perceptions of Belfast at an international level.

In essence, Laganside was about extending the city centre, and this commercialisation of space was resisted at the public inquiry.

To mark publication of the draft Plan, the Belfast Centre for the Unemployeed published an analysis of planning in Belfast, *Belfast Urban Area Plan: Reshaping Space and Society* (Mooney and Gaffikin, 1987). This report criticises the neglect of the issue of who benefits from development, and especially whether planning compensates for or reinforces social inequalities in the city. Work on the new Belfast Urban Area Plan, the authors argue, reflects an anti planning ideology of deregulation and privatisation, without public accountability or any distinction between private interest and the public good. Indeed, rather than about guiding private development in the public interest, it is suggested that the BUAP is harnessed to major public spending initiatives designed to featherbed private development for profit, responding not to social needs but to market opportunities.

Mooney and Gaffikin discuss Belfast's new city centre shopping complex, Castle Court, to illustrate their argument. Criticising the £10 million of urban development grant 'claimed' by developers John Laing, the authors point out that the social case for public subsidy is far stronger for much needed local shops and retail employment in disadvantaged areas of the city. Similarly, the Laganside plan is criticised for putting claims on millions of pounds of public subsidy without any clear social audit of the distribution and nature of benefits. As with Castle Court, although included in the draft BUAP, the Laganside project began to be implemented before the public inquiry into the new Plan.

Mooney and Gaffikin express concern about the type of jobs that will be generated by these projects: often part time, low paid, low or no tech, and dependent on a few powerful commercial and financial corporations, with no local interest other than the return on their investments compared with alternative options. In terms of what they offer to the consumer, the authors argue that it is the comfortably off who will benefit, while the poor will be marginalised. Spending in the poorest areas by 'action teams' is overshadowed by the amount of public funds spent elsewhere and the profits realised by developers and retailers with the prime sites.

Mooney and Gaffikin also criticise the lack of social policy considerations in the BUAP, such as the need for an expansion of childminding facilities, community services for the elderly, and shortfalls in the Housing Executive's budget in the face of major housing needs (as opposed to demand). With regard to transport, the authors comment:

> There is here again an issue of equity. In those parts of Belfast - such as the Southside - where private affluence and mobility would permit residents to visit or have personal access to resources of open space, leisure and culture, there are many amenities on the doorstep. The University, Museum, Parks, Sports Centre, and Theatres are some examples. Whereas, in more depressed and crowded parts of the city where such facilities are more rarely found residents also have less access to private transport to such amenities. They rely on public transport ...
>
> ... The bus service in Belfast offers the public hard seated single deckers even on the busier routes or rush hour. Many are forced to stand squeezed together after a tiring day's work. Parents are obliged to fold down their prams. The 'No Smoking' signs carry little credibility in such limited space. By the mid 1980s the number of yearly passenger journeys on City Bus was less than one quarter of what it was in the mid 1960s. (pp. 61-62)

The BUAP makes no provision to limit the growth of use of private road vehicles in Belfast, proposing more roads, road widening, and car parks.

Mooney and Gaffikin conclude that the Plan aims at achieving a new image for Belfast which contradicts the city's association with conflict and poverty. They note how Belfast's 'neat little terraces' were tarred with the planner's brush in the late 1960s to become 'slums' that had to be demolished: image making which served to legitimise a radical restructuring of the urban area and its region. The authors argue that the new Plan's rehabilitation of the past and its extension of the rules and values of the market into new territory combine to make a strategy for the regressive modernisation of the city: a 'two nations' plan which has little to offer anyone excluded by poverty or disadvantage from the world of modern consumer society and its enterprize culture. Little, that is, other than an image:

> (W)e are asked to discover a collective identity and pride around the inanimate objects that comprise the architecture of selected parts of the city. The cultivation of a distinctive urban image, we are told, will help us to compete more effectively for scarce inward investment. (p. 72)

Behind this exercise, Mooney and Gaffikin claim, is a marked *lack* of planning:

(N)ew 'brightly designed' housing schemes sit without local services amidst the derelict remains of a past age of production. Similarly, the Urban Development Grant Scheme has been organised around specific economic values, which give a priority to securing higher rental returns and a better image particularly for the city centre. Consequently, those areas where need is greatest have been largely ignored. (p. 76)

A marked lack of democracy is also noted:

(T)he Minister of State and his administrative advisors have no particular democratic mandate from the Belfast public. So inevitably 'issues and opportunities' have been identified and policy constructed in isolation of any local endorsement. (p. 78)

In contrast:

(T)he all-embracing and unchecked power of the political administration has allowed the specific requirements of the large property development interests, volume housebuilders, and multiple retailers among others, to be ascertained either directly in negotiation or indirectly through consultative studies. (p. 79)

Conclusion: setting the scene for participation

Mooney and Gaffikin (1987) contrast the ill fated Belfast Urban Area Plan of 1969 with the BUAP 2001. The former involved major road proposals threatening densely populated neighbourhoods, major housing redevelopment and a significant displacement of population. The latter involves nowhere near the scale of restructuring that was planned in 1969 to meet the needs of new manufacturing industry, and instead emphasises the needs of the 'post industrial' sectors of retailing, offices, leisure and tourism:

Understandably, the prospect of the Plan has provoked much less interest and passion that its predecessor. (p. 8)

While true, the past experience of defensive struggles against the costs of planning and housing renewal in working class communities had been behind the establishment of Community Technical Aid to provide community groups with professional backing and a capacity for positive action. One of the founder members of CTA, a community worker in West Belfast, summed up the rationale of the new organisation as follows:

A community group has its own set of interests, its own criteria and its own needs to meet which are often totally different from those of relevant public bodies. In this situation the community group has a right to express its own interests, its own criteria and identify its own needs in a professional and positive manner. (quoted in Blackman, 1988, p. 31)

Many community groups in Belfast had come to see state agencies as having bureaucratic interests quite separate from their own. This has been particularly acute in relation to planning and development agencies, as these functions have tended to impinge more visibly and with greater impact upon whole communities.

CTA was established in 1984 following a conference of community groups the previous year (Blackman, 1988). Funded by trusts, central and local government, the service was managed by a committee elected from a membership of user groups and interested individuals. The intention of the founder members of CTA was that it should have a proactive role about issues as well as providing reactive practical assistance to community groups about housing and planning problems. Various management problems and lack of funding limited the extent to which a proactive role could develop, but with the announcement of the DoE's intention to make a new plan for Belfast CTA saw an opportunity to work for community group involvement in a policy making process.

It was from the experiences of 'planning' in the 1970s that the idea of CTA grew. The case of the redevelopment of the Shankill area in West Belfast is one well documented example of how these experiences of urban renewal, linked to regional restructuring, led to popular action to defend a right to live and work in existing communities (Wiener, 1980; Gillespie, 1983). But it seemed that a crucial lesson emerged from this action: the need to play state authority at its own game, to match the expertise and knowledge used by the state. Without this, it was impossible to contest the claims of impracticality, irrelevance or irrationality levelled at the arguments of ordinary people.

Notes

1. Interviews recorded during September and October, 1988, and carried out by Una O'Boyle, Paddy Carroll and Irene Kennedy.

4 The Belfast Urban Area Plan 2001: mobilising the response

This chapter discusses the Belfast Urban Area Plan 2001 from publication of the Preliminary Proposals through to the public inquiry, where some 2,500 written objections were heard during 37 days of proceedings. The focus of the chapter is on the role of Community Techical Aid in this process. This organisation worked with community groups in Belfast to make a major input to the public inquiry. It was a contribution which challenged many aspects of the Plan. The cases made at the inquiry and their influence on the final Plan as adopted by the Department of the Environment are the subject of chapter 5. The present chapter considers experiences of the inquiry's procedures and draws a number of conclusions about the consultation process as a whole.

The participation of community groups in the BUAP brought a perspective into the proceedings which was at odds with the official planning paradigm. The previous chapter indicated where these alternative planning values came from in terms of local civil society in Belfast and the grassroots experience of planning. During the BUAP, this common set of values about planning brought together many community and special interest groups within a framework provided by Community Technical Aid. Work was focussed on making a credible and major impact on the public inquiry, and there were only two instances of community action outside the public inquiry process. These were a 'planning festival' organised by the Lower Ormeau Residents' Action Group in February 1988, which aimed to get local people involved in a response to the Plan, and a Campaign for Cyclists' Rights demonstration in May 1988, when more than a hundred cyclists rode in convoy around Belfast City Hall and collected signatures for a petition objecting to the Plan's silence on cyclists' needs.

In reading chapters 4 and 5, it will be useful to refer to Figure 4.1 which chronicles the main events discussed.

Figure 4.1 Main events in the Belfast Urban Area Plan and the Community Technical Aid project.

June/July	1985	Notice of intent to prepare BUAP published in the local press and suggestions from the public invited about future development of the urban area. Public response is negligible. CTA establishes working group to look at how it should respond to the Plan.
December	1985	Department of the Environment addresses the Environment Committee of the Northern Ireland Assembly on the BUAP. Work had already started on the Plan.
December/ January	1985 1986	Notice of intent to prepare BUAP sent by Department of the Environment to local councils and suggestions invited. CTA approaches South Yorkshire County Council for assistance in responding to the Plan.
February	1986	CTA meets with DoE to discuss the role it could have in the BUAP.
June	1986	Government announces consultants study of River Lagan. Commercial and leisure development of the riverside would be a 'focal point' for the BUAP's development thrust.
March	1987	CTA holds BUAP response group meeting. Fifty local organisations invited. Seventeen people attend.
May	1987	Department published BUAP Preliminary Proposals and places them on display. CTA criticises the document as superficial and calls for an extension of the consultation period of six weeks.

		CTA with Falls Community Council organises BUAP community conference in Andersonstown, West Belfast. Sixty people attend from 38 organisations.
June	1987	Second community conference for West Belfast organised with Falls Community Council. Local meetings organised for North and South Belfast.
		First information group meeting at CTA.
July	1987	CTA meets the DoE to make case for longer consultation period, funding for community groups and changes to public inquiry procedure.
		Public meeting on BUAP held for community groups in North Belfast.
August	1987	Government press release announces that 1,150 comments received on Preliminary Proposals.
		DoE writes to CTA refusing an extended consultation period.
		CTA chairs meeting in South Belfast. Working group set up.
November	1987	DoE write to CTA offering a grant of £50,000 'to provide technical and professional help to community groups on any aspect of the BUAP'.
		Draft Plan published and exhibited in 11 locations.
		All Belfast conference of community groups organised by CTA. Attended by 140 people. Decision to form a BUAP advisory group.
December	1987	Three temporary planning assistants appointed together with consultants to coordinate the planning team and provide legal representation for CTA and community groups at the public inquiry.

December	1987	First meeting of 16 member advisory group constituted as special committee of CTA.
December/ January	1987 1988	Six meetings held by CTA planners with steering groups in North, West, East and South Belfast.
January	1988	CTA formally submits its objections to the BUAP. Advisory group meets to review results of meetings with steering groups.
February/ March	1988	Eight advisory group meetings review the Plan topic by topic, serviced by CTA planners.
March	1988	Planning Appeals Commission holds three pre inquiry meetings.
4 May	1988	Public inquiry opens to hear 2,500 objections (excluding petitions).
27 June	1988	Public inquiry closes.
September	1989	Planning Appeals Commission makes final report to the Department of the Environment.
December	1989	DoE publishes its Adoption Statement.
February	1990	CTA holds a conference to review successes, failures and future for community action about planning.

Planning paradigms in Belfast

If it had been adopted as a statutory plan, the Belfast Urban Area Plan of 1969 would have ended in 1986. Under the Planning (Northern Ireland) Order 1972, Northern Ireland's Department of the Environment was put under an obligation to prepare a statutory plan for Belfast as well as other parts of the region. In 1985 these factors were the official rationale for initiating a new urban area plan for the period to 2001.

A paradigm is '... a set of concepts, categories, relationships, and methods which are generally accepted throughout a community at a given point in time' (Harvey, 1973, p. 120). It is helpful to think of the BUAP 2001 as prepared within such a paradigm,

68

although the community was not society as a whole but 'officialdom' working within the parameters of government policy. A key question for this book is whether officialdom's paradigm was shared, in general, with the people of Belfast for whom officialdom planned.

Chapter 3 indicated that the concepts inherent in the Plan reflected a coherent paradigm of 'regressive modernisation' which had little to offer anyone excluded by poverty or disadvantage from the world of modern consumer society and its enterprise culture (Mooney and Gaffikin, 1987). The definition of relationships between land use, public services and social and economic policy, the selection of methods for plan making and the procedures for public participation could be expected to be framed by this paradigm. The present chapter concentrates on whether the consultation procedures were acceptable to the public who participated, while chapter 5 will address the question of how land use planning is defined and related to other spheres of social and economic life. Together the two chapters will lead to a conclusion about the legitimacy of the official planning paradigm among those who participated as members of the public in the consultation process and the inquiry. While this excludes the mass of the public who as non joiners or disinterested parties took no part in the process, it is more important to consider the process from the point of view of those who wanted to participate to achieve concrete changes and to contribute their experience and knowledge to planning Belfast.

On 3 December 1985 the Environment Committee of the Northern Ireland Assembly heard two senior civil servants explain the rationale of the BUAP 2001 (Northern Ireland Assembly, 1985). Three issues stand out in this presentation:

(i)   the 'need' to provide land for housebuilding on the urban fringe within the context of a revised stopline or green belt around the urban area;

(ii)   the 'need' to enhance the commercial heart of Belfast, with a particular focus on riverside regeneration for shopping, offices, private housing and leisure;

(iii)   the 'need' for a major review of private and public transportation.

The last issue in particular was a focus of detailed questioning by the Environment Committee, suspicious that a roads ideology still dominated the Department. The reply was, however, that effectively everything was in the melting pot: private consultants had been appointed to review and make recommendations on every aspect of the urban area's transportation systems.

The Department intended to present draft proposals for public consultation by the end of 1986, and to bring forward amended proposals to a public inquiry by the end of 1987. Formal adoption of the final plan was expected by the end of 1988. The Plan fell behind this timetable and following the public inquiry it was fifteen months before the Planning Appeals Commission submitted its final report to the Department of the Environment. The Department formally adopted the Plan in December 1989.

Community Technical Aid (CTA) became aware of the Government's intention to make a new plan for Belfast following the insertion by the Department of the Environment of newspaper advertisements in June and July 1985. The issue was discussed several times during the next few months by a working group of CTA members, one of whom stated very clearly what it had to aim for now it was faced by such a major planning exercise on its doorstep:

> I feel inevitably that CTA (NI) must adopt a prominent and, perhaps campaigning, role throughout this exercise. We talked before about 'mopping up operations' and the BUAP provides CTA with an ideal opportunity. The coordination of community submissions (informed by professional technical support) would involve the establishment of an in-house Planning Unit akin to the Queens University based Popular Planning Unit in the '70s. (1)

The Queen's University unit had involved planning students in work with community groups, and had played a significant role during the 1970s supporting the Save the Shankill campaign and other campaigns against redevelopment by drawing up alternatives to official plans. The Shankill is a working class Protestant area in largely Catholic West Belfast where the experience of 'planning aid' was a formative one for some of the people who later went on to set up Community Technical Aid, as illustrated in the following account by one of the campaign's leading activists:

> The big weakness that we had was an inability to halt the deterioration that was happening in the area; you couldn't ask people to live in atrocious conditions and stick their ground - all the Housing Executive had to do was nothing and we were beaten in fact. It comes down to the big weakness of any community action campaign of this sort - you can stop things happening, it's easy to stop bulldozers, but you don't have the resources to do things. It's OK saying no you won't have any more flats in the Shankill, but it's altogether another thing to get houses of the sort you want...
>
> If I was to look at why we succeeded - because we ought not to cloud the fact that there are four or five phases of new houses which have been built and where people are happy to live and where there's a huge demand - I can identify four

reasons. One of them was the existence of the Save the Shankill campaign which embraced all sections of the community and could mobilise large numbers of people onto the street; it was well organised and had a few people working virtually full time; it had councillors in City Hall which it could educate how to vote. There was one other factor which was of crucial importance and that was the Town and Country Planning Department at Queen's University which we had access to. We could go and we could say 'we don't want these flats in phase 1 we want houses', and we sketched out what we wanted to go back into the area, and the Town and Country Planning Department could draw what we wanted...

One Friday we went out and stopped the bulldozers. On the Sunday night we met the architects from the Housing Executive - fifteen or sixteen of us there with their plan on the wall and above that *our* plan. After half an hour the area of debate had changed from their plan to our plan, and that was the key to us getting terraced housing built in place of nine blocks of flats. There are phases of redevelopment on the Shankill where people today are very happy, and one of the key factors in that was the fact that we had access to someone who could draw an alternative plan according to our specifications. (2)

The Belfast Urban Area Plan 2001 presented, for the first time, the opportunity to involve community groups from all parts of the city in influencing a statutory development strategy for the whole of Belfast. It presented a major new challenge for groups that by definition were locally based.

CTA's board of directors decided that expert planning advice should be sought about the BUAP and the public consultation arrangements. It was recognised that it was beyond any likely resources to draw up an alternative plan if the Department of the Environment's draft plan met with any substantial opposition from community groups. Later on it was also recognised that it would be best to press for changes through clear objections to specific statements in the Plan, rather than to try to present alternative proposals. The planning aid model was relevant in terms of its community based values, but it was felt that these should be used to criticise inadequacies in the BUAP rather than to try and develop alternatives without the time and resources of the Government's planners and their consultants.

CTA was particularly aware that it might be providing the overall public response to the Plan. Belfast City Council had appointed the Town and Country Planning Department in the Queen's University of Belfast to act as their advisors in connection with work on the BUAP, but Council business was threatened with suspension as part

71

of the Unionist protest against the Anglo Irish Agreement. The Council's Town Planning Committee made detailed objections to the Draft Plan after it was published in November 1987. The main elements of the objections were that the Plan was based on a free market philosophy which 'failed to take into account the needs of the majority of people in the City' and that there was a lack of commitment to publicly funded provision (*Belfast City Council Minutes*, 3 May 1988). At its meeting of 21 April the Committee appointed members to represent the Council at the public inquiry, but by the time of the inquiry Council business was suspended and no submission was made (*Belfast Telegraph*, 15 January 1983).

Without urban planners itself, CTA approached South Yorkshire County Council in England with a request to second a planner until the end of March 1986 to help with a response to the Plan. This approach was made because in Northern Ireland the near monopoly the Department of the Environment had of the employment of urban planners meant that local assistance was unlikely; planners would be compromised by helping objectors - including those in private practice and universities because of the Department's importance as a source of fee paying work and employment. It was known that the County Council was due to be abolished along with England's other Metropolitan County Councils by the Local Government Act 1985, and that it had a strong commitment to progressive and participative strategic planning. It was thought that a planner with these values could be available as work was run down before abolition.

Three issues were identified (3):

(i)   ensuring that debate took place about the form and scope of the public inquiry given the lack of democratic control over planning in Belfast;

(ii)   ensuring that the Plan's policies protected and enhanced working class communities in the city, strengthening their areas' economic and social base;

(iii)   making a case for a substantial shift towards public transport as a social service, based on considerations of pollution, accidents, efficiency and car ownership.

It was hoped that the seconded planner would help draw up a bid for substantial trust or Government grant aid to enable the employment of a chartered planner from the end of March to the public inquiry. This post would provide expertise in relation to the issues CTA had identified, provide a resource on which any community group could draw according to their needs, and assist groups present their cases at the inquiry.

It was not possible to achieve the secondment from South Yorkshire as had been hoped, but one of the Authority's planners did make two visits to Belfast with financial support from the

Northern Ireland Voluntary Trust, studying the issues for CTA and meeting with DoE planners and consultants. At a meeting with the BUAP team leader and an Assistant Secretary at the Department of the Environment on 27 February 1986, CTA raised the questions of a Report of Survey and the form of the public inquiry. It was advised that concerns about the latter should be raised in a letter to the Under Secretary. The Report of Survey question was explored at some length. These had been standard public consultation practice in England, preceding production of county structure plans. They bring before the public for consultation the results of pre plan information gathering relating to population, economic and social data and trends.

In a letter from the Department which followed the February meeting CTA was informed that:

> The Report of Survey approach is certainly an interesting one but it may not be open to us - not least because we have a much tighter timetable than an English structure plan - and it may not be practicable to produce a Report of Survey at an early stage. (4)

No report of survey was published. The Department spent £1.9 million on work by consultants for the Plan, of which £1.2 million related to a major transportation study. The reports were difficult to obtain and to read, but were vital to any serious assessment of the Plan's proposals. The transportation study ran to nine volumes and cost £27. These reports were crucial to how problems were defined for the BUAP; they were not just background data. The transportation study, for example, was strongly criticised by Age Concern and the Northern Ireland Council on Disability for ignoring the mobility needs of elderly and disabled people (*Irish News*, 20 May 1987), while the retail study was criticised by an academic for 'irritating' defects, 'dubious assumptions' and recommendations that 'bear little or no relation to the research findings' (Brown, 1987). Clearly these reports had many controversial elements, but they were not easily accessible to the public.

The consultants' reports problem related to the wider issue of the time allocated for public consultation. CTA felt that the Plan was moving ahead much faster than any genuine commitment to public participation should allow. In addition, decisions about the basic approaches of the Plan seemed to be being taken even before preliminary proposals were published. For example, on 12 June 1986 the Northern Ireland Information Service issued a media release announcing the commissioning of a study of the River Lagan, and this revealed that key commitments had already been made:

> The Department said today that it had decided to make the river one of the focal points for a major development thrust in the implementation of the new plan and that the study

would look at the city's riverfront and adjacent lands ... A primary aim of the plan will be to create a climate in which the private sector can invest so as to realise the commercial and leisure potential of the river.

The official paradigm for the BUAP was becoming very clear and CTA realised that it had to match this with a critique drawn from its community group members' perspectives which would have credibility and clout at a public inquiry. It approached a number of charitable trusts for funding to support a planning post for two years to assist community groups influence the Plan and its implementation, but was unsuccessful. Without resources of any significance, and relying initially on one tenacious volunteer, the organisation began work raising awareness about the Plan among Belfast's many community groups.

The Department's *Belfast Urban Area Plan 2001: Preliminary Proposals* was published in May 1987, as required by the Planning (NI) Order. CTA was very critical of this publication, arguing it was superficial and that the Department was pursuing a token public consultation exercise (5). It pressed for an extension of the ten week period allowed for consultation on the preliminary proposals, much more publicity including television advertisements, funds and facilities to support public participation, and the publication of a Report of Survey. It criticised the cost and complexity of the consultants' reports which provided key information about what were seen to be the needs, pressures and strategic options in the urban area. Looking towards a public inquiry, CTA argued that this should exclude legal advocates, have good facilities for lay participants, be presided over by a panel of three inquisitorial inspectors, that there should be pre inquiry meetings for people intending to take part, and that local hearings should be conducted around the urban area. On the policy proposals, CTA argued the following cases:

(i)   The release of green belt land only in exceptional circumstances of housing need and not for speculative building;

(ii)   Mixed land use policies and a strategy for play areas;

(iii)   Proposals for riverside regeneration which were aimed at social needs identified in consultation with local people and not the commercialisation of the River Lagan;

(iv)   A social commitment to developing public transport as an alternative to private road vehicles;

(v)   Enhancement of local shops;

(vi)   Policies for adult education facilities, the Irish language and integrated schools;

(vii)   A demonstration of how the Plan would contribute   to a 'healthy city';

(viii)   Economic   development   proposals   for   specific   high unemployment areas.

CTA concluded its submission on the Preliminary Proposals by calling for the distribution of a more detailed information pack about the Plan and a commitment to local plans:

> When the last urban area plan for Belfast was published in 1969 it was recognised as an urban structure plan in spirit and purpose. It was quite obvious that the next logical step was to prepare district plans within the framework of that urban area plan. In fact the plan's consultants themselves prepared a district plan for Shankill and another for Belfast City Centre. However, with the exception of a district plan for Ardoyne in 1973, no further district plans were produced. As a result, many facilities for local areas, for example clinics, libraries, government offices, etc., have been located in an uncoordinated way.   The relevant government body has found a site, sought planning permission and has been allowed to proceed because since district centres are not being built the planners had no alternatives. In this way the credibility of the 1969 Belfast urban area plan was eroded because the details of the structure were never filled in by the adoption of a complementary system of District Plans.
>
> CTA (NI) hopes that this will not happen with the present Belfast Urban Area Plan. We feel that the DoE (NI) should agree to combining this Plan with a series of District Plans drawn up in cooperation with local communities. In this way, hopefully many inadequacies of planning in the past will be avoided.

CTA circulated this submission to community groups, together with a short questionnaire to collect views about the consultation process and any submissions the group had made to the Department.

Organising responses to the Plan

In March 1987, CTA sent an invitation to fifty community, voluntary, professional and business groups inviting them to attend a 'response group' meeting on the BUAP.   Seventeen people attended. As a result of the meeting press releases criticising the

75

consultation arrangements were issued and a letter was sent to the Environment Minister urging an extension of the deadline for receipt of public comments, consultation about the organisation of a public inquiry and grant aid for community groups wishing to contribute to the consultation process. The Department's attitude was spelt out very clearly in a letter from a Private Secretary to Belfast MP The Reverend Martin Smyth, dated 4 June:

> Anyone who objects to any part of our proposals has *at least* six months between the first appearance of our proposals on 18 May and the need to make his case at a public inquiry. In the meantime the objector may, of course, be so successful in persuading the Department of the merits of his case that his views will be accommodated in the draft Plan which will be published in the autumn ... I hope you will agree that our timetable provides ample opportunity for public consultation.

> To accede to CTA's request would considerably prolong the Plan making process in Belfast and would also prolong uncertainty over many developments and postpone decisions on others; none of which would be in the interest of the citizens of Belfast.

Despite this attempt to present the consultation period as a continuous six months from publication of Preliminary Proposals to public inquiry, the consultation periods were widely perceived to be the ten week deadlines for receipt of comments from the public which followed publication of the Preliminary Proposals in May 1987 and then of the draft Plan in November 1987. The timing of both was criticised; the former overlapped with the June general election and Northern Ireland's traditional July holidays and the latter with the Christmas and New Year holiday periods.

CTA also sent information to the six district councils in the Belfast Urban Area, all Belfast City Council members and relevant Members of Parliament. It continued to issue press releases on the Plan, obtaining reasonable coverage, and to meet with local organisations to discuss their responses to it.

During May and June 1987 two community conferences on the Plan were organised in West Belfast and further local meetings were organised in North and South Belfast. The first West Belfast conference in Andersonstown illustrated the broad range of needs local groups were looking to the Plan to address. Submissions were made on the following topics:

Andersonstown Traders Association on needs regarding traffic congestion, transport, industry, local facilities, general environment and community spirit, and local culture.
West Belfast Taxi Association on the needs of the black taxis which provided a regular public transport service in the area.

Twinbrook Tenants' and Community Association opposing Phase 2 of the Dunmurry By Pass.
The Travellers' Rights Committee on the needs of travelling people.
The Fourth College Committee on the needs of adult education.
Glor na nGael on the need for Irish medium education.
Sinn Fein on revitalising the Lower Falls Road.
The Falls Women's Centre on the needs of women and children.
Divis Residents' Association of the future of the Divis area.
Cathedral Community Enterprises on proposals for the Bog Meadows, an area of marsh and grassland in West Belfast.

CTA's main concerns at this stage were to encourage interest in the Plan, respond to information needs and start to coordinate those groups around Belfast that were beginning to mobilise on the planning issues. A meeting was scheduled for 24 July to bring groups together. Sixty invitations were sent out. Thirteen people attended: five from community organisations, two from voluntary organisations, one from the Northern Ireland Consumer Council, two academics, two from CTA and a volunteer planner. The meeting agreed to the setting up of a small study group of people willing to read and summarise the technical reports relating to the BUAP, and an information group which would have an open membership, meet regularly, disseminate and exchange information, and discuss ways of responding to the Plan. Links were established with other parties working on the Plan, including university researchers that had been commissioned by other voluntary organisations to evaluate its proposals; this was particularly important in accessing research on transportation undertaken for the Northern Ireland Council on Disability, Age Concern and the General Consumer Council, and on economic development.
    CTA was facing a brick wall regarding its call for a lengthening of the consultation period, despite sustained lobbying to try and get the period extended. It became apparent that the Minister would not agree to any such extension. Community groups wrote to local newspapers complaining about the situation. The following example is from Springfalls Redevelopment Association:

> Local groups, like our own, have nether the resources nor expertise to study the proposals and formulate our own submissions yet that is what we have been asked to do by the D.O.E. The planners get two or three years and all the funds and resources they need. What do local communities get? In response, the D.O.E. says that the proposals do not affect every local community but this is misleading in the extreme. The plan isn't just about which communities will be disrupted and which will not. It is more fundamentally about the allocation of finance and resources for the next 25 years. Let no one, and in particular no local community, be in doubt: this plan is about spending money on prestigious

77

projects in the city centre and Laganside but only at the expense of not adequately financing the facilities and services local areas are crying out for. (*Irish News*, 9 July 1987)

There was more success with pressing for talks about arrangements for the public inquiry. CTA was invited to a meeting with senior DoE officials on 2 July to discuss this issue. At the meeting it reiterated its case for extending the public consultation period, but was again told that this could not be accepted and that community groups would have another opportunity to comment following publication of the draft Plan in the autumn (6). CTA made further cases for funding three planning posts to assist community groups, financial aid for local groups researching local issues, three inquiry inspectors, one with experience of community work, and no legal advocates at the inquiry, with the questioning of participants undertaken solely by the inspectors and their specialist advisers. The Department agreed to represent these arguments to the Planning Appeals Commission, and to contact CTA with a decision on the proposals it had tabled at the meeting.

At this point it is relevant to note that payment of legal costs from public funds following the 1977 public inquiry into the transportation review had been recommended by the inspector in his report to the DoE. This, however, was seen as exceptional in view of the 'rather unusual' nature of the inquiry and the 'comparatively limited' amount of legal representation which had made a 'considerable contribution' (Lavery report, 1978, p.190). In chapter 2 it was reported that the British Government rejected a 1986 recommendation by the House of Commons Environment Committee that funding should be available to support the participation of third parties at big public inquiries. It was considered inappropriate to use public funds to support objectors concerned with defending their own sectional interests. So it was difficult to predict what decision the Department might take about the BUAP.

In August, a media release from the Northern Ireland Information Service revealed that 1,150 comments from the public had been received about the BUAP Preliminary Proposals (7). This prompted a DoE spokesperson to state that, 'The public consultation on the Department's Preliminary Proposals has turned out to be highly successful particularly in identifying those aspects of the plan proposals about which there is widespread public concern'. At the same time, the Department wrote to CTA with a response to the 2 July meeting:

> The Public Inquiry will be taken by a senior member of the Planning Appeals Commission. However, he or she will report to the Planning Appeals Commission. All 10 Commissioners will have access to all the evidence and will examine it thoroughly and require to be satisfied about the

recommendations which the PAC will make ... The Public
Inquiry will be preceded by a number of pre-inquiry
meetings, to which objectors will be invited, to endeavour to
discuss the order in which topics will be taken and generally
provide for a smooth running and efficient inquiry ... The
PAC is in principle fully sympathetic to the proposal that
facilities should be provided in the same building for
objectors.

You also asked about legal representation. It is not possible
to deny any party to the Inquiry the right to be legally
represented.

Finally you asked about resourcing the community sector for
the Public Inquiry. Community Groups will not be the only
objectors at the Public Inquiry. The Department would find
it difficult to justify aiding some objectors but not others.

However, the desirability of ensuring that community groups
are provided with professional support on planning and
planning related issues is already accepted by the
Department and is the basis of the Department's grant aiding
CTA. The Department acknowledges that the scale and
complexity of the Belfast Urban Area Plan places an
exceptional strain on the resources of CTA. I think
therefore that we should meet again soon to explore if it is
possible for us to provide any further assistance ... (8)

CTA began a search for independent and experienced professional
help in expectation that this might now be grant aided by the
Department. Through a local contact, a Dublin based firm of
planning law consultants, Reid McHugh Partnership, were
approached. They agreed to work with CTA on a package which
could be presented to the Department for funding. The firm
proposed a procedure which would work as shown in Figure 4.2.
Reid McHugh stressed the importance of relating all the tasks to
the public inquiry where, they urged, CTA had to be legally
represented because other parties would not be precluded from
using legal advocates. A costing for coordinating the project, legal
representation at the inquiry, the short term employment of
planning assistants and the resourcing of meetings and information
dissemination was worked out, and on this basis a request for a
grant of £59,000 was put to the Department of the Environment.
The DoE wrote to CTA on 16 November offering a grant of up to
£50,000 'to enable CTA to provide technical and professional help to
community groups to assist them in preparing, formulating and
presenting their views on any aspect of the Belfast Urban Area
Plan' (9). The size of the grant was disappointing; more had been
hoped for to fund local conferences and distribute information, but

79

Figure 4.2 CTA and Belfast Urban Area Plan: Summary of Suggested Procedures by Reid McHugh and Partners (29 October 1987)

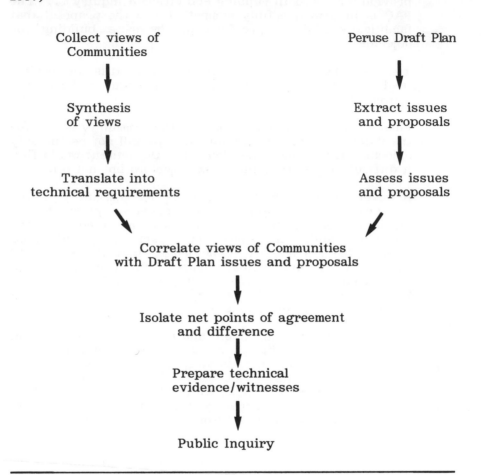

it was enough to commission Reid McHugh and employ three graduate planners.

On 17 November the draft Plan was published, price £5. Some concessions were made to objections received following the Preliminary Proposals: highly controversial proposals for a road through Belvoir Park Forest and housebuilding in 'beauty spots' at Hydebank and Glenmachan were removed. But little else changed, especially relating to the fundamental arguments about social and local needs.

CTA organised an open conference for Belfast community groups on 25 November 1987 to identify issues arising from the Plan, to consider their implications for local communities and special interest groups, and to agree a strategy. This was to be the starting point for distilling objections and evidence for the public inquiry. The conference followed several weeks of intensive work by a few CTA volunteers visiting community groups and increasing awareness about the new Plan. While in some areas, notably West Belfast, many local communities were already fairly well organised, in other areas such as East Belfast the level of organisation and interest was initially low but strengthened later.

Over 140 people attended the November conference from a wide spectrum of interests (see Appendix 1). The organising committee had arranged for briefing papers on all the major topics to be circulated, including transport, housing, industry and commerce, Laganside, environment and conservation, leisure, retailing, health, education, women, and general issues. Following working groups on these topics at the conference, the main points would be published as a report which would form the basis of CTA's response to the Plan. Speakers underlined that a cross community response was essential, and that as far as possible agreement should be reached on issues of a strategic nature, thereby forming a basic brief for CTA's planning team to act upon. Within an agreed position on the Plan's main strategies, it was expected that detailed views on specific or local issues would be formulated by local and special interest groups. CTA's role should be to represent an agreed position on the Plan's strategies through all of the statutory channels including the public inquiry, while individual community and voluntary groups would be free to present their own local or specific cases through the same channels, with or without CTA's assistance. John Reid of Reid McHugh & Partners told the conference that the public inquiry gave community based groups the chance to question the contents of the Plan and how those contents were arrived at:

> It is under the full glare of publicity in a public arena. The DoE will be there speaking with one voice as will private organisations such as companies and commercial groupings. It is absolutely essential that you as a group speak with a single voice. You cannot be seen to be divided among yourselves on major issues ... Community Technical Aid cannot dictate what your views are going to be. It is the mouthpiece of the grouping. You must agree on some administrative or management structure and try to itemise the technical issues seen as important by all the groupings here today. (*Irish News*, 26 November 1987)

The conference agreed to take the following steps:

1.   CTA would represent the views of the conference on strategic issues such as public transport and the green belt;

2.   CTA would be assisted by an advisory group comprising community and special interest groups;

3.   CTA would accept the grant of £50,000 from the DoE but continue to lobby for a more adequate sum;

4.   Issues would be divided into three categories:
      (i)   those on which there was broad agreement;
      (ii)   those on which there was agreement to differ;
      (iii)   those on which there were irreconcilable differences.

CTA would only be involved with (i) and (ii). In the event, there were no major irreconcilable differences between the groups, but this framework was important in enabling the work to proceed on an agreed basis.   There was agreement to differ about breaching the stopline or green belt, which groups in the East wanted protected from proposed greenfield housing, while groups in the West wanted flexibility to help cope with severe shortages of public sector housing for rent in that sector of the city.   It was argued that Government claims that there was enough housebuilding land within West Belfast had 'led to housing being built on every conceivable green space' (*Andersonstown News*, 11 April 1987). The nearest to an irreconcilable difference was opposing the Plan's proposal for a cross harbour bridge and road link which would impact on some 120 acres adjacent to it. The North Belfast Steering Group wanted total opposition, but others regarded it as a *fait accompli* not worth opposing because of an existing clear Government commitment that work on the project would start in 1991 and because local residents did not appear to oppose the project.

Reid McHugh and the three graduate planners were appointed as intended.   The three planners divided up the work according to geographical sector and topic.   The advisory group was formed as a special committee of CTA.   It had the following composition:

Belfast North	2 members
Belfast South	2 members
Belfast East	2 members
Belfast West	2 members
Outer North	1 member
Outer South	1 member
Caring agencies	1 member
Conservation groups	1 member
Socio-economic interests	1 member
CTA	3 members

The area representatives were agreed at public meetings held by CTA. Each representative had a local steering committee which was meant to link them to their 'interest groups'. The arrangement appeared to work well and there were no obvious problems with it.

The first advisory group meeting was held on 9 December to decide the scope and programme of work. CTA's first task was to set out its approach and make a timetable of work up to the public inquiry, which was expected to begin in May 1988.

On 15 January 1988 CTA submitted its own objections to the BUAP along with a number of other groups and political parties, staging the event at the City Planning Office for the media. It was the intention that these objections should dovetail. The full document setting out CTA's objections is reproduced in Appendix 2.

The advisory group process

During December 1987 and January 1988, six meetings were held by CTA in different locations around the Belfast urban area with community groups. At these meetings John Reid explained the planning procedures that would lead up to the public inquiry, and the procedures during the inquiry itself. The planner responsible for the local area of the meeting explained how the plan affected it. Comments and questions were then invited. Meetings were also held during this period with special interest groups, including conservation and women's groups.

CTA prepared a paper on all the issues arising from these meetings, setting out topic by topic the strategic policy objections and area specific objections (the paper is reproduced in Appendix 3). This was reviewed by a meeting of the advisory group at the end of January 1988, helping to inform each member of the issues affecting the others' areas. From February through to March there were eight more advisory group meetings, each devoted to a particular topic or topics. These were housing, transportation, conservation, landscape and green belt, recreation, industry and commerce, shopping, Laganside, health, education and women's issues. A paper was prepared by the planners on one or more topics each week (as an example, Appendix 4 reproduces the paper prepared on housing). Various technical, organisational and procedural points were raised and dealt with at these meetings.

The time available for formulating and researching objections on the ten topics was short, with each having in practice an average time allocation of less than one working week. The topic papers were based on consultations at the local and special interest meetings. Information was also gathered from various other sources, such as the Northern Ireland Housing Executive and the Department of Economic Development. At each of the meetings of the advisory group a draft paper was presented. Following discussion, a position statement on the strategic issues relating to the topic was agreed. This agreement was fundamental to CTA presenting a united community based response to the Plan at the inquiry.

The process placed heavy and exceptional demands on the three planners throughout the process, entailing frequent evening meetings and long hours. A lot of commitment was also demanded from the advisory group members, which formed a vital link between CTA and the grassroots. Some of the members were professional community workers while others worked in the community on a voluntary basis. CTA's planning team commented that without these links into local communities the whole exercise would have been extremely difficult, if not impossible. But it was an uphill task to sustain the commitment of advisory group members during a lengthy and intensive consultation process (10). The experience reinforced CTA's criticisms, made again at the public inquiry, that there was a lack of time and lack of money behind the consultation arrangements.

At the outset of the project, some community groups were unhappy that CTA was funded by the Department of the Environment to 'represent' them. It is evident, however, that during the course of the long advisory group process the planning team came to be trusted by all the groups. Members of the advisory group were interviewed after the public inquiry, and were unanimously supportive of CTA's role and the approach taken in response to the Plan (11). There were some criticisms. A few members felt that CTA was over stretched. The most serious criticism concerned the advisory group meetings. Three members stated they were too long and that it was difficult to digest detailed papers in one evening. It was felt there were too many meetings and some topics were not directly relevant to every member. All the members who made these criticisms, however, said that there was very little else CTA could do given the lack of time and resources.

CTA itself encountered a problem of accessing information. Acquiring statistical data which were often unpublished was a lengthy process. Other information wanted to test the Plan's proposals did not exist, such as transport statistics analysed by gender. Financial constraints meant that CTA could not purchase many reference documents, and visiting libraries was a time consuming luxury. There is also little doubt that the number of meetings that had to be serviced between the November 1987 conference and the last advisory group meeting in May 1988 inhibited the preparation of objections and evidence.

The public inquiry: organisation and assessment

The Department of the Environment sent rebuttal statements to all objectors before the public inquiry. Although meant to answer each objector's points they were in fact standard word processed replies (CTA's is reproduced in Appendix 5). In interviews with thirteen members of the advisory group, these rubuttal statements were widely criticised as failing to answer objectors' cases. Although this is perhaps not surprising, serious criticisms were made that the statements were 'shallow', 'abysmal', 'provocative' and 'distortions of the truth'. Six respondents, however, felt that they provided some insight into the way the Department was likely to develop its case at the inquiry. Overall, the rebuttal statements seemed to serve little purpose.

The Planning Appeals Commission organised the pre inquiry meetings CTA had pressed for. Three meetings were held during March 1988. Eight of the thirteen members of the advisory group interviewed said that these meetings were *not* useful. They were criticised as being poorly organised, confusing and 'an insult to people's intelligence'. Although the Planning Appeals Commission treated the pre inquiry meetings as largely about timetabling topics and appearances at the public inquiry, the *perception* of many people who attended them was that the inquiry process had begun. They were therefore frustrated when technical matters could not be raised. One of the members of the advisory group commented that the meetings were poorly handled and did not inspire confidence in the PAC. Much more attention should have been paid to these pre inquiry meetings, not least to present the PAC as 'user friendly' and independent of the officialdom of the Department of the Environment. The CTA planners commented that most of the community groups going into the public inquiry did not perceive the PAC as a body that could help them or be sympathetic, regarding the commissioners with suspicion. Very few, if any, they believed, perceived the public inquiry to be an objective or just forum for hearing their objections. The pre inquiry meetings almost certainly contributed to this feeling.

There was no negotiation with objectors prior to the inquiry. The nearest to negotiation that took place was a suggestion at a pre inquiry meeting that detailed discussions about development proposals in the Jordanstown area would take place as part of a local plan, and that widening of the Lower Ormeau Road could be avoided by passing a route along the Ravenshill embankment. Objectors resisted these suggestions, believing they should not be led into playing off one area against another when fundamental policy issues were at stake. While negotiations might have helped to arrive at some mutually acceptable solutions, they would have been unacceptable once the draft Plan was published precisely because objectors were then faced with arguments that houses and road traffic routes had to go somewhere. The time for negotiation had been when problems were being defined before the Preliminary Proposals, such as whether traffic congestion was a problem of road capacity rather than control of road vehicles and enhancement of public transport. This was one reason why CTA considered the early stages - when it had been arguing for publication of a Report of Survey - to be too rushed; events had been precipitated towards the public inquiry, where the situation was inevitably not only adversarial but perceived to be unfair because no one had been consulted about the definition of problems and issues.

Despite this, both the PAC and the Department urged that the inquiry should be non adversarial. 'Cross questioning' was to be preferred to 'cross examination' during the inquiry to indicate dialogue rather than conflict. While hardly a court room drama, the inquiry discourse was not one of dialogue and often a community group would put its case without comment from the DoE. It would even be a relief not to be cross examined; many found the prospect to be highly intimidating and unfair - it seemed as it they were on trial when it was the DoE's Plan that was under examination. In most cases community groups appeared at the inquiry as a small panel with members of the group's committee and often some local residents, businesspersons or an elected representative; the prospect of cross examination was easier then because questions from opposing counsel were directed at the whole panel rather than one individual. Two groups had their own legal representation, one stating that they used a barrister to avoid putting themselves in front of the DoE's counsel. The impression of the CTA planners was that the few groups which did use legal representation - including calling on CTA's barristers - seemed to have their cases treated more seriously by both the DoE and the PAC. This may have been because arguments become more structured and this in turn led to a more formal atmosphere. It it difficult to decide whether this actually influenced the commissioners' recommendations.

The public inquiry opened in Central Hall, Belfast, on 4 May 1988 (use of the City Hall had been refused by Belfast City Council as part of its protest against the Anglo Irish Agreement). The CTA team was accommodated at the front of the hall opposite the DoE team and with the same facilities. Its agreed role was to present proofs of evidence on all the topics that had been identified as important at the November conference, and which were subsequently discussed at the advisory group meetings. A month had been spent following these meetings recasting the revised advisory group papers as proofs of evidence, justifying and sourcing the evidence in them. While many community groups presented their own cases, the months of pre inquiry planning paid off in ensuring that these complemented CTA's submissions. In CTA's opening submission, the weaknesses of the consultation process were highlighted:

> CTA ... is concerned that detailed proposals could have been formulated for particular parts of the Belfast Urban Area without a single consultation with local people by either the Department or their consultants ... The extent to which

even the representations made on the Preliminary Proposals were considered by the Department could also be questioned. The period which elapsed between the closing date for receipt of such representations and the date of the publication of the draft Plan was a mere 15 weeks. The draft Plan comprises complex technical documents produced to a most detailed specification in terms of printing technology. That these documents were materially amended during such a short period of time, on foot of representations received, is doubted. (13)

The inquiry ran for just over seven weeks from 4 May to 24 June. During the inquiry CTA presented its various proofs of evidence on housing, transportation, conservation, landscape and green belt, recreation, industry and commerce, shopping, Laganside, health, education and women's issues, as well as case studies and single presentations on behalf of geographically based groups. This typically involved one of the planners reading out the proof of evidence, followed by an opportunity for questioning by the DoE's legal representatives, and finally an opportunity for CTA to question the Department.

The continuous presence that CTA had at the inquiry meant that it could brief people calling in about how the inquiry was progressing, timetabling (which was flexible during the inquiry), cases already presented and provide last minute advice. Above all, as they saw it, CTA could reinforce its arguments by using the opportunity at the inquiry to speak in opposition to objectors whose cases conflicted with CTA's; this was particularly important with regard to the Glenmachan housing zoning objection (see chapter 5).

Interviews with advisory group members revealed general satisfaction with CTA proofs of evidence. Its permanent presence at the inquiry was found to be useful and reassuring. The arrangement was a model that should certainly be considered for other major inquiries.

The permanent presence of CTA also helped to overcome a problem with the consultation procedure whereby although the draft Plan is published and advertised, the locations and nature of objections are not. It was thus possible for someone to have inspected the draft Plan, considered it acceptable, but then for an objection unknown to them to threaten fundamentally new proposals for their area. This was the only aspect of the consultation process which the PAC criticised, recommending that all objections be made public in time for representations to be made on them.

Interviews with the thirteen advisory group members after the inquiry revealed mixed opinions about its procedures and facilities. Four respondents were generally satisfied with all aspects, one involved in the transportation issues felt they were rushed, three members stated that the facilities were poor, two felt that the procedures were intimidating, two criticised the timetabling, one felt that not all objectors were treated equally, and one stated that the DoE were patronising. Several comments were made about the absence of a creche. Most of the respondents welcomed the provision of a photocopier for use by objectors, but it was stated that more than one machine was needed and that placing such facilities in the office used by the PAC intimidated some users. It was also claimed that there was a failure to advertise the facilities.

Eleven of the thirteen advisory group members described the inquiry's atmosphere as formal and intimidating, mainly due to the setting in a city centre public hall and the presence of barristers. Comments made about this atmosphere included references to 'men in suits', 'legal heavyweights', that the inquiry 'belittled people' and an observation that 'the DoE don't have to do anything', that is, it was the objector who felt under examination:

> I felt I had to defend a position. You shouldn't have to defend yourself. It should be up to the DoE to defend themselves. They are putting forward the proposals.

Respondents stated that the atmosphere varied from adversarial to non adversarial depending on the objector and the circumstances. One respondent felt that people were treated differently depending on their 'social class', and that decisions to cross examine were not consistent, depending on the timetable. Two positive comments were made that the commissioners were 'very good, flexible and non adversarial', and that the atmosphere at the inquiry was 'friendly but formal, and semi non adversarial'.

Overall, then, we have a picture of a formal official process conducted in public with two commissioners hearing whatever people had the will and ability to say about the Plan. The fact it was in public seemed largely irrelevant; despite a crowded hall for the first few days, by the second week attendance had fallen to very small numbers indeed. In fact, for at least some people, the public hall setting added to the intimidating atmosphere rather than facilitating public participation.

Conclusions

Chapter 5 discusses the cases made by CTA and the community groups at the inquiry, and examines how far the final Plan as adopted by the Department of the Environment reflected these arguments. The present chapter has focused on the history of CTA's involvement in the Plan and its strategy for involving community groups in the public inquiry. Two major conclusions about the consultation process emerge from the chapter.

First, the consultation process was inadequate due to a failure on behalf of the the DoE actively to encourage participation, especially in the critical stages prior to the Preliminary Proposals when the issues and problems which the Plan should address were being defined. The grant to CTA was belated and extracted only after lobbying. Above all, at £50,000 it was a trivial sum hardly able to put the DoE and community groups on an equal footing at the public inquiry when the former had spent three years and £1.9 million on work by consultants on *their* proposals (12). It was also hardly compensation for the complete absence of local democratic control over the planning authority.

It seems impossible to involve the mass of the public in planning. Ash (1979) concludes that participation exercises in planning should therefore focus on encouraging the formation and participation of voluntary grassroots associations, and this was what largely happened in the BUAP exercise. Months of community work and networking through specifically constituted area committees by the CTA planners, tapping the accumulated knowledge and experience of community and special interest groups around the urban area, was distilled into a series of formal objections and proofs of evidence at the public inquiry. The Planning Appeals Commission recognised the many groups which contributed to the public inquiry as 'representative' (PAC, 1989, p. 3).

The DoE went through the motions of press notices, consultations with statutory bodies and public displays as required by statute. Publication of the Preliminary Proposals and six months later the draft Plan, each followed by consultation periods of only several weeks, fragmented what should have been continuous dialogue with individuals and organisations invited to take a positive part in plan preparation right at the beginning as partners and consultees in the process. The restricting of public participation to narrowly defined land use matters for no apparent reason other than bureaucratic convenience was also a source of fragmentation and dissatisfaction among groups who wanted to raise issues about all the public services for their localities, an issue discussed in the following chapter.

The present chapter's second conclusion relates more directly to the public inquiry. This was a formal process perceived accurately by lay participants to be part of 'officialdom' (the DoE and the commissioners were not distinguished from each other in this respect). The public hall environment and quasi judicial process were intimidating and inimical to ordinary people contributing their own experience and knowledge, and feeling that their voices could be heard; something appreciated by Sheffield City Council in its decision to use small groups rather than a public inquiry to examine its City Centre Plan (see chapter 2). The lack of participation in the making of the draft BUAP meant that inevitably the public inquiry was an arena for a confrontation between the 'official point of view' and the community perception of the environment and its problems. Officialdom was the repository of power and this in itself meant that the officialdom-people division was a real and unequal one at the inquiry and in the whole planning process. As Arnstein (1969) concluded:

> participation without redistribution of power is an empty and
> frustrating process for the powerless. It allows the
> powerholders to claim that all sides were considered, but
> makes it possible for only some of those sides to benefit. It
> maintains the *status quo*. (p. 176)

Whether much was achieved by way of influencing the final Plan for
Belfast is the subject of the next chapter. However, whatever the
inadequacies of the public inquiry, it meant that the draft Plan was
examined in public issue by issue and area by area with an
opportunity for all objectors to be heard. This fact acted as a
major focus and stimulus for CTA's participation exercise. The
draft Plan and the public inquiry were things that everyone could
relate and build up to.

CTA's role mitigated some of the most serious defects of the
consultation process and the public inquiry. Much of this work
occurred well before the inquiry itself. Considerable effort was
necessary to outline to all parties the statutory procedures for
making a plan and submitting written objections, and informing
groups of where the draft Plan could be inspected or purchased
from. The provision of planning and legal advice was highly
successful in supporting the preparation and presentation of
submissions which community groups wished to make. CTA had a
vital role in translating diverse needs and ideas into planning
arguments that could stand up at the public inquiry. Much time
was spent advising groups and individuals about how the inquiry
would be organised, what kind of atmosphere to expect, how to
present objections and supporting evidence, what objections to
highlight, how the Department might question the group, how they
should respond, and in turn how they might question the
Department.

Although in making its argument for three commissioners and
publication of the reasons for their appointment CTA was concerned
that only one commissioner would preside at the inquiry, two
presiding commissionsers were appointed and this seemed to work
well.

Reade (1987) argues that 'planning aid' has become 'merely a way
of educating the public into the way in which the planning system
works' (p. 100). This, he suggests, contributes to the ideology
that planning is a technical activity rather than about the politics
of locating and allocating urban resources. However, the danger
with this argument is that it implies that education about public
policy making processes is not important compared with raising
political awareness about class bias in state actions. Knowing how
the system works is not only essential to pragmatic community action
and politics aimed at winning benefits within the system, but also
to developing alternatives to it. There is already often a high
degree of awareness among deprived and oppressed groups about

class and social bias in state actions as a result of direct experience of such bias. No groups who participated in the BUAP inquiry, for example, expected anything other than a process heavily weighted towards the proposals of the draft Plan. Although all of the members of the advisory group believed that the Plan could be influenced or changed, this was strongly qualified by 'realism': '90 per cent of the Plan is set in concrete and only 9 or 10 per cent might be changed'; 'forces are stacked against us'; 'there is not much hope for change'; 'there will be minor changes to maintain a democratic image'; 'bits and pieces'; 'cosmetics'; 'small things - a PR exercise'; and 'people do not believe themselves capable of achieving any changes' were commmments made before anyone knew the outcome of the public inquiry (14). People from groups in largely Protestant and less deprived East and South Belfast were more confident of winning changes than people from groups in largely Catholic and more deprived North and West Belfast.

In a conference organised by CTA in February 1990 to assess the successes and failures of the project, one of the main achievements was felt to be that many people now knew how the planning system worked. A bureaucratic process had been demystified by playing the public inquiry game. CTA spent a large amount of time with individuals and groups explaining the planning system and its legislation before it was possible to translate local views into planning arguments. The demand for such advice was considerable, and there was not enough time for this process. Centralising the work through CTA was not particularly popular with the community groups, especially initially when there were some early communication problems, and one member of the advisory group reflected after the inquiry that the groups should 'have done their own thing to a greater extent'. But at the end of the project twelve of thirteen advisory group members interviewed were positive about CTA's role as the only way to coordinate and sustain a response from community groups. Comments included, 'there was a lot of openness in CTA's approach', 'there were opportunities to meet other groups concerned with the Plan', 'a genuine attempt to represent grassroots feelings', 'if it had been left to the groups it would have gone down the drain', 'it ironed out a lot of differences' and 'it was a feat of sheer endurance to get everyone in the same room'.

Notes

1. Paper by Brendan Carolan, undated.

2. From a tape recording of a speech by Jackie Redpath to a conference on community technical aid in Magee College, Derry on 7 May 1983. CTA (NI) was launched following the conference.

3. Report prepared by the Principal Chief Planner, South Yorkshire County Council, 19 December 1985.

4. Letter to J Larkin from D McIldoon, 27 March 1986.

5. Submission made by Community Technical Aid (NI) to the Department of the Environment (NI) on the Belfast Urban Area Plan - Preliminary Proposals, undated.

6. The Belfast Urban Area Plan - Report of a Meeting held between the Department of the Environment and Community Technical Aid on 2 July 1987 in Clarendon House.

7. Northern Ireland Information Service, *Belfast Urban Area Plan*, 27 August 1987.

8. Letter to L Allamby from D McIldoon, 26 August 1987.

9. Letter to C Morrison from D McIldoon, 17 November 1987.

10. Accounts by the CTA planning team made during September and October 1988.

11. Interviews with advisory group members recorded during September and October 1988 carried out by the CTA planning team, Una O'Boyle, Paddy Carroll and Irene Kenedy.

12. Written answer No. 67 for 9.3.88 from Mr Needham (Environment Minister) to Mr. Peter Robinson MP (Belfast East), 16 March 1988.

13. Preamble: Proof of Evidence presented at public inquiry into Belfast Urban Area Plan 2001, May 1988, Community Technical Aid (NI).

14. See note 11.

5   The outcome

> CTA claims that the views which it will put forward at this
> inquiry are a product of a proper system of public
> consultation which, if incorporated into an amended BUAP,
> will produce a Plan that will obtain broad public acceptance
> and will more property satisfy needs and utilise opportunities
> than that Plan currently on the table. (1)

Thus concluded CTA's preamble in the opening stages of the BUAP
inquiry. In a long initial submission CTA summarised the objections
it would be making. Its strategy of concentrating on researched
objections rather than submitting alternatives to the Plan's
proposals was immediately challenged by the DoE's counsel who
accused CTA of criticising the Plan without presenting any such
alternatives. CTA's response was to state that it was appearing at
the inquiry to present its objections; it was the Department's
responsibility to provide alternatives (*Belfast Telegraph*, 11 May
1988). This was not especially satisfactory, but CTA had little
choice given the absence of time or resources to demonstrate in
detail how its objections should be met, and the adversarial set up
of the public inquiry, which facilitated criticism and invited attack
from the Department on any alternatives presented by objectors.

The BUAP is a strategic development plan. But while similar in
scale and purpose to an English county structure plan, it is more
precise in locational terms. This led to controversy about some key
objections which objectors considered relevant to a Plan of this
nature, while the Department, and in almost all cases the Planning
Appeals Commission, judged them to be matters for local plans or

local development control. There was also no comprehensive commitment to local plans from the Department; it had stated that these would be produced 'where the scale of development in any particular area made it desirable' (2).

The inquiry ended on 27 June 1988. In June 1989 the Planning Appeals Commission reported to the Department of the Environment its views on the objections, the evidence and consideration of them by the two presiding commissioners relating to housing proposals and green belt issues. The Commission took a different view to its appointed commissioners on three of the housing proposals. In September the Commission reported its findings on public transport and highways, taking a different view on restraining the use of private cars and two aspects of the road proposals. These findings are discussed below. On all other matters the Commission was in full agreement with its appointed commissioners. In December the Department of the Environment published the 486 page report of the Commission together with the Department's Adoption Statement (Planning Appeals Commission, 1989; Department of the Environment (NI), 1989). The Adoption Statement sets out in summary form the Department's decisions on the objections considered by the Commission and based on the report of the public inquiry.

The present chapter considers the objections and evidence from community groups at the inquiry and in CTA's submissions. This is done analytically to draw out the implications of the arguments and the response to them by the Planning Appeals Commission and the Department.

The fundamentals: what can planning do?

In preparing the ground for the range of objections relating to social needs, CTA had to argue for these to be considered planning matters. An important thrust of its whole argument was that the Plan should address social issues as an integral aspect of land use. At the inquiry CTA pointed to the statutory rules which govern town and country planning in Northern Ireland and which are modelled on their English equivalents, the Town and Country Planning (Structure and Local Plans) Regulations. In Northern Ireland, the Planning (Development Plan) Regulations 1973 (No. 365) set out thirteen matters to which development plans are required to relate 'as the Ministry may think approptiate':

1.   Population
2.   Employment
3.   Housing
4.   Industry and Commerce
5.   Transportation
6.   Shopping
7.   Education

8.   Health and Personal Social Services
9.   Other Social and Community Services
10.   Recreation and Leisure
11.   Conservation, Townscape and Landscape
12.   Utility Services
13.   Any other relevant matters including minerals

The Regulations require that a development plan should indicate 'as the Ministry may think appropriate ... The regard the Ministry has had to social policies and considerations'. A critique of the neglect of social policies and considerations challenged the official paradigm of the BUAP. This was not purely the coordination of land uses. It was underpinned by an economic strategy based on stimulating sectors in which growth was occurring nationally. As Frank Gaffikin, quoted in Wilson (1988, p. 16), explains:

> To call it a land use plan and at the same time to acknowledge that it has accompanying it fairly detailed investment proposals for Laganside, for the retailing sector, among others - which go far beyond the traditional land use strategy approach to specific proposals for development - is to deny that it is in part underpinned by a key economic strategy. The strategy, like many other similar strategies for riverside cities, for old dockland cities, is to assume manufacturing is in some kind of irreversible decline as a source of jobs and investment, and that the alternative on the agenda seems to be retailing, tourism and general leisure activities, and therefore we need expansion of those.

The concern of CTA and many other objectors was that this growth, if it was sustainable in Belfast, would not close the gap between the most deprived sections of the city and the comfortable, and may indeed widen it. It was also feared that among the external costs of growth would be damage to the environment.

Many community groups searched the Plan in vain for means of social and economic development and qualitative improvements planned for their areas. And although there were such stated aims as 'to create a physical environment and framework for social and economic activity which will enhance the quality of urban living', no social policies were spelt out in the Plan (Department of the Environment (NI), 1987, p. 7). Falls Women's Centre, for example, objected that the requirements of women for the provision of health care, local shops, public transport, local recreation and community employment were not addressed by the Plan. The Lower Lenadoon Housing Action Committee objected that their needs for sheltered housing, improved public transport and community workshops were unmet by the Plan. The Lower Ormeau Residents Action Group objected to the Laganside proposals as marginal to the many social needs of its adjoining area. They presented their own *People's Plan* to the inquiry which argued against the widening of the Lower Ormeau Road and documented needs for play and recreation facilities, shops and new development by the Housing Executive (Northern Ireland's public housing authority).

Two of the steering groups made a series of submissions to the inquiry about the social and economic needs of their areas. The North Belfast Steering Group argued that needs for public sector housing, improved public transport and better recreation provision in the area were ignored in the Plan and objected to the lack of proposals on health. The West Belfast Steering Group objected to the paucity of proposals for health, education, women, local shops and industrial development, and argued the need for planned public sector housing for rent rather than speculative housing for owner occupation. It objected to the failure to address the problems of travelling people and to consider the role of West Belfast's shared black taxis in public transport services. Conservation was highlighted with a defence of the green belt and an attack on the failure to control damage to Black Mountain and heavy pollution caused by quarrying. A failure to list and protect historical and cultural monuments in West Belfast was also criticised.

The Gaelic League, Glor na nGael and the Irish language schools made a joint submission objecting to the Plan's absence of a policy for the Irish language, calling for West Belfast to be designated a bilingual area and for land to be zoned for Irish language facilities. The presiding commissioners agreed to hear part of the submission in Gaelic and provided an interpreter. This action was fiercely criticised by Unionists who saw it as giving a platform to Sinn Fein, and led a Unionist City councillor to reverse the decision not to address the inquiry and attend to make a submission on tourism in French (*Belfast Telegraph*, 11 May 1988). The CTA planners felt the submission by the Irish language lobby to be over long and have only tenuous links to the Plan; this made it easier for the Planning Appeals Commission to conclude that Irish language and culture were not matters for a strategic development plan (Planning Appeals Commission, 1989, p. 329).

CTA complemented all these objections with evidence on social and economic needs which it argued the Plan should address. On women, for example, it pointed out that the Royal Town Planning Institute, the Town and Country Planning Association and many local planning authorities in England had drawn up statements on women's issues. The BUAP did not recognise these issues and as a result its policies were indirectly discriminatory. For instance, 30 per cent of the land zoned for recreation in the Belfast Urban Area was golf courses and a further twenty per cent was playing fields, both catering for overwhelmingly male pursuits. These uses were included in the land area to population ratios on which the Department based its argument that the recreation needs of the urban area were catered for, yet this totally disregarded the specific needs of women for leisure provision. CTA also argued for a strategic policy on play; for example in West Belfast, an overcrowded area with 40 per cent of its population under 16, there were only three equipped play areas. The argument was partially won with the Planning Appeals Commission. It made a rather weak recommendation that, 'included in the Plan there should be a statement which would remind those authorities and all others charged with or involved in, local plans and development proposals to take serious account of the special needs of women in all aspects of life in the Greater Belfast Area (Planning Appeals Commission, 1989, p. 336). The Department of the Environment, however, rejected the recommendation in the Adoption Statement, stating that women's needs are 'not an appropriate matter for a strategic land use plan' (Department of the Environment (NI), 1989, p. 23).

More success was achieved by the objections calling for a health policy in the Plan. CTA highlighted the role for planning in promoting health. This was recognised by the presiding commissioners, who were prompted by information received after the inquiry about Belfast's membership of the World Health Organisation's Healthy Cities initiative. Belfast's Healthy Cities Working Group in fact included representation from the Planning Service. The Commission recommended that the Plan should 'endorse' the aims of the project (Planning Appeals Commission, 1989, p. 323). The Department of the Environment accepted the recommendation, amending the Plan to include objectives of improving the physical environment to promote the general health of the population and supporting and facilitating the Healthy Cities project in Belfast (Department of the Environment (NI), 1989, p. 22). However, this apparent commitment to health was not reflected in changes to any of the existing proposals in the draft Plan on health grounds. For example, the Lower Lenadoon Housing Action Committee, the West Belfast Steering Group and CTA had argued that continuing quarrying operations at Black Mountain were damaging the health of local residents. In their consideration, the presiding commissioners ignored the health issue, referring only to 'amenity problems' caused by the quarrying, while the Adoption Statement referred to the need to protect 'the scenic and amenity importance of the Belfast hills' but rejected the Housing Action Committee's argument that quarrying should be stopped at this location (Planning Appeals Commission, 1989, pp. 257-258; Department of the Environment (NI), 1989, p. 15).

Overall, the Commission accepted a role for the inquiry in hearing evidence about social and economic needs, but felt in all but a very few cases that they were issues to be referred elsewhere. Thus:

> We take the view that in reporting on those matters which on strict interpretation would be found to be outside the remit of the Inquiry, we are providing the Department and other implementing authorites with a preview of the concerns and aspirations of many representative groups throughout the

97

Greater Belfast Area which preview, we trust, will serve as a guide to further action, particularly at local level. (Planning Appeals Commission, 1989, p. 3)

As long ago as the Skeffington report (1969) it was recognised that people who participated in town planning would also be concerned about public services in their areas. The Skeffington Committee recommended that when issues about, for example, refuse collection were raised in public meetings about development plans, the appropriate department should be notified of the issue - an approach reflected in the PAC report on the Belfast Urban Area Plan. The same principle was also applied to questions such as provision for children's play, which was considered to be a matter for local plans and development control at neighbourhood level rather than a subject about which there should be a policy in a strategic development plan. The Adoption Statement summed up the DoE's position:

> The Department has noted the views expressed on wider political, ecological, social or economic matters and the comments of the Planning Appeals Commission relating to these issues. It notes that the Commission has offered no specific advice and the Department is satisfied that the BUAP has the flexibility necessary to accommodate change within the plan period. It is not the purpose of a strategic land use plan to deal with the social, economic and other aspects involved. Some aspects, such as sites for the 'Travelling People' or for other community purposes, can be best handled through the development control process, or where appropriate in the context of a Local Plan; other subjects such as Irish Language Schools are primarily a matter for the education system. However, the Department notes the strength of feeling expressed at the Inquiry and will draw these issues to the attention of the statutory bodies concerned. (Department of the Environment, 1989, p. 2)

The position maintained by the Department at the public inquiry was that its role in health, education and other public services was largely one of leaving the planning to the local health and education authorities and processing individual planning applications from them through the local development control system. The formal recognition of the Healthy Cities project included a new policy that local plans would facilitate meeting land needs identified through the project. But in general the arguments made by many community groups that the BUAP and local plans should be used as vehicles for consulting about and planning for a wide range of needs failed.

The issue was confused because in certain areas the Department used the Plan to address 'needs'; this was explicit with regard to land for recreation for example, and the green belt was justified to protect rural areas from 'considerable development pressure unrelated to the needs of the local community' (Planning Appeals Commission, 1989, p. 250). With regard to shops, however, need is subordinated to the 'economic realities' that shopping provision will be a function of an area's spending power, and no policy was proposed to tackle the regressive effects of this in terms, for example, of health and diet. The Plan's policy for retailing focused on the vitality of the city centre, a symbol of Belfast's regional capital status and recovery from the high level of unrest in the 1970s, and a locale identified by consultants as now offering attractive returns on investment. Even creche and nursery facility provision by retailers, where it might be possible to introduce a strategic development control policy, was rejected as 'outside the remit of the Plan' (Planning Appeals Commission, 1989, p. 292).

The issue was raised again at a conference organised by CTA in February 1990 to assess its role and that of the community groups in the BUAP (3). Representatives of the Department of the Environment were invited and responded to these criticisms by stating that the Plan was a facilitator not a provider. Even if the Planning Service chose to zone land for, say, recreational use, if there was not the money to purchase it for recreational use then such a zoning could be challenged by a developer applying for a certificate of alternative development.

Much of the frustration with the whole issue of local need arose from an absence of coordination of services across the city. This had been recognised as a problem in Scottish local government by the Paterson Report (1972). The Bains Report of the same year criticised a perception of local government

> limited to the narrow provision of a series of services to the community ... It has within its purview the overall economic, cultural and physical well-being of the community. (Bains Report, paras, 2.10, 2.13)

The Bains and Paterson reports advocated restructuring based on installing strong corporate management 'to achieve a situation where the needs of a community are viewed comprehensively and the activities of the local authority are planned, directed and controlled in a unified manner' (Paterson Report, 1972, para. 5.3). These recommendations were widely adopted in Britain, although not without criticism as undemocratic 'people management' (Cockburn, 1978). However, the ability of local authorities to act comprehensively and autonomously was severely cut back by Conservative government legislation from 1979 (John, 1990).

In Northern Ireland, although local government was reorganised in the early 1970s, the impact of the conflict and the decisions to remove major powers from local councils meant that all purpose authorities never materialised and that distinct and separate administrative structures were set up for groups of related services: area boards for health and social services and education and libraries; a regional Housing Executive for housing; the Department of the Environment for planning and infrastructure; and district councils for some environmental and recreational activities (Birrell and Murie, 1980).

So it was not surprising that so many community groups - by definition groups that looked comprehensively at the whole needs of their areas - wanted the BUAP to relate to these needs and propose strategies for tackling them comprehensively. It is clear that when people are participating in making a land use plan they are not satisfied with being excluded from planning for all the public services that affect them (Ash, 1979). In Belfast, social policies were pursued quite separately from the BUAP even when these were geographically based. For example, a package of proposals to improve employment, health services and the environment in West Belfast was announced a few weeks after the end of the BUAP inquiry, proposals which could have been integrated into the Plan and examined in public (*Belfast Telegraph*, 19 July 1988).

Laganside

The riverside redevelopment of Laganside was an acknowledged focus of the 'development thrust' of the BUAP. Through the Laganside Corporation the Government sought to concentrate public expenditure on schemes aimed at enhancing land values along the river to attract developers to sites believed to be unprofitable without public spending. An explicit planning objective in the draft Plan was:

> To encourage the development of a mixture of new commercial, residential, recreational and cultural uses which will complement and enhance the existing established riverside uses and create a new and visually exciting waterfront. (Department of the Environment (NI), 1987, p. 96)

There was considerable and critical interest in Laganside among the community groups CTA worked with and the Irish Congress of Trade Unions, and several submissions of objections and evidence were made to the inquiry. These related to a lack of consultation, the commerial emphasis of the redevelopment, and the failure to address local needs for social housing, jobs and recreation directly. In their report, however, the presiding commissioners stated that Laganside 'carried the status of established Government policy' and therefore the principle of the project could not be considered, only the various components of the development scheme (Planning Appeals Commission, 1989, p. 3). Even so, while the inquiry was in session the first site for commercial development was put on the market by the Laganside development company. In a press report

100

the Environment Minister

> rejected a suggestion that the project was only for Yuppies
> and said: 'This is not something being imposed by
> government, it is something which the whole community of
> Belfast demand and want and deserve'. (*Irish News*, 3 June
> 1988)

It appeared that no public consultation was necessary to establish
this. The commissioners' consideration of the Laganside objections
stated:

> While we acknowledge as patent the evidence of need of these
> particular communities and the urgency of effective remedial
> action, we would also affirm the overriding importance of the
> Laganside proposals ... The success of many
> dockland/riverside development schemes elsewhere in the
> world convinces us that Laganside has a vital role to play in
> the physical, economic and social enhancement of Belfast.
> (Planning Appeals Commission, 1989, p. 309)

Laganside illustrates the key aspect of the official paradigm of the
BUAP: to bring about investment by private investors and
developers. The PAC's faith in the urban development corporation
approach to riverside regeneration reflects a rather unexamined
ideology. Howes (1988), for example, concludes that, 'Increasing
the supply of land and stimulating the demand for its use will not
automatically guarantee needed development' (p. 65). Howes
therefore argues for the close involvement of the public sector, a
view partially echoed by the PAC, but which in both cases ignores
the issue of what development is *needed* rather than can simply be
attracted, and in particular what social benefits will be *guaranteed*
as a condition for millions of pounds of public investment. The
latter issue was examined in the Third Report of the House of
Commons Employment Committee (1988), which concluded that UDCs
should be charged with 'greater responsibility for ensuring that
communities both in the areas covered by UDCs and in the
neighbouring areas benefit from regeneration' (p. xxix).

Despite the BUAP consultation process, the public inquiry, the
nature of the many objections made to Laganside, and its role as the
'focal point' for the Plan's 'development thrust', mechanisms to
achieve such social guarantees were not considered or proposed by
the PAC. This is clearly a strategic question, albeit one of a social
strategy for the BUAP. The Department of the Environment's
position in the Adoption Statement that consultation about the issues
raised by objections at the inquiry could be achieved through the
planning application process for individual sites reinforced the
almost total exclusion of a social strategy in the official paradigm for
the Plan. That a House of Commons Employment Committee could

address at least some aspects of this issue, while the PAC chose not to, lends credence to the points developed in chapter 2 that the public interest ideology underpinning planning inquiries will not extend to asserting the public's interest in the bundle of rights that comprises private property beyond such conservative objectives as preventing harm to officially defined amenity considerations.

Although Laganside had an unsatisfactory consideration in the PAC report, it may be that the public inquiry served a purpose of informing Government about potentially destabilising alienation at the grassroots; it would not be good for Laganside to develop in an atmosphere of unmanaged conflict. Subsequent to adoption of the BUAP, the development company agreed to work with CTA in establishing a consultative forum with local community groups, but this was not successful. It remains a showpiece project, which will probably have more significance in disguising the scale of Belfast's decline as an industrial city that in contributing to any sustainable growth.

Housing

Housing and transport were the central topics considered at the BUAP inquiry. For CTA, the main housing issues were to defend the green belt against speculative housebuilding and to promote a commitment to public sector housing solutions in areas where housing need existed. CTA argued against the 'capacity approach' of the Department of the Environment. This involved estimating builders' demands for land up to 1993 by taking the current rate of housebuilding in the urban area and increasing it by almost 50 per cent to derive the 'need' for both urban and greenfield suburban land and a choice of sites.

The Department argued that the capacity approach would provide for a rate of housebuilding that would stop families moving out of the Belfast Urban Area. However, while the BUAP sought to reduce or halt population loss, the Area Plans for some adjacent districts appeared to assume continuing significant out migration from the BUA (Planning Appeals Commission, 1989, p. 18). The 1969 Belfast Urban Area Plan had estimated that there was enough land to house up to 630,000 people; by 1986 the population of the urban area had declined to 495,000. Despite this, the DoE identified a further 400 hectares of housing land zonings beyond the existing built up edge of the urban area to cater for housebuilders' demands to 1993, and a further long term reserve of suburban development land for the period to 2001. Together, this was expected to provide a housing stock capable of accommodating up to 510-520,000 people by 2001. This capacity figure was not based on population projection, which the Plan stated was unreliable. It was based on what land could be developed for housing before damage to the environment, principally to surrounding hills, was judged by the Department to occur:

The plan proposals were not formulated on the basis that 520,000 was the target population to be achieved by 2001 but rather that on the basis of the development of lands judged environmentally acceptable such a population could be accommodated. (Plannings Appeals Commission, 1989, p. 16)

It just happened that this population figure married with the population projection for Belfast made by the *Regional Physical Development Strategy*, a coincidence about which the presiding commissioners were very sceptical. They also expressed scepticism about the Department's commitment to the green belt in the light of certain development control decisions (Planning Appeals Commission, 1989, p. 56) and its broad brush approach to delimiting it (pp. 251-255). The main reason for zoning attractive suburban sites, however, was to stimulate speculative housebuilding in line with Government housing policy for expanding home ownership:

An increase in private housebuilding and provision of choice of housing sites in convenient locations were important features of Government policy which would be difficult, if not impossible, to achieve were the existing Stopline to be adhered to rigidly. (Planning Appeals Commission, 1989, p. 16)

Such a rationale in terms of Government policy obviously provided the argument that to reduce the number of sites would conflict with Government policy and was therefore outside the consideration of the inquiry! These houses had to go somewhere either in the urban area or the 'green belt'.

CTA confronted this situation by arguing that standard planning practice had not been followed. A population projection had not been made as a basis for deciding on the future need for housing land. This argument was rejected by the Planning Appeals Commission and the Department on the basis that even if accurate projections from past trends could be made, the BUAP housing strategy and the housing zonings in the 'green belt' were 'interventionist' in seeking to reduce or halt the trend of population decline in the BUA (a trend in fact induced by policies of regional decentralisation and city centre commercialisation pursued in the 1960s and 70s).

CTA was equally unsuccessful with its argument that housing tenure should be considered in allocating housing sites. The PAC considered that, 'On the crucial point of the split between public authority and private sector housing, we accept that this is fundamentally a matter of wider Government policy outside the remit of a Development Plan' (Planning Appeals Commission, 1989, p. 20).

Green belt zonings for housebuilding presented the possibility of substantial profit taking by landowners and builders in easy to develop and attractive sites on the urban edge. As discussed in chapters 1 and 2, the state plays a major part in forming land values by restricting land use while not taxing inflated values resulting from this public rationing. At the BUAP inquiry, developers and landowners employed objections to press for more zonings, particularly in desirable parts of the south and east Belfast suburbs. Planning consultants and barristers were used to press their cases. The director of the Federation of Building and Civil Engineering Contractors argued for more land releases on the outskirts of the city in general:

> people wanted to live in certain areas, and it was up to the builders to try and meet that demand ... there was limited interest in inner city sites and ... most demand was for houses on the periphery of the city ... the private building industry played a key role in the Ulster economy, and if it could not get land to build in the right places then jobs would ultimately be lost. (*Belfast Telegraph*, 16 May 1988)

The focus by speculative builders on desirable outer city sites can easily be seen to be implicated in the sociospatial polarisation of the urban area. Indeed, the choice to live away from the inner city or proximity to public sector housing estates was an important element in some of the cases made by developers. In the urban area, high walls already separated some of the new private housing from adjoining public sector estates. The planning requirement stipulating low housing densities in green field locations also means that these zones will be largely 'exclusive' when developed.

Proposals in the draft Plan to zone five major sites for housing on the slopes of the Dundonald Valley were opposed by the Dundonald Green Belt Association with arguments that these would be visually intrusive, breach a natural physical boundary and destroy the ambience of the area. The Association submitted a petition with over 4,000 signatures opposing the proposed housing sites. Greenfield housing proposals were also opposed for similar reasons, including the destruction of natural habitats, by the Hightown Residents' Association, the Hilltop Environmental Committee and Jordanstown Residents' Association (the last employed its own counsel and a series of expert witnesses to oppose housing and road proposals). The Ulster Trust for Nature Conservation also made objections to greenfield housing developments.

The Old Holywood Road, Glenmachan and Belmont Green Belt Association appeared at the inquiry to contest objections by developers calling for the reinstatement of a housing zoning in the 'green belt' at Glenmachan. This zoning had been removed from the draft Plan following some 5,000 public objections at the Preliminary Proposals stage. The developers argued at the inquiry that public pressure was not a valid planning argument; if the site had initially been accepted as suitable for housing, then that still had to be the case. At the inquiry, the planners were accused of

ignoring the demand for luxury homes (*Irish News*, 14 May 1988).
Counsel for the objectors argued vociferously that a statement by
the Environment Minister in February 1987 announcing that these
housing proposals would be withdrawn from the Plan had seriously
prejudged the issue in attempting to court political support. The
commissioners considered that the public objections had led the
Department to reassess existing planning considerations and arrive
at a new conclusion that amenity factors outweighed demand. They
did not accept this conclusion, however, and reinstated the zoning:

> if the sole issue was the landscape character of the lands and
> their contribution to the setting of the city the proper
> response would be to exclude these lands from housing
> development. (A)rguments that the well-to-do can look
> outside the BUA for their homes or that more weight would
> attach to the housing argument if the need were generated by
> those presently without a home, do not commend themselves
> ... We therefore conclude that there is a demand for low
> density housing which is unlikely to be met in any meaningful
> way if the objection lands remain within the Green Belt ...
> (Planning Appeals Commission, 1989, pp. 47-48).

The overriding consideration employed by the PAC in assessing
housing objections was that of stemming population loss from the
Belfast Urban Area. This meant that housing zonings could not be
purely on the basis of demonstrable need for new housing but on
the basis of evidence that there was a market demand, principally
for relatively expensive low density housing, in areas where amenity
would not be seriously damaged. The zoning of green field land
at Rosemount also illustrated their thinking, which went against a
very substantial public protest. This single proposed site for 25
dwellings generated 300 of the 2,500 objections made to the draft
Plan. There were also objections seeking an extension of the
housing area into the proposed green belt. The commissioners
decided that there was a market demand for housing in this area
since new houses built in its vicinity had 'sold readily' but rejected
the objections seeking a more extensive zoning. This overrode
amenity considerations that would in the normal course of affairs
probably have led to a rejection of a planning application:

> if the issue was purely the determination of a development
> control application we would tend towards rejecting housing
> development on these lands ... However ... it is our opinion
> that, on the finest balance of consideration, the adverse
> effect on the landscape will not be of such magnitude as to
> justify the rejection of these lands from residential zoning.
> (Planning Appeals Commission, 1989, p. 112)

The Commission was not happy with the presiding commissioners' recommendations for housing zonings at some of the sites, and overruled them for Glenmachan, land at Old Holywood Road and some of the lands at Carnmoney Hill, a natural feature within the BUA. While developers won eighteen extra zonings following their objections at the inquiry, they failed to win another twenty five, and four zonings in the draft Plan were successfully opposed by community groups. This brought the zonings back to the DoE's total land requirements estimate, so did not challenge the strategic goal of building houses to stem population loss. However, in its Adoption Statement the Department noted the presiding commissioners' view that more land was required and made some additional provision at sites confirmed by the Commission. Development Control Guidance would be required for the greenfield sites.

There was widespread support among all the community groups for opposing housing zonings in the 'green belt'. Given the rather narrow range of interests which appear to benefit from green belt controls, notably green belt owner occupiers, it seems odd that there is such widespread support for this planning concept. Private ownership of land severely restricts the recreational value of such large areas, as one planning consultant was quick to point out at the BUAP inquiry:

> Objectors' claims that development (at Rosemount) would remove an area of great recreational value for walking and picnicing were groundless - the lands were private property with no proposals to acquire them for public use. (Planning Appeals Commission, 1989, p. 105)

The role of green belts in diverting development pressure from the outer city to regenerating the inner city is also empirically unproven (Rydin and Myerson, 1989). This is often used as a social policy argument because it is believed that inner city regeneration will deliver more social benefits than outer city expansion. But Neill and Singleton (1990) suggest that if the role of housing policy is to deliver affordable housing rather than inflated asset growth for existing owner occupiers, then major suburban land releases may achieve social benefits by damping real rises in house values which only benefit existing owner occupiers. In addition, as West Belfast has experienced, failure to release suburban land can damage the quality of life within the city as recreational and open spaces are built upon.

The green belt, however, has considerable ideological significance as a symbol of the public interest by which planning seeks legitimacy. As Rydin and Myerson (1989, p. 473) comment:

> Green belts are perceived to be 'all things to all men', to offer something to every interest group, to be in the 'public interest'.

They argue that popular attachment to the green belt is about two underlying concerns, and these were strongly echoed in objections to greenfield zonings at the BUAP inquiry. Firstly, containing the spread of urbanisation, which reflects a long standing anti urban association of countryside with quality of life. Secondly, fears about the destruction of an often imagined sense of community by over development. The Dundonald Green Belt Association, for example, argued that Dundonald 'has already borne more than its fair share of Belfast's expansion but retains a sharp sense of its own independence which is under grave threat by the present proposals', only to have the commissioners reply with regard to what they called 'the sociological arguments' that, 'Dundonald no longer possesses an identity as a separate community but functions as an integral part of the Belfast Urban Area' (Planning Appeals Commission, 1989, pp. 60, 84). These deep rooted social values motivated many people to object to the BUAP's green belt housing proposals.

Transport

The draft Plan's strategic highway measures were based on public investments to improve traffic flows across the River Lagan and along the main corridors of travel from the south and east into Belfast, the so called Southern and Eastern Approaches Highway Strategies. The main thrust of CTA's objections was to control private road traffic and to enhance public transport, especially for those such as low income households and disabled people whose accessibility to urban resources is disadvantaged by present policies.

The evidence on transport submitted by objectors was the most well researched evidence presented to the inquiry, and CTA itself used two English consultants as expert witnesses. In contrast to housing, the BUAP transportation strategy was largely non interventionist. Road proposals sought to accommodate without restraint a projected growth in traffic of up to forty per cent by 2001, while just 'maintaining' public transport services. There was to be no coordination between bus and rail because this 'could result in less competition'. The issue of prioritising public or private transport brought the competing versions of public interest promoted by the Department and the community groups into direct conflict.

The Department argued at the inquiry that their strategy met the needs of the eighty per cent of daily trips made by private road vehicles. Objectors, on the other hand, argued for the fifty per cent of Belfast households without ownership of a car who had a very different experience of getting about the city, and the social divisions and environmental damage that would follow a roads based strategy. Objectors reworked official statistics and unpacked DoE submissions to show how 'the facts' had been biased in favour of the roads lobby. The Department had, for example, included spending on concessionary fares as a captial item to justify equivalent spending on roads. Without a single member of the public stating support for the roads strategy, the Department stated at the inquiry that it was doing what the public wanted. Evidence that they had not done what the 1978 Lavery Report on the transportation inquiry had recommended - a 55:45 expenditure split for roads:public transport - was presented by the General Consumer Council, who argued that since 1978 only 15 per cent of available expenditure had gone directly to public transport in Belfast. The Department's response to objections is best summed up by these short extracts from its argument:

> Social measures were not matters for a land use Plan but Governmental decision ... (R)estraining the use of the private car would have adverse effects on city centre growth ... The preferred transportation strategy would substantially reduce congestion and give 'good value for money'. (Planning Appeals Commission, 1989, pp. 391, 399)

The DoE had spent £1.2 million on work by consultants to identify the transportation problems faced by Belfast. Objectors were not impressed. The cross harbour links had already been approved following the transportation inquiry in 1977, and the road congestion problems identified in East Belfast and Lower Ormeau were already widely known. There had been no costing of the disbenefits of road investment. Given that the consultants themselves recognised that congestion would still follow a new road for the Eastern Approaches, a bus priority or light railway solution was needed.

Dr Martin Mogridge, one of CTA's consultants, argued that the transportation model used by the Department's consultants was flawed because it assumed that extra road capacity would relieve urban congestion. His evidence was that this did not happen. Public transport was not only a solution for people with no access to a car, but had to be enhanced to attract people from their cars by making it a quicker alternative in terms of door to door journey time.

The Commission accepted many of the arguments made for an enhanced role for public transport. It recognised the extent of need among non car users and the need for investment to attract car users to public transport, including a further reassessment of investment in light rail and discouragement of city centre parking. It recommended the establishment of a Transport Review Authority (also recommended by the Lavery Report in 1978). While stating that concessionary fares for the elderly were beyond the remit of a planning inquiry, it reported on the arguments made by objectors for more generous concessions because the DoE had included a statement on concessionary fares in the draft Plan. It recommended that black taxis should be fully assimilated into the overall structure of public transport services, and for 'monitoring' of the needs of cyclists. Thus all objectors' points were recognised, although the recommendations were not particularly strong. The Department's Adoption Statement revised the Plan to state a general policy of strengthening public transportation links with the city centre and Laganside, but it rejected discouraging city centre parking. It dealt with the concessionary fares issue by deleting reference to them. The proposal for a Transportation Review Authority would receive consideration.

The inquiry examined road proposals one by one. The Lower Ormeau Residents' Action Group, the Ballynafeigh Community Association and the North Belfast Steering Committee opposed the environmental and social costs they argued would follow widening the Lower Ormeau Road, a component of the Southern Approaches Strategy. The commissioners were 'impressed' by their case. But they were also unhappy about the whole Southern Approaches Strategy: 'a problem had been identified to which the plan did not seek to provide a solution' (Planning Appeals Commission, 1989, p. 465). They considered that radical improvements to the road network would be needed much earlier than the draft Plan envisaged. The Commission therefore urged a complete reassessment of the whole Strategy, and this was accepted by the Department who stated in the Adoption Statement that new proposals would be brought before another public inquiry. The groups that had campaigned against the Lower Ormeau scheme were very dissatisfied that they had not been allowed to win decisively. Considerable effort had gone into their submissions at the BUAP inquiry, and now they faced the prospect at some future indeterminate time of having to make their case again.

The Eastern Approaches Strategy was dominated by a proposal to build a new road, Comber Route 1, through East Belfast along a disused railway line to link commmuter suburbs with the city centre. Part of the route had been turned into a park, the Beersbridge Nature Walk, winner of the BBC Wildlife Award in 1987. The nature walk would be destroyed by the proposed road. It was opposed by the Stop the Bypass Campaign, the Alliance Party, the Civic Trust, the Royal Society of Ulster Architects and Ballyhacamore Traders. Some objectors argued that a light rail link should be reinstated along this corridor. The commissioners' consideration was again an interesting assessment of the public interest:

> All in all we are satisfied that the existing and potential contribution which these lands make to the quality of life of the local community cannot be lightly set aside ... (T)he claim of objectors that 'our amenity will be grossly impaired largely to facilitate commuter traffic which has no interest in

109

our locality' is understood. However we consider that many of the fundamental objectives of the BUA require that access towards the central area be improved and that congestion levels do not increase to a level where the core of the BUA loses attraction through accessibility limitations. In this wider sense the needs of road space for commuters is a significant factor. The weighing of these many considerations leads us to the conclusion that the best interests of the public generally would be served by confirming the Comber Route 1 proposal though in doing we acknowledge fully the price to be paid by the more local community along and around the proposed route. (Planning Appeals Commission, 1989, pp. 466-467)

Taken together with the housing strategy, a version of the public interest can be seen to be emerging which is defined in what Gottdiener (1985) has called 'abstract space'. To prioritise personalised social space - the local environment of human relationships, buildings that meet common needs and relationships with nature - would make impossible the imperative of growth and the overriding significance of metropolitan centres to wealth creation. The fragmented space of the Belfast urban area, with commuting from an outer city to the city centre at the cost of communal social spaces, reflects the built product of modern capitalism rather than of conscious human purpose. Strategic planning relates to the scale of the urban economic system rather than of real people, and in doing so manages the capital accumulation process, legitimising this as in the public interest. In this way, rights the public have in the 'bundle of rights' that consitutes private property can be expropriated by officialdom 'in the public interest'. Gottdiener (1985, p. 227-228, 247) concludes that:

> the forms of space are produced ... by the articulation between Late Capitalist structures and the actions of the property sector, especially the effects of select groups and the state in chaneling the flow of social development into specific places and shapes ... The sum total of this receptivity to development coupled with public subsidies organized by the ideology of growth is often referred to as a good business climate.

Gottdiener argues that a good business climate may be at the cost of a commercial expropriation of public life:

> on the one hand, everyday life transpires inside the individual suburban home, where only family members and select friends meet. On the other hand, public activities no longer take place in a ludic village center, with its particular

social space and civility. They occur increasingly in the
large malls or shopping centers under the auspices of the
property owners. (pp. 248-249)

Thus, the planning of Belfast in an 'abstract space' and the
commercialisation or destruction of real spaces are features of the
official paradigm of the BUAP 2001 even though the spatial
restructuring is not as dramatic as was proposed by the BUAP of
1969. Against this are the social concepts and relationships through
which people perceived the Plan. These largely localised contexts
of day to day experience often conflicted with the planners'
identification with a larger abstract space - a Belfast urban system.
This logic was in many respects being imposed on the variety of
local populations and places in Belfast. It was a planning paradigm
that could not build a common purpose out of social diversity, and
that used an open public sphere - the inquiry - not to democratise
the planning process but to state the public interest defined in the
abstract space of officialdom.
  Where the strategic interest is better met by an alternative, the
commissioners can justify overriding specific strategic proposals in
the interests of preventing damage to a locality. While the loss of
Beersbridge Nature Walk was a price that had to be paid,
improvements to another East Belfast route, the Upper Newtownards
Road, did not justify damaging a golf course and the views enjoyed
by car commuters when they would not solve the traffic problem:

> From the evidence presented we consider that, if traffic flows
> were below the high scenario figure of 40%, the scheme of
> junction improvements to the Upper Newtownards Road might
> just cope with anticipated demand but at a very high cost in
> terms of quality of life for those living along the road. The
> loss of many mature trees to Knock Golf Club would be in
> our view loss of amenity not only to the local community but
> the wider public who travel the route. If this were the only
> means to meet the expected traffic volumes it might be a price
> to be, however reluctantly, paid ... Weighing the various
> arguments and evidence advanced it is our opinion that such
> would be the adverse environmental impacts of the proposed
> improvements to Upper Newtownards Road the scheme should
> not be confirmed at this stage. (Planning Appeals
> Commission, 1989, p. 467)

The Castelreagh Roundabout Action Group also won their case
against a flyover, which they argued would cause loss of amenity,
visual intrusion, vibration, noise and fume pollution, because the
commissioners considered it not to be an effective solution to the
wider traffic problem in the general area. The commissioners were
therefore able to recommend deletion of the project in 'the wider
community interest' (Planning Appeals Commission, 1989, p. 470).

Similarly, objections by Carrick Hill Residents' Association, North Queen Street Recreation Centre, Sinn Fein and the North Belfast Steering Group were successful in removing a new city centre road from the Plan. The community affected lived in one of Belfast's worst housing ghettos - Unity Flats - which was due for redevelopment on the basis of a plan drawn up with local residents by the housing authority. The new road would inhibit redevelopment. The commissioners established that the road had 'very low priority' and recommended its deletion from the Plan. The North Belfast Steering Group was less successful in removing another city centre road scheme, Frederick Street. This was an 'essential element' and 'must proceed ... the wider public interest in this instance must prevail' (Planning Appeals Commission, 1989, p. 482).

Nature conservation

It might be thought that a paradigm that was based on the expropriation of social space for strategic objectives in abstract space would also subordinate the natural world to these objectives. The main issue in this respect at the BUAP inquiry was proposals to zone for industry important natural habitats in the lagoons area of the harbour. This was opposed by the Belfast Lough Nature Conservation Committee, the Belfast Urban Wildlife Group, the Royal Society for the Protection of Birds and the Ulster Trust for Nature Conservation. All these major environmental groups in Belfast were represented on a panel which submitted evidence on the harbour estate zoning, as well as arguing that nature conservation had been neglected in the Plan and that the need to recycle waste rather than burying it was ignored.

The Harbour lagoons issue revealed serious inadequacies in public consultation under the Nature Conservation and Amenity Lands (NI) Order. The complexities of the issue are not relevant to the purpose of this book, but what is significant is that the commissioners recommended *legislative change* to bring consultation arrangements in line with planning legislation. This exhibited an interesting distinction in the commissioners' conception of their remit; they felt able to recommend legislative change in this instance, while often elsewhere referring to Government *policy* as the reason for arriving at certain decisions. In assessing arguments for and against 'green belt' housing zonings, for example, 'account was taken of government policies which favoured house building and job creation' (Planning Appeals Commission, 1989, p.62), while in recommending the zoning of part of the edge of the Lagan Valley Regional Park for housing the commissioners took into account 'Government requirements regarding disposal of surplus assets' (Planning Appeals Commission, 1989, p. 227). While the commissioners felt able to criticise the adequacy of legislation governing consultation they at no point criticised legislation relating to substantive matters of policy.

The Harbour lagoons presented the commissioners with reconciling nature conservation arguments, which they accepted, with the 'overriding' and 'crucial' need to allow the Harbour 'to expand and modernise to meet the industrial/commercial challenges which the Province must face in an increasingly competitive world' (Planning Appeals Commission, 1989, p. 316). This was sought by recommending that a Local Plan for the area should pay attention 'to the future viability of Belfast port' while being 'sensitive to the importance of wildlife interests in the general area' (p. 317).

Conclusions

> Although the Commission has expressed some reservations on various aspects of the BUAP, it does comment that overall the Plan offers the Belfast Urban Area (BUA) a framework within which its many laudable objectives can be achieved to the enrichment of the environment and the benefit of all its citizens. (Department of the Environment (NI), 1989, p.1)

This conclusion was not shared by CTA or the community groups at the inquiry. For them the Plan remained largely superficial and irrelevant to the needs that they considered demanded a comprehensive plan. The BUAP 'marketed' Belfast to visitors and prospective investors, but it had failed to win any significant expressions of public support. While restricted by statue, much of the conservative nature of the Plan's actual proposals derives from an ideology of Belfast's planners. This is that planning is purely about 'securing the orderly and consistent development of land', rather than intervening in the production of space with clear social purposes derived from the needs and aspirations of the city's residents. Government policy is not made democratically in Belfast, and the PAC could have had a role in considering the appropriateness of Government policies to meeting such social purposes.

CTA's approach to the outcome of the exercise was to identify those commitments made in the amended BUAP which were potentially important to community groups in the city. These commitments varied from preparing local and area plans to monitoring changes in population, housing, traffic and shopping provision to assess whether the Plan was meeting its objectives. Certainly at least some of these commitments resulted from CTA's evidence to the inquiry.

Many of the arguments made by community groups about local facilities were considered by the PAC to be matters for local plans rather than strategic policy. The DoE was committed to preparing local plans for the city centre, the Lagan Valley Regional Park, Castlereagh, the Harbour and Newtownabbey, and certain recommendations were made by the PAC about how they should address objectors' concerns. The Lower Ormeau neighbourhood was to be included in the local plan programme. A major overhaul of the Southern Approaches Strategy to include possible public transport measures would result in a future consultation exercise and inquiry. Various other commitments were made, such as for example minimising the loss of amenity resulting from building the highway along the former railway in East Belfast. Development control guidance would be published for new suburban housing sites.

For CTA these commitments raised questions about how consultation would be built into the monitoring exercises, whether local studies such as of shopping in North and West Belfast would be open to public comment, whether the various 'schemes' that had been proposed would go through statutory consultation processes, what role community groups would have in local plans and making further proposals, and how consultation would be built into regional policies. The organisation considered it had an important role in these issues.

As noted above, CTA organised a conference in February 1990 to review the outcome of the inquiry. It was felt that an important outcome was that people would be less intimidated by planning in the future, but:

> Many workshop participants were cynical about the whole planning process following their experience of it. Some participants felt we needed a more flexible planning process that could take people's views into account, liaising with local communities. Planners had to plan for diversity. Some who had taken part in the Public Inquiry had felt it to be a very sterile experience and that the period of feedback was much too long for people to keep up an interest in the process ... Strategic proposals should be brought to local groups ... Over a million pounds was spent on consultants' reports which ended up of very little value, while money spent on public participation was paltry in comparison ... Not even the city council was in a position to represent effectively the views of ordinary people. (4)

Although the commissioners were recognised to be flexible and accommodating during the inquiry, many participants at the conference considered that the PAC report of the inquiry was superficial and failed to address objectors' evidence point by point. The poor accountability of the Department of the Environment was widely felt. The inquiry had been useful for making public arguments and for getting some issues recognised for future local and transportation planning in particular, but the narrow focus of planning left participants feeling that the system had not met their needs.

Notes

1.   Preamble: Proof of Evidence presented at public inquiry into Belfast Urban Area Plan 2001, May 1988, Community Technical Aid (NI).

2.   The Belfast Urban Area Plan - Report of a Meeting held between the Department of the Environment and Community Technical Aid on 2 July 1987 in Clarendon House.

3.   Community Technical Aid: Belfast Urban Area Plan 2001 Conference, 15 February 1990 - Summary of Proceedings.

4.   See note 3.

6 Conclusion: new horizons for planning

At one level, the story of the BUAP is one of professional judgement imposed on public opinion. Professional judgement need not, of course, be imposed. The whole idea of planning aid and organisations such as Community Technical Aid is to break down the separation of people with specialist expertise and knowledge from the larger public, especially oppressed and disadvantaged groups. In political terms, professionals working as part of grassroots civil society are 'organic intellectuals' (Gramsci, 1971). Their work is mental labour but it is grounded in everyday life. In planning, this ideally goes further than the BUAP project, not just formulating objections and compiling evidence but working up alternative proposals based on new ways of thinking, challenging accepted wisdom where it offers no solutions and providing guiding theory. New ideas then develop as integral aspects of popular culture, lifestyles, language and traditions. In this way, a conception of the city or society as a whole is no longer reserved to the experts and administrators but becomes a popular phenomenon.

The BUAP was certainly not a popular phenomenon. Chapter 5 introduced the concept of 'abstract space' to understand how professional planners made their strategic plan for Belfast. Their work was not grounded in everyday life yet it required legitimation through the process of public consultation and the inquiry. To enable this, an ideology of public interest governed the process. There is a direct association between 'abstract space' and 'public interest': both are ideological, abstract and legitimations of state action at a largely unaccountable scale.

Planning in abstract space entails a set of concepts, categories, relationships and methods which constitute a paradigm. It was argued in previous chapters that at the BUAP inquiry there was opposed to this paradigm not a disparate bundle of objections from community groups but an alternative paradigm reflecting quite different concepts and relationships. Figure 6.1 schematises these and compares them with the official paradigm.

Figure 6.1   'Officialdom' versus 'community':   opposing
              paradigms at the BUAP inquiry

	Official paradigm	Community paradigm
Key concepts	Growth of urban system Relating land use to market forces	Quality of localities Intervention in social and economic determinants of land use for stability and equity goals
Key categories	Order and efficiency City centre and private transport	Living areas and community facilities Accessibility by public transport
Key relationships	Land use, growth and commuting	Land use and community development/ social policy
Key methods	Plan emerges from officialdom within Government policy parameters	Plan emerges from public consultation and systematises local needs

---

Property: the key to a paradigm shift

Chapter 1 discussed the importance of the concept of property to planning. This concept is central to understanding the BUAP's official paradigm and urban planning in general. Through the controls of the planning system the public have a share of the bundle of rights which comprises private property. Decisions about the use of property are thus made in the public sphere by planners employed by the state and with opprotunities for the public to participate in the process.

Planning, however, cannot extend the 'public interest' so far that private property no longer exists in any meaningful sense. The existence of private property is central to the economic system of capitalism on which the existence of the capitalist state itself depends (Jessop, 1982). The modern economic system is similarly dependent on state intervention to manage economic crises and instability arising from the market mechanism.

The state is a 'public power' separated from the immediate control of the people over whom it exercises control. Its agencies act within the limits and pressures which arise from the basic requirement to maintain the conditions of capital accumulation. Thus, planning authorities may impose controls on land use which prevent the realisation of exchange value as if land was a pure financial asset, but no planning authority could generally oppose the exploitation of space for financial returns without causing a collapse in business confidence and legal and political intervention to reestablish conditions for capital accumulation.

In rolling back the state from direct provision to create more market opportunities, Conservative Governments in Britain extended the sphere of private property relations and in doing so have relegated democracy. This is because the more private property relations extend into the use of land, capital and labour, the less any person can decide what is to happen in society and the more this is decided by market forces. As Ryan (1987) puts it:

> The more developed the forms of property and the more perfect the market the less any actual person can decide what is to happen in the world, and the more it is decided by things. This is not, of course, to be taken literally. My factory does not literally start itself up at 7 am on Monday morning, whatever I do to prevent it. Rather, I am faced with a world in which my factory merely represents a certain stock of captial, and one in which I have to maximize the return on my capital or perish. (p. 119)

It is difficult to deny that capitalist property relations are highly efficient if our conception of efficiency is to get the maximum production out of people and materials. But an alternative conception of efficiency is 'social efficiency' where the objective is not to maximise production and growth but *welfare*.

Welfare became associated with statism and bureaucracy in Britain's post war period. This was an inevitable consequence of creating welfare agencies as 'exceptional' institutions in a society otherwise based on inequality and competition (Williams, 1983, pp. 83-101). The old concepts of 'relief' and 'insurance' were inherited by the post war welfare state and during a period of rising incomes the continuing currency of these concepts eroded the idea of common social provision, which was interpreted as selective entitlement and burdensome cost.

More recently, bureaucratic regulation and an elite perspective on need has been undermined by mass perspectives on the 'quality of life' - what living conditions people actually want in the pursuit of satisfaction and happiness (Mukherjee, 1989). Interestingly, the evidence from quality of life studies suggests that conventional indicators of need may be poor bases for fomulating policy. Health and family and neighbourhood stability appear to be of greatest importance to most people, yet these are difficult variables to quantify. In general, the social environment seems to be more important to most people's conception of the quality of life than physical and economic dimensions (Ley, 1983, pp. 327-367).

It seems inappropriate, however, to break down an all embracing concept such as quality of life into separate dimensions as if these are autonomous. As discussed in chapter 1, the existence of private property is itself dependent on an ideological separation of legal, political and economic spheres. This makes impossible the pursuit of policies based on social interest, community or welfare, which embody collective principles of communal administration, other than in exceptional and bureaucratically regulated spheres of society. These extended interests of community and welfare have a temporal as well as spatial dimension as awareness grows about the rights of future generations to enjoy continuing access to sustainable resources. This cannot be reconciled with individual self seeking. It necessitates planning based on shared management, and explicit social and economic aims which express a sustainable equilibrium between production, consumption and the natural environment. Thus Williams (undated, p. 32) writes:

> We need to restore the old linkage between opposition to the exploitation of people and opposition to the exploitation of the natural world. Our most positive value will be that respect for life-forms and land-forms which makes it impossible to treat any of them as mere raw material. Instead of production as the dominant objective of a social order, we shall emphasise livelihood: that more rounded and diverse conception of practical life. We shall end the false separation of products and by-products, effects and side-effects, insisting on seeing all products and effects as following from nameable processes, and thus as necessary, objective material in assessing, monitoring and investing in them.

The thrust of Williams' argument is to unite the economic and political. This he sees as necessary if conscious choices are to be made to support and enhance life rather than cause damage, or run the risk of damage. The concept of livelihood captures for him the idea of a practical society based on self management, sustainability and people caring first for each other. It is, in essence, a way of life rather than a mode of production.

State institutions and a conception of the public or social interest are still necessary to this project because there will always need to be negotiated coordination between sectional and social interests. Devine (1988) explicates the idea of negotiated coordination in economic planning as an alternative to market mechanisms or central planning. This is in essence negotiation between sectional interests represented on 'coordination bodies' existing at local, regional and national levels. Representation on these bodies would be cross cutting so that included would be Devine's 'planning commission' and other organisations representing a more general interest, as well as production units and communities directly affected by them. These bodies construct definitions of the social interest in relation to the decisions facing them, with access to both quantitative and qualitative information about the issues. Devine sees the coordination bodies as complementing elected representative assemblies which determine 'the overall social interest and allocate resources accordingly'. Interest and cause groups would have representation in 'chambers of interest' linked to the assemblies. Overall, he argues that:

> Negotiated coordination ... allows decentralized decision making that is able to take account of all the information available and arrive at a coordinated aggregate response that reflects the interests of all those affected. (Devine, 1988, p. 237)

The major obstacle to broadening democracy in the way argued by Williams to be not only desirable but crucial for ecological reasons is private property rights. The separation of these rights from the 'externalities' caused by exercising them is one reflection of the difficulty of achieving stability and equity through the intervention of democratic state institutions when the social interest is subordinate to powerful sectional interests. Claims for private property rights imbue law and policy to constrain planning on the basis of an ideological argument for their greater legitimacy. Yet, as argued in chapter 1, all rights - of which property rights are part - are conditional on the popular franchise.

Representative democracy, though, is crude democracy. By individualising social issues as private concerns decided every few years by one person one vote it is difficult to represent the real extended interests beyond individuals of which concerns with community and environment are part. The market mechanism is incapable of dealing with this. The market has exploited both environment and community as costless resources. They are indeed difficult to monetize and their value has to be decided democratically.

The planning system does this, very imperfectly. Professional judgements are made, for example, about the value of 'amenity'. Such concepts, however, serve to restrict a potentially very extensive public share of the bundle of property rights which is presently largely vested in the hands of the private owner. This potential arises from the effective nationalisation in Britain of the right to develop land for urban uses.

At the BUAP inquiry, the community groups argued for planning control to be extended to embrace values of community and welfare. They argued for these values to be defined through public consultation. But without any legal underpinning for the concept of shared community property rights which their arguments implied, it was difficult for officialdom to respond even if it was predisposed to do so. The institutionalisation of such rights would pose a direct challenge to the development industry and the dynamic of capital accumulation through investment development, speculative housebuilding and contracting. At present, the social costs of supporting and enhancing the development industry's conditions for accumulation are manifest in such examples as the huge shifts in unearned wealth through land development profits, the diversion of capital from investment in industry to property speculation, and the marked sociospatial polarisation of cities reflected in housing, shopping and health inequalities.

Urban planning is nevertheless unusually open to social activism. This brings local perspectives into conflict with officialdom's pursuit of strategic objectives. A fundamental argument of this book is that the local perspective should have greater legitimacy than the strategic perspective because it is more rooted in people's concerns and experiences. The problem was revealed by the BUAP inquiry but not resolved by it because, without strategy developing from local roots, change arising from the public inquiry can only be tokenism or incorporation of local needs by a larger scale authority in which power lies. Whilst the BUAP inquiry called the state to account, a not insignificant feature in Northern Ireland, it could not turn upside down a process that had begun in 1985 and was basically largely completed by the time of the inquiry in 1988.

The public inquiry: an instrument of government

Despite appearances, the public inquiry is not an open and democratic public sphere that can broaden democracy to reflect the interests of all those affected. It serves to provide a bureaucratically regulated opportunity for people to represent their views to officialdom so that decisions 'in the public interest' appear to have public legitimacy.

In Belfast, community action about urban renewal and planning was known to be a disruptive phenomenon. Although it was unlikely that the Department of the Environment would have made an effort to involve community groups in the BUAP, it was not surprising that CTA's lobbying secured financial assistance to organise community action about the Plan. As CTA itself had emerged out of community groups' own experiences of planning struggles in the 1970s, both sides felt it in their interests for the contest of views to be organised. For CTA this was pragmatic radicalism; for the DoE it was a small token to participation which would keep the whole process within the rules of the game and, certainly as some civil servants saw it, facilitate the expression of a legitimate set of interests.

The decision to fund CTA reflected a number of changes to public inquiry procedure in Britain aimed at improving the management of inquiries, principally the 1988 rules requiring written statements of case. As discussed in chapter 2, urban planning is a physical basis for conflict and the planning inquiry is a quasijudicial instrument for managing conflict. This entails an inquiry discourse designed to identify the public interest in a 'fair' way. All parties are in principle given the opportunity to put their cases and to answer all significant points against them. This assumes, however, that the inquiry is adjudicating between competing sectional interests; an assumption employed to justify the British Government's decision as a matter of policy not to provide funding to support the participation of third parties at big public inquiries.

At the BUAP inquiry CTA was, in terms of the linkages and coherence evident in its objections, actually proposing a version of the public interest. This was negotiated by a coordinated synthesis of local and sectional interests. It has to be pieced together when reading the PAC report because the objections are abstracted from any consideration of political and social philosophies which is taken to be beyond the remit of the commissioners. CTA also played down these broader arguments in an effort to target problems with specific proposals in the Plan, which was how the public inquiry game should be played. Nevertheless, an alternative paradigm underpinned CTA's objections and thus these added up to an alternative version of the public interest to that of the BUAP. The inquiry commissioners were faced not with deciding where the public interest lay in relation to competing sectional interests, but with deciding between competing versions of the public interest.

The resolution of this problem was not difficult. Chapter 2 concluded that Governments as centralised as the UK's can only tolerate one version of the public interest, that expounded in Government policy and ministerial rhetoric. Sovereignty is concentrated in central government rather than decentralised, and this reinforces the claim that central government is the sole legitimate guardian of the public interest.

Public inquiries are a suitable instrument of such a form of government because their discourse suppresses social values and political debate. The merits of Government policy are excluded from consideration, and although inquiries can consider whether policy should be applied in a particular case, these arguments are easily politicised and thus rendered irrelevant. With an adversarial format, it is more easy to present third parties as sectional interests in conflict, thus demanding an adjudication by central government, advised by its inquiry inspectors. The inspectors give an often unfair contest between unequally resourced and represented parties an ideological gloss of 'fairness'. Government decisions may then be justified according to the tenets of bureaucratic rationality which uphold 'professional judgement' rather than 'public opinion'. The latter can be portrayed as an emotional response to economic realities and bureaucratic rationality itself. As Williams (1983) writes:

> Emotions, it is true, do not produce commodities. Emotions don't make the accounts add up differently. Emotions don't alter the hard relations of power. But where people actually live, what is specialised as 'emotional' has an absolute and primary significance ... There are still good and bad emotions, just as there are good and bad forms of rational intelligence. But the habit of separating the different kinds of good from each other is entirely a consequence of a deformed social order, in which rational intelligence has so often to try to justify emotionally unacceptable or repulsive actions. The deformed order itself if not particularly rational or intelligent. It can be sharp enough in its specialised and separated areas, but in its aggregates it is usually stupid and muddled ... It has succeeded in the hitherto improbable combination of affluent consumption and widespread emotional distress. (pp. 266-267)

Community groups at the BUAP inquiry were carriers of broad concepts which were not the separate creations of either emotions or rational intelligence alone. It was therefore impossible for a procedure meant to separate one from the other to cope with these concepts. While chapters 2 and 5 suggested changes that could make the procedure more user friendly, these are likely only to worsen the problem that the planning system as presently constituted is largely incapable of accommodating public aspirations.

It is possible, though, to use the planning system to secure social objectives in the form of weighing up the social costs and benefits of development. But this is a difficult and grey legal area with the room for manoeuvre becoming more restricted by Government regulations and guidelines. The judiciary has established as unreasonable attempts to use regulatory planning powers to achieve ulterior objects not related to the needs of the development in question. Legislative change is necessary if planning authorities are to use planning controls to achieve wider positive social and economic objectives. This also raises major tax and compensation issues as landowners will argue that controls made for social reasons prevent realistic economic uses.

The Northern Ireland case

Chapter 3 considered how comprehensive land use planning was adopted in Northern Ireland to facilitate the physical restructuring necessary to serve the conditions of existence of modern capital accumulation. The Matthew Plan also served the political interests of the ruling Unionists in the Stormont government, but from 1972 planning was under Direct Rule by British ministers. During the 1970s urban renewal in Belfast imposed considerable social costs, principally on working class populations affected by the Belfast Urban Motorway.

A reprieve arose as a result of the worsening situation of the UK economy. Revised transportation strategies were examined in public at the 1977 inquiry. Community groups formed to fight redevelopment opposed the roads plans through the Community Groups Action Committee on Transport. This pressed for a 'fourth strategy' based on the results of public consultation about the needs of local areas in the inner city.

The Action Committee won a two month adjournment to help prepare a fourth option but this proved an impossibly short time. Without resources, nothing had been prepared by the time the inquiry resumed. The inquiry inspector recommended a compromise strategy balancing road building with improvements to public transport. Few improvements to public transport were made by the time of the BUAP 2001, although several road schemes had been completed.

The inspector at the 1977 transportation inquiry doubted the representativeness of the Action Committee. But it was the inability to table alternative proposals which was more serious and a source of the initiative to establish Community Technical Aid in 1983. Although initiated with funding from a charitable trust, CTA attracted grant aid from the Department of the Environment itself. Representative, professional and with notable cross community support, it fitted in with a Government ideology of self help and might assist in translating policies and plans into terms community groups were less likely to resist for 'irrational' reasons (Blackman, 1988).

The bureaucratic rationality of the BUAP 2001 did not arise from a need for urban restructuring on a large scale but from the imperative to market Belfast in an era of image consumption sometimes styled 'postmodernism' (Lash and Urry, 1987). There was no context of regional modernisation, only strategic city marketing goals: to reverse population decline, strengthen the city centre, attract private investors and visitors, and generally impress with a post industrial image.

The remarkable feature of CTA's participation exercise with a multifarious community and voluntary sector was the coherence of its final case. CTA's role was one of providing both organisational and technical resources to enable arguments across many topics to be synthesised and framed in planning terms. CTA was both critical of the statutory planning process and provided the resources for community groups to work within it. It challenged the fundamental philosophy of the BUAP as well as specific proposals.

The impossibility of CTA's task, basically to replace the BUAP with another plan, was evident at an early stage. The presentation of Laganside as a *fait accompli* illustrated the centrality of this type of 'planning' to the philosophy of the BUAP. The failure to meet any objections to the Plan that would mean fundamental changes was prefigured in the refusal to publish a Report of Survey at the early stages of plan preparation or extend the time for public consultation. Even the decision to grant aid CTA could be interpreted as a reflection of the general pressure to get the Plan adopted as soon as possible and smooth its path through a public inquiry. While the motive for this was also probably partly corporatist - to try and establish community groups as partners in the planning process - this could not work successfully in the context of an adversarial public inquiry where it is very difficult to negotiate a definition of the social interest in relation to each issue. The us and them situation which marked consultation was apparent at many stages and was reflected in the practices of both sides, including the tone of the Department of the Environment's rebuttal statements and the format of the Planning Appeals Commission's pre inquiry meetings.

What the Department's decision to fund CTA did establish was that consultation exercises can work well when they encourage the formation and participation of voluntary grassroots associations. This needs to be supported by expertise and resources accountable to such associations. While consensus is not of course always likely, it was achieved in Belfast, where perhaps expectations would be that consensus is all the more difficult to secure. With this input to the inquiry, the problem of the absence of an all purpose authority for Belfast, with participative mechanisms to support policy making, was exposed. The city's separate administrative structures meant that the Plan was powerless in many areas of urban life. Finally, the overall outcome of the inquiry, in the face of a range of coherent objections arising from public consultation, showed very clearly how the share the public supposedly has in the bundle of rights that comprise private property is expropriated 'in the public interest' by an officialdom acting as the instrument of the central state.

Some theoretical considerations

An implication of the above consideration of the past five chapters is that the BUAP is a one sided and thus distorted plan. Public inquiry discourse facilities this one sidedness because its discursive rules are not designed to establish common need interpretations and thus a generalizable interest. For this to be achieved particular attention has to be paid to the process for establishing such a generalizable interest. This has been a central element of the work of the social theorist Jürgen Habermas, and in order to point in some possible directions for reform this section considers how some of his ideas might be applied to the problem of planning. A recently published review of Habermas' recent work by White (1989) guides much of this discussion.

Legal regulations are a fundamental coordinator of planning. Habermas is critical of what he sees as a vast increase in legal regulations throughout society, which he calls 'juridification'. McAuslan (1980) identifies this trend in planning. Juridification induces people to define their public life in terms of relationships to bureaucracies so that everyday situations can be subsumed under legal categories. This is a requirement of administrative control and professional 'expertise' claimed in relation to the legal categories. The overall result is dependency and the definition of norms not by people themselves in everyday life situations but by administrators and professionals.

Juridification is for Habermas a feature of 'modernisation', and a cost of modernisation is 'cultural impoverishment'. This is caused by:

> the elitist splitting off of expert cultures from the contexts of everyday practice ... (I)ncreasingly specialised forms of argumentation become the guarded preserve of experts and thereby lose contact with the understanding processes of the majority of individuals'. (White 1989, p. 116)

The consequence, Habermas concludes, is that planners and policy 'experts' make a wide range of decisions which affect norms in everyday life but claim that these have professional justification. This organisation of knowledge and practical deliberation actually undermines a rational society which, for Habermas, would make these decisions through rational discursive procedures.

At a public inquiry many people express what they perceive to be their needs. The satisfaction of these needs are normative claims: no need is legitimate objectively because needs are always interpretations or *norms*. For policies that meet these needs to be incorporated into a plan they should be generalizable. This means that an individual proposing a need or norm as legitimate should subject this proposal not only to rules of fair argument but also to a critical assessment of the need which is being claimed. Habermas calls this the test of reciprocity and he proposes it as a rational discursive procedure for deciding on need.

The test of reciprocity requires each individual to interpret his or her needs in relation to others who may be affected by these needs being met. For a need interpretation to be legitimate it has to be capable of being universalised or 'communicatively shared'. Thus the need for more roads cannot be communicately shared if it leaves the mobility needs of non car owners unmet. By this means Habermas argues that need claims may be discursively tested as to their acceptability to all participants.

It is an important element of Habermas' model that all parties represent their own needs, and so the test of reciprocity relies on all relevant parties voicing their needs. At a public inquiry the test of reciprocity would be a communally followed procedure involving all those affected by a proposed norm. In effect, this forces an exchange of roles of each party with every other.

The major problem with Habermas' ideal is that it expects a lot of individuals to subordinate their interests to an ethics of reciprocity. Why should an unemployed tenant place him or herself in the role of a millionaire developer, and vice versa? It is not plausible to conceive of individuals freely willing a wholesale questioning of what they claim are their needs. Furthermore, the requirement that all those affected participate in the process is a tall order. It is a utopian perspective, but one which nevertheless suggests principles for public participation in planning.

The abandonment of such a utopian ideal leaves little else to coordinate action than money and power. For Habermas, money and power have led to an effective neutralising of the 'public sphere' as a site for effective citizen participation. As a consequence, 'money and power increasingly infiltrate spheres of social life in which traditions and knowledge are transferred, in which normative bonds are intersubjectively established, and in which responsible persons are formed' (White, 1989, p. 112).

The achievement of a planning system based on the negotiated coordination of interests in which needs are tested for reciprocity must entail a subordination of private property, money and power to the social interest in a much more definite way than at present. The negative controls of the current planning system would need to be augmented by major positive powers. These positive powers would employ zoning, taxation, compulsory purchase and a wider range of conditions attached to planning permissions to provide each locality with the infrastructure and community facilities it needs. The taxation of land use could be employed to create a financial framework for realising the socially agreed pattern of land use in the localities and across the city. Land use taxation could be introduced as part of a package to reduce or phase out income tax, including new taxes on wealth and the consumption of non renewable resources.

Devine (1988) considers the problem of transition to such a rational society. It is of course a project for political struggle. This is primarily a struggle for an acceptable form of state and a hegemonic position in society for the concept of social interest. Otherwise, decentralized control can open the way for discrimination, sectionalism and stalemate. Dominant groups in society are then likely to lead a return to state authoritarianism and/or market forces. Perhaps this is why the community groups involved in the BUAP project wanted to make the exercise with CTA work. There was manifest evidence of the wider failure in Northern Ireland to reach agreement about fundamental issues. The BUAP was a concrete situation where an effort could be made to interact and define together a social interest amid a wider social crisis. Government refused to acknowledge the greater legitimacy of a social interest so defined compared with the public interest ideology used by its officialdom. This was a wasted opportunity. Some part at least of a solution to the wider social crisis might have been built out of this exceptional effort across many of the city's community and voluntary groups to establish a shared social purpose for the BUAP.

Final conclusions

This book has been about how encouraging and supporting grassroots community and voluntary groups animated public participation in planning. It has described a largely successful model of providing planning aid within a conventional consultation process. The experience suggests a potential for urban planning in democratising urban policy making. But while in Belfast community groups rose to the challenge, the ambit of planning was too narrow to respond to the many legitimate needs which were expressed through the consultation process. This limitation was a consequence of planning law, planning ideology and the absence of an all purpose authority for Belfast.

There is a strong case for considerably broadening the ambit of urban plans beyond the coordination of end land uses so that the adequacy and appropriateness of the *social geography* of cities can be publicly examined and agreed. This would involve statutory agencies coordinating change and development with the urban plan process in a similar way to how service departments in local government presently coordinate their expenditure with corporate medium term plans for budgetary and taxation purposes. The urban plan would thus invite comment and bring forward proposals across the range of public provision and economic development as well as addressing issues of urban form, segregation, urban activity and the quality of urban life. To have teeth, it would have to be a basis for land use taxation. The technology of geographical information systems could be used to present pictures of the social geography of the city under different scenarios.

Reform of the planning system would have to be related to changes in government structures to create multifunctional authorities at suitable scales, preferably interlinked by overlapping representation as advocated by the minority report of the Royal Commission on the Constitution (Kilbrandon, 1973). Thus, the long overdue establishment of regional governments would include giving local government representation in their second chambers, while regional government would be represented in the second chamber of a reformed national parliament. This democratisation of sovereignty would ideally be complemented by financial arrangements which placed expenditure under regional and local democratic control, while ensuring a fair redistribution of national tax revenue to promote a broad equality of living standards across the country (Tyne Wear 2000, undated). In Northern Ireland at least, besides power sharing arrangements, regional government would have to be underpinned by a bill of rights (Labour Party 87, 1988).

A fundamental tension evident at the BUAP inquiry was between local and strategic perspectives. This book has argued that the conventional approach which accords greater legitimacy to the strategic should be reversed because the local is more real than the abstract space of strategic policy making. This should not be a retreat into localism but a process whereby local needs are incorporated into the plan as legitimate through a test of reciprocity to establish their universality. In this way, localist traditions are combined with a sense that we are all members of a wider community. The social interest in relation to each issue and decision is established through negotiated coordination. Instead of strategic policies for improving road traffic flows along arterial routes for example, there would be universal policies for meeting the shared need for accessibility. This may involve changing land use patterns to reduce the need to travel rather than catering to growing commuter flows in a fragmented urban system.

The book has highlighted problems with the conventional public inquiry as a vehicle for popular participation. Participation needs to start at an early stage of problem formulation and work through local meetings supported by community development resources at which people speak for themselves. Machinery for negotiated coordination similar to that developed by CTA needs to be put in place. This has to be backed up by media advertising and community based planning aid to encourage interest in the plan and provide support throughout the consultation process. A programme of quantitative and qualitative research should support the public meetings with information on all the issues, including public opinion. The final draft plan should be brought to a public inquiry without intimidating quasi judicial procedures, but restructured as a forum for achieving agreement on policies. It would have to be flexible, allowing for interaction and for initial positions to be modified. It would search for common values and norms, while attempting to recognise real differences in specific solutions. The plan, with any irreconcilable differences, should then be the subject of a referendum, with the final plan having to win at least two thirds support among those who choose to take part.

These are the directions in which reform might go. It is an agenda for discussion and for a struggle to realise the ideas that emerge. The book has been written in the spirit of critical discussion but it is meant to be positive about what has been achieved and what can be done.

Appendix 1

List of Participants at the CTA Conference on the BUAP, 25 November 1987

Name	Organisation
Acheson, Michael	Bryson House Better Belfast Project
Aiken, Hazel	East Belfast Community Council
Alcorn, Derek	Community Technical Aid
Bains, Bridget	St. James Housing and Environmental Association
Bankhead, Judith	Ulster Trust for Nature Conservation
Bass, Mrs.	Individual
Bennett, Isabel	Sydenham Environmental Group
Black, Mary	Eastern Health and Social Services Board
Black, Tony	Forum for Community Work Education
Blackman, Tim	University of Ulster
Bowers, Maggie	Dee Street Community Centre
Burke, Michael	Old Hollywood Road, Glenmachan, Belmont Green Belt Association
Burns, Bridge	Individual
Byrd, Paddy	Wheatfield Tenants Association
Campbell, Ann	Belfast Community Services Belfast City Council
Campion, Jane	Individual
Carroll, Paddy	Community Technical Aid
Casey, John	West Belfast Parents Youth Support Group
Christie, Susan	Ulster Trust for Nature Conservation

Collins, Brian	General Consumer Council
Conway, Pat	Social Services North and West Belfast Unit
Couvert, Cathy	Lower Ormeau Residents Action Group
Coyle, Yvonne	North Queen Street Community Centre
Davison, Rowan	Community Technical Aid
Delahunt, Michael	N.I. Council on Disability
Devon, Norman	Stranmillis, Belvoir
Doherty, John	Belfast City Council Community Services Department
Doran, Dan	Belfast City Council Community Services Department
Dornan, Cathy	Belfast Trades Council
Dunbar, Louis	N.I. Graphical Association
Dunlop, Dorothy	Belfast City Councillor
Ellison, Cecil	Donegal Pass Tenants Association
Emerson, Peter	Ecology Party
Fairley, Pat	Carlisle Tenants Association
Fenton, Michael	Greater West Belfast Community Association
Finlay, Henrietta	Wandsworth Residents Association
Fletcher, Ms	Individual
Frew, Andy	Community Technical Aid
Gaffikin, Frank	Centre for the Unemployed
Geyer, Hans	Community Technical Aid
Gillen, Mr.	Irish Congress of Trade Unions
Glendinning, Will	Help the Aged
Guertler, Sally	Individual
Hanlon, Kathy	Ballynafeigh Community Development Association
Hannna, Gloria	Bryson House Better Belfast Project
Hanvey, Dr. J.	Suffolk Community Services Group Residents Association
Hinds, Moya	North Queen Street Community Centre
Hughes, Joanne	Queens University Researcher
Hurst, Mr. G. M.	Lower Ormeau and Botanic Environmental Group
Johnson, Billy	Individual
Jones, Mervyn	Councillor
Kane, Mrs	Ardoyne Housing and Environmental Group
Kennedy, Irene	Community Technical Aid
Lavery, Irvine	Age Concern
Leary, Colleen	Individual
Mackin, Brendan	Belfast Centre for the Unemployed
Maguire, Ann	National Union of Students Union of Students in Ireland
Marshall, Marie Isabel	Individual
Maskey, Irene	Forum for Community Work Education
Mellon, Clive	Belfast Urban Wildlife Group
Moffat, Lawrence	Shelter N.I.

Morrison, Cedric	Community Technical Aid
Muller, Janet	Lower Ormeau Residents Action Group
Murphy, Carol	Belfast Centre for the Unemployed
Murphy, Chris	Royal Society for the Protection of Birds
McAlornan, Seamus	North Belfast Steering Group
McBride, Ann	Belfast City Council Community Services
McBride, Victoria	Individual
McCallum, Frank	Belfast Trades Council
McCavona, Carmel	West Belfast Parent Youth Support Group.
McClean, Edmond	Equal Opportunities Commission (NI)
McCrea, Stephen	St Georges Youth and Community Workshop
McEvoy, Ann	Falls Womens Centre
McGarry, Martin	West Belfast Parent Youth Group
McGill, Paul	Education Correspondent Belfast Telegraph
McGrath, D.	Lower Lenadoon Housing Action Group
McIlhennon, Laura	Sydenham Environmental Group
McKernan, William	Individual
McKetterick, David	Ulster People's College
McKnight, Sean	Markets Tenants' Association
McManus, Patrick	Lower Ormeau Residents' Action Group
McMullan, Mary	Falls Community Council
McQuade, D.	Individual
Noble, Mr.	Dundonald Green Belt Association
NiChléirigh, Noírín	Glor na nGael
O'Boyle, Catherine	Community Technical Aid
O'Boyle, Úna	Community Technical Aid
O'Brien, P.	Lower Ormeau Residents' Action Group
O'Connor, Sharon	Centre for Neighbourhood Development
O'Halloran, Chris	Suffolk Community Services Group/Residents' Association
O'Hara, Mary	St James Housing and Environmental Association
O'Neill, Maura	Markets Tenants Association
O'Prey, Monina	North Queen Street Community Centre
Price, Jocelyn	Ulster People's College
Price, Silvia	Conservation Society
Rainey, Michael	Belfast Exposed Community Photography Group.
Reid, John	Reid, McHugh and Partners Planning Consultants
Robinson, Victor	Individual
Rudner, Frances	Community Technical Aid
Shearan, Alan	Tenants Participation Advisory Service
Simon, Ben	Ulster Trust for Nature Conservation
Simpson, Arthur	Belfast Civic Trust
Slevin, N.	N.I. Council on Disability
Smyth, Dr. Austin	Individual
Snoddy, Andy	N.I. Graphical Society
Stewart, Jean	Individual

Sutton, M.	Lower Ormeau Residents' Action Group
Sweeny, Paul	N.I. Voluntary Trust
Turkington, B.	Individual
Turner, Eileen	Wandsworth Residents Association
Uprichard, Eileen	North Queen Street Community Centre
Walker, Jim	St Georges Youth and Community Group
Walsh, Elsie	Morton Community Centre
Wells, Jim	Royal Society for the Protection of Birds
Wilson, Noel	Belfast Civic Trust
Winterbauer, Marcus	Photographer (CTA)
Wood, Stephen	North Belfast Steering Group
Workman, Mr.	Ballynafeigh Community Development Association

Appendix 2

CTA's Objections to the BUAP

Community Technical Aid
(Northern Ireland)

Registered Office
74, Dublin Road
Belfast
B12 7HP

14th January 1988

Belfast Urban Area Plan,
Town and County Planning Services,
Department of the Environment (NI),
Bedford House,
Bedford Street,
Belfast, BT2 7FD.

Re: Belfast Urban Area Plan 2001:

Dear Sirs,

Pursuant to the provisions of Part III of the Planning (Northern
Ireland) Order, 1972, we hereby make objections to the Belfast
Urban Area Plan 2001 as it has been published in accordance with
Article 6 of the said Order.

The said objections are dealt with below in the following sequence:

Conservation
Public Health
Housing
Industry and Commerce
Laganside
Recreation
Retailing
Transportation
Women
Education
Local Plans
General Comments

Conservation

The present attitude towards waste disposal is totally unacceptable in environmental terms. This whole area should be re-examined and the Department of the Environment should act as a central body to co-ordinate, in conjunction with local councils, a recycling scheme as a service to the people of the Belfast Urban Area and beyond. It is ironic that in this, the European Year of the Environment, the Department of the Environment is still giving permission for dumping in the Belfast Lough Area which is extremely important for the numerous waders and wildfowl and other wildlife which use it. This is symptomatic of an environmentally insensitive waste disposal policy. Recycling of many forms of waste can make sense also in economic terms and should be seen as a potential job creator and to some degree an alternative form of energy. This may also prove an effective method of cutting down on imports of timber, paper, fertilizers, etc.. The Plan offers no positive way forward in terms of dealing with the waste issue. It seeks only to find new areas to dump the evergrowing volume of waste and does not address the root of the problem.

The Belfast Urban Area is fortunate in possessing some very interesting and important wildlife habitats, foremost among them being the Belfast Lough and Harbour Area. It is essential that the importance of this area is recognised and that it is given permanent protection in the form of a Nature Reserve. The present designation of the area as an ASSI (Area of Special Scientific Interest) is welcomed but the fact that dumping continues shows that this status is inadequate. This valuable natural resource should be developed for the benefit of the people of Belfast and further afield. It should be opened up for educational purposes and promoted in a sensitive way and not, as at present, hidden from the public eye. Other areas of particular significance include Belvoir Forest, Hydebank Wood and the Bog Meadows. Here too the Department of the Environment should bear in mind that these areas are positive assets to the environment of Belfast and should be treated as such. Where possible, methods for increasing access to them should be developed in consultation with local conservation groups.

Throughout the Belfast Urban Area there are some small green areas, pockets of woodland, etc. which are also very important in conservation terms. These also play a crucial role in terms of recreation and education, particularly for children in certain areas of the City where access to larger, more peripheral areas is very restricted. Many such small areas are being swallowed up, for example, in West and North Belfast for private housing and in East Belfast the road proposal following the nature walk along the old Comber railway line (recently acknowledged for its contribution to urban nature conservation and community involvement).

Concern is felt that when referring to pollution caused by traffic, the Plan is restricted to considering noise pollution only. This is totally inadequate as the problems of fumes, carbon monoxide and lead pollution, together with the issue of damage to health due to accidents, must be considered. This is particularly important in the case of children, who are more susceptible to such danger. Exhaust fumes from vehicles also contribute to problems such as acid rain and create a generally unpleasant atmosphere.

It is considered that environmental pollution could be lessened considerably through the development of public transport alternatives. There should be more consideration of and encouragement given to the most environmentally sensitive forms of private transport especially the use of bicycles and walking.

Safeguards should be included in the Plan whereby Cave Hill is not commercialised or deformed. It is too important and too prominent a part of the City setting.

As a general principle the Green Belt should not be broken. Only in exceptional circumstances should deviations be permitted from this basic principle. In every such instance the provisions of Articles 8 and/or 22 of the said order should be applied.

The preservation of the Urban Area's character in all parts of the Area is felt to be of importance and every effort should be made to keep buildings of character intact. If this is not possible, an attempt should at least be made to preserve the facade. Access for the disabled should be carefully considered and ramps, etc. should be designed tastefully and in the correct style. The social usefulness of buildings should be taken into account when considering possible demolition, for example, Ormeau Baths may be such a case. Every effort should be made to take into consideration the conservation of working class areas of interest which may also be of value and of historic or cultural significance.

Public health

It is considered that the Plan deals inadequately with the vital matter of Public Health. There appears to be a lack of communication between the Department of the Environment and the health and education services.

It is considered that the question of reducing the numbers of people in institutional care and a proposal to build up services in the community is not dealt with adequately.

Concern is also felt regarding the effects of a roads-dominated transportation strategy on health. Building more roads leads to an increase in noise and petrol fumes. It also encourages more people to use roads, thus increasing the level of environmental and health problems. The building of bicycle lanes should be investigated, which would actively encourage people to use an alternative form of transport that was pollution free and health-enducing.

The detrimental effect of poor housing and overcrowding on the health of communities must be taken into account in the plan and strategies developed to alleviate these problems.

Housing

It is felt very strongly that local people should have a greater say in the choice of housing type and mix and also the design of the houses.

Housing development has been concentrated into certain areas of Belfast and this has had several detrimental effects. Residential areas have become devoid of other facilities. In certain areas of Belfast, for example the West, nearly all the vacant space has been used up. Hence there is a severe lack of industrial recreational sites, etc. It was felt that a lot of residential areas lacked amenities such as shops, chemists, general practitioners, post offices. Such amenities have a very important role in neighbourhood economies as well as in community life. While the conversion of residential units to offices in certain areas of the City should be discouraged, a degree of urban mix is desirable to avoid areas being deserted at certain times of the day and night. The lack of recreational space in residential areas is a particular

137

problem.

It is felt strongly that the local community's housing and other needs should be taken into consideration in the Laganside Development.

It is felt that the housing needs of certain minority groups have been ignored. It is suggested that there should be an increased provision of suitable affordable housing for single people, disabled and the elderly. It is felt also that current sites available for travelling people are unacceptable and there should be moves to resolve the problem as soon as possible.

It is generally considered that private house building has been favoured at the expense of public housing. Cuts in the Northern Ireland Housing Executive's budget have led to a very inadequate public house building programme. The Executive should not sell off land in its possession to private developers. The private developer's interests will most likely lie in the more profitable suburban sites, particularly on the edge of the City. Sites must be positively identified for public housing.

There is a need for greater assessment of land needs and agreement about housing density standards so that the real housing land needs can be ascertained. It is considered that in many parts of the Urban Area there are opportunities for infill development which would reduce the need for incursion of new housing into the surrounding rural areas.

Industry and commerce

There appears to be no economic rationale behind the policy statement on Industry and Commerce. The plan contains policies similar to those of the 1969 Plan which proposed that an infrastructure and environment be created which would attract foreign multinational investment. In today's circumstances this is not a viable strategy. The Plan also intends to designate simplified planning zones which are based on the principles of enterprise zones. However, enterprise zones have been shown to be a failure with 3% job loss in these areas and with 60% of the jobs located there merely being relocated from elsewhere. The Plan also presumes the Northern Ireland and Great Britain growth rates will be along similar lines. This is questionable.

It is felt most strongly that the policy statement on industry does not properly take into account local need. The allocation of industrial land does not correspond to local need and there is no proper addressing of the problems of severe local unemployment.

It is felt most strongly that the policy statement on industry does not properly take into account local need. The allocation of industrial land does not correspond to local need and there is no proper addressing of the problems of severe local unemployment.

It is felt that it is not enough merely to allocate land for industry. There is nothing in the industrial strategy to prepare people for work. It is believed that facilities to train people for work should be provided in addition to allocating land for industrial purposes.

It is felt that industry is located too far out of the Inner City and that sites allocated in the suburbs are often inaccessible by public transport.

It is felt strongly that some industry should go back into the City Centre, perhaps into the ring outside the inner City.

There is too much emphasis in the Belfast Urban Area Plan on private investment. The Plan sees the private sector as the engine of economic growth. However, the private sector in Northern Ireland is not dynamic despite the huge sums of money pumped into it, a large proportion of the private sector being dependent on the State.

It is felt also that there was too great an emphasis on the retailing and services sector in the Plan.

Laganside

The major area of concern with regard to the Laganside concept is the almost total zoning of residential land along the Lagan for private sector as opposed to public housing. It is felt that such housing would become the preserve of the more affluent, pushing out the indigenous population, and therefore transforming the social composition of these areas. It is considered that housing on the Laganside must provide a balance between private and public sector investment and that the housing, employment, health, recreation, retailing and community requirements of the indigenous population receive priority attention.

Recreation

Recreation provision within the Belfast Urban Area Plan is felt to be insufficient and inappropriate to the needs of the population of the Belfast Urban Area.

The provision of tourist facilities will be of minor benefit to the local population and the use of the Green Belt for recreation, constrained by land owners and access to it from the Inner City, will be limited.

The changing concept of leisure and recreation has not been developed sufficiently in the Plan. Merely to provide open space is not enough, neither is the provision of sports centres used by the able bodied. Such centres are often outside walking distance of the local population.

A new approach is needed which considers leisure as an essential social provision comprising anything that is relaxation rather than essential activities.

More localised leisure, play and recreation provision is needed, accessible to the local population both physically and financially and catering for the various local needs. A recreation policy should consider in detail the needs of the local population, looking at, for example, the numbers in the area, the age profile (existing and projected) and the number of unemployed, pensioned, single and handicapped people within the area.

Community and local plans should be prepared based on surveys carried out to assess what facilities exist and what are needed. The implementation of such plans would require an interagency approach with co-operation and co-ordination between the statutory and non-statutory agencies such as the Department of the Environment, Belfast City Council, BCC Parks Department, BCC Community Services, Befast Education and Library Board, Northern Ireland Housing Executive, Playboard and various involved community and voluntary groups.

Retailing

The retailing strategy in the Plan is considered to be totally inadequate. It is believed that the current proposals focus on retailing in the City Centre and ignore the smaller, local retailer.

In certain areas that the provision of local shopping facilities is totally inadequate. It is considered that there is a major problem today with the closure of local shopping facilities on arterial routes. This current Plan reinforces the 1969 Belfast Urban Area Plan in removing shops from arterial routes and encouraging them to move to district centres.

As a result of such policies not only do local businesses suffer but so do local communities. Shops act as social meeting places particularly for older people and people confined to their homes due, for example, to unemployment or caring roles.

There has been instead a steady rise in suburban shopping centres, which, while they offer cheaper commodities, they are very often

140

inaccessible for the elderly and mothers with young children. There has also been a growth in the garage shop with its excessive prices; it has long opening hours but caters chiefly for the motorist.

There is a need for conveniently located and reasonably priced shops, for example, co-operatives, and community shops for those without cars and with low disposable incomes. Such shops should provide creches and drop-in centres so as to help to restore a sense of community.

It is considered that the increase in traffic on certain roads is discouraging people from stopping to shop. Roads are having a bad effect on traders.

The Plan has identified retailing as the most active sector of the economy and is based on the premis of growth in this sector, yet the Plan itself predicts little or no growth in retail turnover.

Transportation

The transportation strategy, orientated towards private transport (favouring the car user), is considered to be out of date, inappropriate and out of balance with the transportation needs of the population of the Belfast Urban Area.

Despite low car ownership levels, the roads orientated consultants' brief means the Plan takes the form of a road building strategy with disruptive environmental effects rather than a transportation strategy.

Existing public transport systems, particularly buses, are inadequate, have an inappropriate route network, insufficient frequency and suffer from the lack of integration between bus and rail services.

The Plan fails to address the transport requirements of the disabled and elderly and the needs of women and children particularly with respect to public transport.

The Plan fails to consider the environmental and health implications of an improved road system such as the loss of natural habitats, loss of amenity (as on the old Comber railway line) noise and fume pollution and road injuries or deaths.

Concern is felt over the environmental effects of road widening, for example, on the Albertbridge Road (part complete) and Lower Ormeau Road and the potential effect on local traders.

There is an overwhelming need for an increase in the availability, accessibility (physical and financial) and efficiency of public transport which should be recognised as a consumer orientated public service which need not be profit based.

It is felt that alternative methods of transport are not given sufficient, if any, consideration. The role of black taxis is virtually ignored. Other alternatives such as smaller buses with more flexible routes, dial-a-ride schemes, light rail transport, cycle lanes and more pedestrianization of streets are ignored.

It is felt a wider brief encompassing all transport issues and methods should have been issued to the Department's transportation consultants.

Various benefits accruing from a more balanced transportation system should be investigated such as the more efficient movement of all the Belfast Urban Area population, less pollution and energy savings through the reduction in the number of vehicles required.

Coupled with improvements to public transport, measures to restrict the private car from the City Centre through more expensive car parking and pedestrianisation should be formulated.

There is a need for a Transport Review Authority with public accountability to ensure the transport needs of the whole of the population of the Belfast Urban Area are met.

Women

There should be greater provision of public housing for women. Women, because of generally lower income levels have less access to the private house market.

Women, whether by choice or not, are generally more home-centred than men. The design of their houses and neighbourhoods should, therefore, ensure that their environment is a pleasant and safe place in which to live and work.

Creches, toilets and feeding facilities for nursing mothers should automatically be provided in retail outlets. The extent of provision could, perhaps, be in proportion to square footage of retail floor space.

It is not good enough merely to provide open space and label it as recreation; the concept of recreation must be developed with regard to the needs of women and their children.

Bus stops should be well lit and shelters provided, so women will feel safe using public transport particularly at night.

Community based employment and training programmes should be established near housing estates and in suburbs where there are few employment opportunities.

Design of housing estates, it was felt, must take account of the personal security of women. Planners should ensure, through the development control system, that developers take security matters into consideration.

Education

The Plan acknowledges that school enrolments in the Urban Area are dropping but makes no mention of other educational needs such as adult educational requirements at local level. Likewise there is no mention of particular educational needs such as Irish language or integrated schools.

Local plans

The need for developed local plans as the appropriate basis of any strategic document was identified thus involving people on a much wider basis in the planning process.

The Plan as it stands is broad brush in its scope and coverage. There is a need for local plans to be prepared so that a comprehensive, integrated and sensitive approach can be taken in the planning of local areas. The Plan makes no committment to a programme of local plan preparation in which the public can participate.

There is a need for 'community plans' covering all areas of the Belfast Urban Area and resources should be made available to local groups to help prepare them.

General comments

Any submission made in relation to preliminary proposals will be accepted with regard to any inquiry whether or not they have been resubmitted.

It is considered that the Department of the Environment's consultation process has been inadequate. It is felt also that there was a lack of time for consultation.

It is felt the Plan is directed towards more affluent members of the population, neglecting working class communities.

Much of the Plan is cosmetic in approach and does not tackle the roots of the problems.

It is felt that the aim should be to preserve and enhance existing communities - Belfast should be planned as a city of 'urban villages' - with houses, shops, jobs, health and community facilities.

The interpretation of the Plan by lay people is very difficult. The Plan does not make clear how proposals at strategic level would effect people and their environment on the ground. For example, a road widening scheme will mean land being taken away to facilitate it, but where? Accordingly, it is difficult for people to object to the Plan on issues that would affect them on a local level.

The Plan is not concerned with social issues but is merely a land use Plan. The Plan ought to address social issues as planning is fundamentally a distributor of scarce resources.

We are concerned that in the period purportedly made available for consideration of the Plan by the public, there have been Government announcements that major components of the Plan will definitely be proceeded with. Such components include Castle Court, Laganside and the Cross-Harbour Link.

Conclusion

The above is a summary only of our objections and is as detailed as can be made, given the deadline and the timing of that deadline set by the Department for the receipt of objections.

In the absence of resolution of our objections and in the event of the Department causing a public inquiry to be held, we hereby request to be heard at such an inquiry.

Yours faithfully,

Rowan Davison
Chairman CTA(NI)

Appendix 3

Belfast Urban Area Plan: Paper for Second Meeting of CTA Advisory Group to Review Objections, 25 January 1988.

Introduction

The purpose of the second meeting of the BUAP Advisory Group is to review objections drawn from the seven local and special interest group meetings.
These objections will be reviewed under the following headings:

I.	Conservation
II.	Public Health
III.	Housing
IV.	Industry and Commerce
V.	Laganside
VI.	Recreation
VII.	Retailing
VIII.	Transportation
IX.	Women's Issues
X.	Education

Strategic Policy Objections will be discussed under each heading. This will be followed by Area Specific Objections discussed under the following subheadings (where appropriate):   Outer North, North, West, Outer South, South and East. Finally other objections put forward by CTA will be stated.

I.   *Conservation (natural and built)*

Strategic policy objections

* Present waste disposal policies are wasteful and environmentally insensitive. They show absolutely no imagination in terms of recycling, etc.
* The DoE's perception of pollution as caused by traffic is extemely restricted and misleading as it refers only to noise levels. This should be rectified.
* The small natural green areas remaining in the built up areas of the BUA are very important locally.
* There is one area in particular within the BUA, the Belfast Harbour Lagoons which is of international significance. There should be a policy of ensuring the protection of this area. It should be dezoned immediately and designated as a nature reserve.
* A policy of encouraging better public transport provision and promotion of cycling and walking would help protect the environment. The Plan should seek to facilitate such transport alternatives as opposed to the biased and outdated roads based strategy it has adopted.
* Failure to show the relationship between the proposed Greenbelt inner edge and the Matthew Stopline was a serious omission from the Plan in terms of its influence on people's perceptions of exactly what had been proposed in this area.
* To give the Greenbelt concept strength, any developments within it should be more strictly monitored to prevent abuses of the needs criteria and ensure adherence to the recently introduced design standards. The BUAP does not propose at present to break the greenbelt in areas of any great significance in conservation terms, the most important areas under threat having been removed with the publication of the Plan.
* All rivers within the BUA should be the focus of attention for water quality and general environmental improvements, in particular, the River Lagan.
* Conservation policy has a bias toward those buildings and areas reflecting the values and attitudes of the wealthier members of our society. This should be redressed and the listing of buildings or designation of Conservation Areas should seek to accommodate the history and culture of working class people also.
* To maintain the character and vitality of traditional shopping areas, there should be a policy designed to control the conversion of ground floor retail outlets to nonretail uses such as banks, buildings societies and estate agents, which has been destroying not only the character of traditional

frontages but threatening the future viability of such shopping areas.

Area specific objections

Outer North *   Green Belt breaches of Matthew Stopline in North Belfast to cater for private residential development should not be permitted while derelict and vacant housing land still remains in the north of the city. Excess supply of land zoned for industrial use in North Belfast should be considered for housing use. Proposed breaches for housing at Hightown, Lyndhurst, Ligoniel and Colin Glen should be excluded from residential development.

* Housing at Carnmoney Hill should not be permitted as this is an area of archeological and high local amenity value.

* Cave Hill should remain unspoilt by insensitive development though use of this natural asset and appreciation of the area's archeological significance should be promoted and access to it improved. The reference to chairlifts in the Plan could not be termed 'sensitive development' for this most prominent view.

* The many small green areas of shrubland and woods in North Belfast should be identified and protected from destruction by residential or industrial use. This has not been happening and the Plan does not appear to remedy this.

* Belfast Lough and the North Foreshore are important in terms of scenic and wildlife value. They should be strongly protected by designation as a Nature Reserve and opened up to allow the public to fully appreciate their significance.

* Once listed, a building should only be considered for de-listing under very exceptional circumstances. There are areas in North Belfast worthy of special protection that have not been given it in the Plan, for example, the People's Home at Clifton Street and thatched cottages at Ballysillan.

* Recycling waste has great potential which is being ignored to the detriment of the environment. It is noted that the BUA intends to export its waste to other areas of Larne; this is hardly justifiable. Dumping on the foreshore should stop at once. The quality of sewage

147

being pumped into Belfast Lough is felt to be suspect, yet the Plan proposes no measures to combat this problem.

West * From Lyndhurst all the way to Colingrove the Greenbelt line should be brought inward to coincide with the dotted line indicated as the 1993 development limit. Continued development further up the mountainside in West Belfast would remove one of the few areas of natural environment within reasonable access to local people. To increase this access, footpaths should be constructed.

* Great concern is expressed about the quarrying operations above Colin Glen which is detracting from the high scenic value of the area, destroying its natural beauty.

* The continuing pollution problem of noxious smells caused by the sewage treatment plant at Kennedy Way should be dealt with immediately as it continues to cause considerable distress in the area.

* The Bog Meadows should be protected as a nature reserve. The area should have improved access to allow enjoyment of the area by local people.

* There are only a few buildings of any architectural or historic interest left in West Belfast. All the more reason that some buildings of great local historical significance should be recognized and listed, for example, the Falls Road Library, the house of James Connolly, St. Dominic's High School.

South * The Annadale to Grahamholm Link through Belvoir Forest Park will endanger a vital wildlife habitat near the city.

Outer South * The potential of reopening the old canal at Lisburn should have been looked into by the Plan.

* The Deriaghy River Valley zoning should have been extended right down to the river.

* Some feel that the status of the Lagan Valley Regional Park is not that much different from general Greenbelt land and its separate designation on the development strategy map is misleading.

East * Objections to proposed road through old Comber railway, now a Nature Walk managed by Conservation Volunteers.

* The Greenbelt should not be broken at Old

148

Holywood Road as it is a natural part of an undeveloped hillside and development here would made the Glenmachan area with its wildlife reserves more vulnerable to future development. The area in question also forms part of a natural break between Holywood and Belfast, preventing these built-up areas from merging together.

* In inner East Belfast in general there is a need for the development of more local nature conservation areas.

* The DoE's decision to drop proposals for housing development in the Gothic Wood, Hydebank and Glenmachan areas is to be commended. These areas should remain free from any such development in the future due to their importance in nature conservation terms.

II.   Public Health

Strategic policy objections

* The Plan deals inadequately city wide with the vital matter of public health, illustrating a lack of communication between the DoE and health and education services. Poor housing, overcrowding, noise, air and water pollution, and inadequate access to health, community and recreation facilities for all members of the population(both able-bodied and disabled) have a detrimental effect on the health of the community. However, Plans and strategies to alleviate these problems and raise community awareness through health, education, etc. have not been put forward.

* The Plan does not mention the "Healthy Cities 2001" campaign of the World Health Organisation.

* The Plan's road dominated transportation strategy will encourage more people to use these roads, thus increasing noise, lead and carbon monoxide pollution and associated health problems such as injuries and deaths.

* Bicycle lanes and other pollution free, health inducing forms of transport such as walking have not been investigated.

* The waste disposal policy contained in the Plan is environmentally insensitive, with no attempt to encourage or develop waste recycling, possibly incorporating energy provision.

* The Plan lacks effective pollution control with respect to the dumping of effluent and waste into Belfast Lough. A review must be provided with the aim of controlling it.

Area specific objections

North   *   Residents of North Belfast object to the lack of effective pollution control in the Plan, particularly with respect to the dumping of effluent and waste into Belfast Lough.

West   *   People in West Belfast object to the lack of planned community and health facilities, particularly for the elderly, in their area.

South   *   Groups and individuals in South Belfast oppose the Southern Approaches Roads Strategy as proposals contained within it, such as widening the Lower Ormeau Road and the Annadale Embankment, pose serious questions as to the future health and safety of the population.

                *   The Plan fails to provide information on how toxic soil in the gasworks site will be tackled, or how the River Lagan will be improved.

East   *   The majority of residents of East Belfast oppose the Eastern Approaches Roads Strategy, including the widening of the Albert Bridge Road, the Connsbank Link, the construction of the Comber Route (1) Bypass and the Ballygowan Road/Castlereagh Road Flyover. Their objections arise from the danger of noise and fume pollution, health risk and associated loss of amenity.

                *   The Plan also fails to earmark neighbourhood clinic facilities in the Ballyhackamore area.

Other CTA objections

*   The question of reducing the numbers of people in institutional care and a proposal to build up services in the community is not dealt with in sufficient detail.

III.   Housing

Strategic policy objections

*   Housing development on greenfield sites should be limited for a number of reasons:
  a)   Developing more and more housing on greenfield sites creates problems of access. This often results in roads being proposed through existing housing areas to accommodate the new population.
  b)   Building on greenfield sites more often than not degrades the scenic value of the area.

150

c)   When infill sites are available in other parts of the city, developing greenfield sites is seen to take away from regenerating the centre of the city.

d)   It leads to large private profits being made at public expense.

*   The 'whiteland' between the limit to development line 1993 and the edge of the Greenbelt does not offer sufficient protection from development. In certain areas the inner edge of the Greenbelt should be drawn into the limit of development 1993.

*   There is a lack of clarity in the Plan as to what exactly the housing proposals are.   Clarification is needed on the following:

a)   What is the availability of infill sites (including sites with capacity for 10 or fewer) and vacant/derelict land?

b)   What is the balance between public and private housing and where will these developments take place?

c)   Have all proposals for housing been indicated in the Plan? This query arises because people have heard of developments going on in their area that have not been indicated.

*   There should be more control over what sort of industry, institutions, and so on are allowed to locate near residential areas.   The public should have this information made available to them.

*   There is an overemphasis on private housebuilding.   This does not take into account the most needy: those on waiting lists, the homeless.

*   The NIHE Housing Programme does not take into account the changing demographic composition of the population, particularly the aged and single parents. Cuts in the NIHE budget also negate some of the housing policies stated in the Plan.

*   Traveller's needs and the needs of other minority groups have been ignored.

*   Housing development in the Laganside scheme will not take into account the housing needs of the local people.

Area specific objections

Outer North *   A group from Jordanstown objected to the housing proposals at Jordanstown and Monkstown. Its development would give rise to access problems. They believed the N10 road proposal was proposed to cater for accessing this site. This road development in turn would be detrimental to Jordanstown.

*   An objection was raised to the housing proposals at Hightown, which would be visually intrusive

151

and result in a loss of amenity. The site is also 180 metres above sea level.

North   * The housing development between Glebe Road and Carnmoney Hill was objected to: it was felt that such a development would be visually intrusive and take away from the scenic value of the area.

         * The group objected to building in the Green Belt particularly because of the supply of infill sites in the North Belfast area. More statistics should be made available on the availablility of infill sites in this area, including those with a capacity for 10 or fewer.

West   * The Plan lacks clarity as to what is proposed as housing and what is not. Some people knew of housing development that was being or going to be carried out but that was not shown.

         * The Plan did not clarify whether the housing was to be private or public. Private housing in West Belfast, it was believed, would lead to an influx of people from outside the area and not cater for the local people's housing needs.

         * The needs of Travellers in West Belfast have been ignored.

Outer South * The representative objected to the lack of clarity in the Plan as to what is proposed as housing and what is not. He wished to know whether there was housing development planned at Arema Estate.

South   * In the North Parade area there was an objection to the lack of control over change of residential use to other uses. There is a particular concentration of psychiatric homes in this area.

         * The group objected to housing in the Cairnshill area. This was considered inappropriate because local people at present are unable to get housing in that area. The development also created the necessity for the Annadale to Grahamholm Link, so in effect it was a self fulfilling prophecy.

         * The Laganside development will not provide housing for local people; rather, it will provide housing for short stay residents.

East   * There is little control over the location of noxious businesses near residential areas.

         * Suburban housing should not be developed in East Belfast. It is essential that where housing development does take place that it adheres to maximum density figures.

         * There is an inappropriate balance between public

152

and private housebuilding. The concentration on private housebuilding will not cater for the changing social composition of the population of East Belfast.

* Housing development should not go ahead at Knockagoney as this would destroy the countryside break between Belfast and Holywood. It would also destroy an area of high scenic value.

Other CTA objections

* Local people should have a greater say in the choice of housing type and mix and also in the design of the house. This point is reinforced considering the plight of Divis residents.
* Housing development in certain areas of Belfast is overdeveloped and too dense, resulting in all vacant space being taken up and leaving very little appropriate land for other land uses. A mix of land uses in residential areas would be more satisfactory.
* Density standards of housing development should be clarified in order that the exact amount of land is zoned for housing. It is only through this that the real demand for housing land can be assessed.

IV. *Industry and Commerce*

Strategic policy objections

* The Plan does not locate industrial land in suitable locations. There is a need to review the distribution of industrial sites to ensure that there are sites available within reach of all sections of the urban population.
* The Plan relies on multinational investment which has already been shown to be inappropriate.
* The proposals merely follow the present government's fiscal policies: the government provides land, buildings, infrastructure, etc. and the private sector provides jobs, investment, etc. However, more public funding is needed to tackle the problem of unemployment and to target the areas of most need.
* The Enterprise Zone is not appropriate as a large percentage of the jobs located in Enterprise Zones have merely been relocated from other areas and are not new businesses.
* The Plan ignores the importance of local community initiatives and does not make use of the skills and talents in these communities. There is a greater need for small multi-purpose units in local areas.

153

* Noxious or inappropriate industries should be confined to industrial sites.
* The concentration of office facilities in the city centre has a detrimental effect on the community/linear development of shops and businesses and for local employment.
* The Plan has not provided facilities for community initiative.

Area specific objections

North
* Proposals to designate York Street as a Business Development Area do not make clear whether this would be appropriate for the skills and employment needs of the local community.
* Despite so-called shortages of large industrial sites in the inner city, the government have allowed the prime industrial site of Gallaghers to be transferred to a retail development.

West
* Not enough suitable industrial land has been allocated for smaller workshop units in West Belfast. Certain industrial sites should have been given over to the community to manage.
* There has been no attempt to bring service jobs into West Belfast despite the fact that 53% of the people in Northern Ireland who are employed work in the service sector.
* Conway Mill was not mentioned in the Plan.

South
* There is no provision made in the Laganside proposals for employment designed to meet local needs.
* In South Belfast there should be realistic job creation, by surveying local skills and providing small workshop units.
* The effect that concentrating shops and office facilities in the city centre has on the development of shops and businesses and hence, local employment in the South Belfast area needs to be examined.

East
* The Plan should ensure that noxious or inappropriate industries do not encroach upon residential areas in East Belfast.
* The Lagoon area should be dezoned.

Other CTA objections

* The Plan does not make clear the role of the IDB, LEDU, YTP and CBI, etc. It is believed that none of these agencies are meeting needs.
* It is not enough merely to allocate land for industry. There is nothing in the industrial stragegy to prepare people for

work.
* Certain types of appropriate industry should be moved back into the city centre.
* The conversion of residential areas to a predominantly office use in certain areas of the city should be discouraged to avoid loss of residential units.

VI.   Recreation

Strategic policy objections

* Recreation provision within the BUAP was felt by all groups to be insufficient and inappropriate to the needs of the BUA population. It fails to address recreation and leisure as a necessary social service whereby the zoning of appropriate land, not just on the edge of the city but also at a local level, particularly in inner city areas, ensures its protection from inappropriate development.
* To simply provide open space (if any), however, is not enough. Neither is the provision of major sports/leisure centres used by the affluent and able bodied, often outside walking distance of the local community. Emphasis must be put on meeting the recreation and leisure needs of all members of local communities and ensuring access to such facilities is both physically and financially adequate.
* An increase in facilities geared for the tourist will be of minor benefit to the local population.
* The proposed use of the Greenbelt and some of the hills surrounding Belfast for informal recreation will be constrained by land owners and access to these areas from the inner city. The Plan makes no mention of rights of way, public paths, etc. which councils have the power to ordain.

Area specific objections

North   *   For accessibility and sectarian reasons, large areas of North Belfast are deprived of open space or leisure/recreation facilities. To help remedy this, the BUAP suggests a leisure complex in the Cliftonville area. However, this would also prove inaccessible for many people and alternative sites, such as the Waterworks, could be identified. Small local park areas must also be identified and protected.

West   *   Groups and individuals in West Belfast object to the lack of informal open space and local

155

recreation facilities zoned in their area, particularly in the vicinity of McCrory Park, Brooke Park, the Bog Meadows, Black Mountain and Divis Mountain.

* They also object to the removal of 15 feet from one of the few park areas, Dunville Park, to facilitate road widening.

Outer South * Concern has been expressed that the boundaries of the Derriaghy River Valley Park are inappropriate and should extend to merge with the Lagan Valley Regional Park.

South * The BUAP gives insufficient attention to facilitating financially and physically accessible play and recreation facilities for the Lower Ormeau area.

* Groups and individuals from South Belfast also object to the Southern Approaches Roads Strategy which would destroy recreation and leisure in the Belvoir Park and along the Annadale Embankment.

East * The BUAP's lack of local playspace and community facilities provision is opposed in East Belfast, as is the proposed loss of the Beersbridge Nature Walkway to the Eastern Approaches Roads Strategy, which would result in a serious loss of amenity in East Belfast.

* The Plan fails to suggest the extension of the Redburn Country Park through Glenmachan to Stormont.

VII. *Retailing*

Strategic policy objections

* There is a bias in favour of locating shopping areas in the city centre. This has resulted in a poor provision of local shopping facilities, which in turn directly affects the most disadvantaged and vulnerable sections of the community.

* Adequate retail floorspace should be provided in all new housing estates and old housing estates where land is available; rent and rate concessions should be made available to small retail businesses to encourage this.

* There should be less dependence on national retail chains and a greater development of cooperatives and community shops.

* Adequate parking facilities should be provided for existing linear shopping centres.

* Public transport should service retail areas.

* The encroachment of offices into local linear shopping areas is decreasing the amount of retail floorspace. Office

156

development therefore should be more strictly controlled.
* Certain road proposals in the Plan will have detrimental effects on shopping in local areas.

Area specific objections

North   * North Belfast contains only 6 percent of the available retail floorspace in the BUA. This has led to a dependence on the city centre for shopping which is inconvenient for the disadvantaged and vulnerable sections of the community.

          * Grants should be made available in all areas of North Belfast to ensure the retention and enhancement of prime shopping frontages.

          * Parking facilities should be provided along the existing linear shopping development.

West   * West Belfast wants to see the development of a local shopping centre in the Divis street area opposite the Falls Baths.

          * Traders in Andersonstown have been ignored, particularly regarding parking provision. Traffic congestion in this area is a major problem.

          * There is a need for small shop units in housing estates in West Belfast, and the development of local shopping centres is also needed in this area.

South   * The proposed road expansion along the Ormeau Road will take away from local shops and traders. This in turn will have a detrimental effect on the local population.

East   * There is a lack of local shopping facilities, particularly around Ballyhackamore.

          * The roads proposals in this area go against the development of self-sufficient urban villages.

          * There has been an invasion of building societies, insurance offices and estate agents into the local shopping area. This has limited shopping choice for local people.

Other CTA objections

* Because shops act as social meeting places, particularly for older people and those confined to home, the degeneration of shopping in local areas also affects the morale of the community. The Plan has not taken this social aspect into account.
* The Urban Plan has identified retailing as the most active

157

sector of the economy and is based on the premise of growth in this sector. Yet the Plan itself predicts little or no growth in retail turnover.

*   Groups are concerned about the extent to which local traders will be consulted in the drawing up of local plans for shopping.

VIII. *Transportation*

Strategic policy objections

*   The BUAP Transportation Strategy is considered to be out of date, inappropriate and out of balance with the transportation needs of the population of the Belfast Urban Area.
*   In the form of a private transport-orientated strategy (favoring the car user), it attempts to tackle congestion by building more roads or widening existing ones. A more appropriate solution would be to improve public transport and encourage car drivers not to use their vehicles for work journeys through more expensive car parking and pedestrianisation.
*   The Transportation Strategy virtually neglects the needs of those dependent on a public transport system (particularly bus transport), which is currently inadequate by nature of its inappropriate route network, insufficient frequency and lack of integration between bus and rail services. This lack of interest in public transport reflects the Transportation consultants' report and ultimately their brief, which was drawn up without consultation with the people of Belfast. Their consequent research, which was trip-based, rather than needs-based, thereby automatically excluded those who do not or cannot use public transport.
*   Public transport should not be profit-oriented (i.e. minimal subsidy) as in the Plan, but should be a consumer-oriented social service that is flexible, efficient, safe (particularly at night), and both physically and financially accessible to all members of the population, particularly the disabled, the disadvantaged, the elderly, parents with young children, and women travelling alone - all of whose needs are not satisfied at present.
*   The Transportation Strategy fails to show any interest in alternative forms of transport to those already in existence, such as mini-buses, flexi-buses, shared taxis, dial-a-ride for disabled people, light rail transit, Park and Ride, cycle lanes, cycle parking, transfer ticketing, bus lanes, and a failure to recognize the role of Black Taxis in North and West Belfast's transport system.
*   The Transportation Strategy is incoherent in that it fails to

158

recognize the need for integration between all existing and proposed transport systems, and the need also for a publicly accountable Transport Review Authority to ensure the transport needs of the whole population are met.

* The BUAP fails to consider the environmental and health implications of an improved road system, such as the loss of natural habitats, the loss of amenity (as on the Old Comber railway line), noise, lead and carbon monoxide pollution, road injuries and deaths. Neither does it encourage environmentally sensitive forms of transport such as walking and cycling.

* The BUAP lacks a Transportation Technical Supplement.

* The Plan fails to discuss how land now used for car parks to be released following the construction of multi-storey car parks will be used or zoned.

Area specific objections

Outer North * Residents in the Jordanstown area oppose the BUAP N10 proposal for a new traffic route, Lynda Road, to link the Jordanstown Road and the Circular Road including a flyover, over the railway line. This new route will destroy a wooded area, attract traffic wishing to avoid the local level crossing and will facilitate new housing developments on the outskirts of Jordanstown which are also opposed by local residents.

North * Groups and individuals in North Belfast object to the Carlisle Circus/Regent Street project (W6) which involves major traffic management alteration, as it benefits only the car user while disrupting nearby communities. They believe the scheme will encourage more traffic and more traffic-related problems, such as pollution and health risks. It also uses land that might better be used if appropriate to rehouse the people of Unity Flats.

* Residents also object to the Cross Harbour Road Link which, in their opinion, would stimulate commercial and domestic traffic in North Belfast, disrupting communities, lowering the quality of life for the people of Sailortown and destroying housing land that could be used to rehouse people from the New Lodge area.

* Groups and individuals also object to the Plan's failure to improve the Citybus and Ulsterbus route network in North Belfast.

West * The widening of the Falls Road from Albert Street to the Grosvenor Road (proposal W13) is

159

strongly opposed as it will mean the demolition of existing buildings and taking a 15-foot slice off Dunville Park.

South   *   Unanimous opposition exists in South Belfast to the Southern Approaches Road Strategy, and in particular:

     (a)   to the deferred Annadale-Grahamholm Link (S18) through Belvoir Forest which will be opposed now and at any time in the future;

     (b)   to the widening of the Annadale Embankment (B11) which will increase noise and fume pollution and destroy a public walk amenity; and

     (c)   to the widening of the lower Ormeau Road, as residents believe it will result in the isolation of one part of a community from another, increase noise and fume pollution from increased traffic, increase the risk of accidents, particularly for the young and elderly, and may result in the loss of homes, amenities and jobs.

East   *   The Eastern Approaches Road Strategy is vigorously opposed as it offers no improvement to the limitations of the existing public transport system but time savings for the motorist. Community groups and individuals object to the following aspects of this strategy:

     (a)   the widening of the Albertsbridge Road, which will have adverse environmental effects on adjacent communities and will potentially disrupt local traders;

     (b)   the proposed Connsbank Link; and

     (c)   the proposed road classified as Comber Road (1) running along the Old Comber Railway, as it is believed this will cause major environmental problems in East Belfast, such as increased traffic, noise and fume pollution, and the loss of the Beersbridge Nature Walk, one of the few such amenities available in this part of the city. This new route will also potentially isolate communities from facilities along the Newtownards Road and the Holywood Arches area.

   *   There are further objections to the Castlereagh Road/Ballygowan Road flyover as it would prove visually intrusive, attract more traffic, encourage more speeding and increase noise and fume pollution.

IX.   Women's Issues

Strategic policy objections

*   The needs of the family and of women and children in particular have been ignored in the Plan.
*   The transportation needs of women have been ignored.
*   Women are vulnerable to sexual and physical attack; however, their safety has not been considered in the Plan.

Area specific objections

Area specific objections were not made in the submissions or in the meetings with the six geographical areas.

Other CTA objections

*   There should be greater provision of public housing for women. Women, because of their generally lower income levels, have less access to the private house market.
*   Women, whether by choice or not, are generally more home-centered than men. The design of their houses and neighbourhoods should, therefore, ensure that their environment is a pleasant and safe place in which to live and work.
*   Creches, toilets and feeding facilities for nursing mothers should automatically be provided in retail outlets. The extent of provision should perhaps be in proportion to square footage of retail floor space.
*   It is not enough merely to provide open space and label it as recreation; the concept of recreation must be developed with regard to the needs of women and their children.
*   Bus stops should be well lit and shelters provided, so women will feel safe using public transport, particularly at night.
*   Community-based employment and training programmes should be established near housing estates and in suburbs where there are few employment opportunities.
*   Design of housing estates must take account of the personal security of women. Street lighting must always be sufficient. Planners should ensure, through the development control system, that developers take security matters into consideration.
*   Clinics and health centres should be located in housing estates within easy access of the residents.

X.   Education

Strategic Policy Objections

*   Under the Education section, the Plan does not mention the needs of particular groups, for example, those requiring Irish language schools or integrated schools, or the needs of adult education. Because of this land is not identified for such uses.
*   Land zoned for education purposes should be shown on the Development Strategy map.

Area specific objections

North   *   Lack of adult education provision in North Belfast - the Plan makes no attempt to provide for this shortfall.
West   *   There is an obvious demand for education in Irish language schools in the West of the city which is not being met.
            *   There is a need for an adult and community college in West Belfast.
East   *   Need for a permanent local library, possibly incorporating a Citizens Advice Bureau at Ballyhackamore.
            *   This area also suffers from a lack of adult education facilities and nursery school education.

Appendix 4

Belfast Urban Area Plan: Paper for Fourth Meeting of the Advisory Group to Review conclusions of CTA Team on Housing, 10 February 1988

Introduction

The purpose of the fourth meeting of the BUAP Advisory Group is to review the CTA Team's conclusions on the topic of Housing arising from the Conference of 25 November 1987 and subsequent meetings and consultations together with a perusal of the Draft Plan and technical reports.

The following is the agenda of matters for discussion:

    I.   General Matters
    II.   Housing Demand
    III. Housing Supply
    IV.   NIHE Programme
    V.   Inner City
    VI.   Infill Sites
    VII. Locational Impacts
    VIII. Access
    IX.   Specific Areas

In common with previous meetings, the structure that will be followed will consist of a general overview followed by specific topics leading through to particular locations as appropriate.

I. General Matters

Housing is one of the most important of all urban land uses because of the following factors, amongst others:

* together with food and clothing, shelter forms one of the three basic human physical needs;
* it will affect the total need for urban land more than any other land use;
* it is vulnerable to injury by other land uses such as industry or major roads;
* the balance between infill and greenfield development will affect the overall looseness or tightness of the urban fabric;
* it will create a demand for many associated land uses such as schools, shops, recreation;
* it will create a demand for infrastructure such as water, sewerage systems, transportation;
* it will create a demand for services such as health, welfare, education
* it is where most people spend most of their lifetimes;
* it is a land use to the ownership of which more people aspire than to that of any other land use.

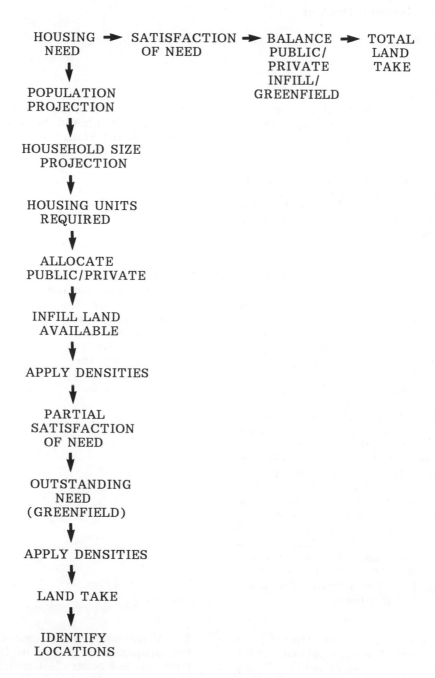

HOUSING NEED → SATISFACTION OF NEED → BALANCE PUBLIC/ PRIVATE INFILL/ GREENFIELD → TOTAL LAND TAKE

HOUSING NEED

↓

POPULATION PROJECTION

↓

HOUSEHOLD SIZE PROJECTION

↓

HOUSING UNITS REQUIRED

↓

ALLOCATE PUBLIC/PRIVATE

↓

INFILL LAND AVAILABLE

↓

APPLY DENSITIES

↓

PARTIAL SATISFACTION OF NEED

↓

OUTSTANDING NEED (GREENFIELD)

↓

APPLY DENSITIES

↓

LAND TAKE

↓

IDENTIFY LOCATIONS

II. Housing Demand

Problem   *Proposal*

Demographic Trends:
The Plan claims that there is a trend within society toward the formation of small households of one or two persons. There is no explanation in the Plan as to how they calculated the decrease in household size from 2.8 in 1986 to 2.53 in 2001.

The calculations used to reach such figures should be made explicit in the Plan.

The NIHE District Housing Plan 1987-88 states there were signs that the nature of demand as expressed on the waiting list was changing character, with higher proportions of the applicants being single persons and a concomitant fall in the percentage of large families and large adult households. Research into the characteristics of these newly-forming households indicates that for a large number, the public sector is the only real housing option available. The Plan has not identified this demand for public sector provision for these new households. Rather, it plans to use the private sector to satisfy the demand for small dwelling units.

The Plan must look at the needs of those on the waiting list to see how the different groups on it can best be accommodated. It should be more sensitive to demand illustrated by the waiting list and not solely demand illustrated by market trends.

The Plan states there is a demand for more private sector housing development. They justify this by saying that

The Plan must justify logically the proposals it makes in the Plan and not contradict trends identified by the NIHE.

166

owner occupation levels have increased. The NIHE, however, state that home ownership levels have reached their peak.

A population projection has not been made.

A population projection should be made to justify the demand for housing land.

Unfitness and Disrepair:
The Plan gives scant attention to problems of housing unfitness and disrepair despite housing renewal being a top priority for the NIHE housing programme.

The Plan should whole-heartedly accommodate the priorities identified by the NIHE.

Local Need:
Neither the housing objectives, housing strategy or housing policies specify the particular housing needs of each geographical area. The technical supplement refers to the waiting list by area, housing tenure by area, etc. but no specific proposals are made in the light of these differences. The Plan also ignores the social problems of certain areas. While houses may not be considered unfit by the NIHE definition, there may be other problems, for example, a high degree of unemployment/vandalism, that are being overlooked.

Data on the specific needs of individual areas need to be collated. Then, proposals specific to that area can be justifiably made.

The NIHE district housing plan, for example, has looked at the level of overcrowding in certain areas, the type of household that predominates in certain areas in order to establish the different needs of each area. The Plan,

The Plan should have considered more closely the role of housing associations.

however, has ignored these and other variables that will affect the housing needs of different areas.

Special Interest Groups:
The Plan does not make any reference to the housing needs of Travellers of homeless people or disadvantaged groups.

The Plan must assess the needs of all disadvantaged groups and then make provisions for them in the Plan.

III. Housing Supply

Problem

Proposal

Proposed Level of Private and Public Housing:
The BUAP has identified sites for:
24,500 dwelling units:
 8,500 are public sector
10,000 are sites within the urban area (Matthew Stopline). These will be predominantly for private development.
6,000 are peripheral sites that fall outside the Matthew Stopline. These will also be predominantly if not exclusively for private development.
The Plan is therefore largely satisfying the demand for housing through private development.

More land should be set aside for public sector housing.

Public sector housing is not identified on the map. However, by area:
East Belfast will receive 26% of public sector housing
South Belfast - 12%
West Belfast - 13%

The Plan should first of all clarify local housing need and then propose public sector housing according to that need.

North Belfast - 49%.
It is not clear whether this level of public sector provision will satisfy local demand because no attempt was made to establish the particular housing needs at a local level. The Plan does not provide waiting list figures for these geographical areas so provision cannot be related to these local areas.

The vast majority of proposed housing is for the private sector. The Plan states, "The growing trend in home ownership places increasing importance on the role of the private sector in the housing market" (BUAP, p. 25)
There are several criticisms of this conclusion:
- The NIHE district housing plan 1987-88 states that the NIHE house sales have fallen despite incentives to retain the demand.
- The co-ownership scheme was the single biggest factor leading to a much higher level of private sector housebuilding. However, there are signs that both the co-ownership scheme and private sector building may have passed their peak.
-According to the Housing Strategy Review 1988/89, 1990/91, private sector developers are moving to up-market developments because the bottom end of the market is over supplied.
The Plan's argument is therefore not justified in light of trends identified by the NIHE.

The Plan should base housing proposals primarily on social need and not solely on market trends.

The Plan does not seek a public sector alternative. None of the objectives in this section look at social need. There is an automatic assumption in favour of private development. The Plan states that private housebuilding rates have increased since 1983. If building continues at current rates, land will become exhausted in five years in certain parts of the city "There is therefore a need to provide an increased supply of sites in a variety of locations to meet market demand" (BUAP, p. 25).
Several criticisms arise:
- The Plan assumes that private housebuilding rates will remain at current rate. The NIHE have, however, identified trends to suggest they will not.
- There is an automatic assumption that private housebuilding should continue. No public sector alternative is proposed.

Proposals not included in the Plan:
The Plan does not make clear what housing is being shown on the Development Strategy Map or in the BUAP 2001 preliminary proposals on housing.
The former document shows no public sector housing; it shows some housing sites within the urban area, some sites that have been rezoned for housing and all the peripheral housing sites. It

The Plan should develop a public sector housing alternative and not automatically make a presumption in favour of private development.

The Plan should explain very clearly what is the content and purpose of each document on housing. There should be one source to which people can refer in order to obtain a comprehensive list of how much and what type of housing is proposed in their areas.

170

is, however, not made clear the exact function of the map. The latter document is incomplete and omits housing sites that have been proposed in certain area plans (e.g. the Lisburn Area Plan). Again, the function of this book is not made explicit. An introduction is not included in the book so it is not clear to the reader that it is incomplete.

Density and Population Projection:
A population projection was not made in the Plan. Rather, a capacity calculation was made that limits the population to 520,000 within the inner edge of the greenbelt. By limiting land supply so much, this may well force land prices up and reduce choice. However, this is very hard to judge whenever the population by the year 2001 is not even known. The Plan's zoning policy is therefore very unclear.

A population projection must be made in order to make sense of and justify the land zoned for housing up to the year 2001.

NIHE Housing Programme

Problem

Proposal

Housing Programme in the Plan:
The housing section in the Plan makes little reference to the NIHE Housing Programme. Certain aims in the Plan would seem to contradict the programme.

The Plan should coordinate much more closely with the NIHE Housing Programme.

171

Needs of the Elderly:
The needs of the elderly in the Plan have largely been ignored. The NIHE District Housing Plan very clearly states the quantity of sheltered dwellings that need to be provided in the BUA. From 200 to 500 units must be provided in each of the 7 districts of the BUA (a total of 1,991). The Plan, however, makes no reference to the percentage of old people in different areas. Certain areas, for example, East Belfast and the inner city, contain a higher than BUA average population of elderly people. No provision is made for this.

The Plan must take into consideration the needs of the elderly. It should identify where this population is and make proposals accordingly.

Needs of Single People:
The NIHE District Housing Plan 1987-88 states that there are signs that the nature of demand as expressed by the waiting list was changing character with higher proportions of the applicants being single persons and a consequent fall in the percentage of large families and large adult households. Their research into the characteristics of these newly-forming households indicates that for large numbers of these households the public sector is the only real housing option available.
However, the technical supplement states that there is a clear opportunity for the private sector to deal with smaller households by providing small housing units either for rent or sale.

The Plan must take into account the social needs of single people identified by the NIHE District Housing Plan. More public sector housing land should be identified for this group as private housing is clearly not going to satisfy the need.

172

Clearly an emphasis on private housebuilding will not meet the needs of single people.

The Plan maintains that the "success of recent private housing schemes in the city centre indicates that there is a demand for small dwelling units and apartments in suitable locations" (BUAP, p.25). This does not provide sufficient evidence to propose private housebuilding as a solution to the housing needs of single people. No attempt was made to identify what socioeconomic group bought these houses. What are their terms of success?

The Plan should justify its successes with hard statistics.

Budgetary Implications for Housing Programme:
The Draft Plan is supposed to be a strategic plan. However, strategic planning for housing requires greater stability and predictability in housing expenditure. Due to cuts in the NIHE budget, the Executive has had to omit some of its programmes. The relationship between the NIHE and the DoE is unclear and it is difficult to see how the Plan can make strategic housing proposals into the year 2001 while the NIHE must assess its financial situation yearly and make modifications in the light of this.

There should be a longer cycle allowed for the NIHE budget.

173

V. Inner City

Problem

About 5,000 young professionals, young single people and young married could be accommodated in *new* dwellings in the city centre. This does not include building conversions to flats and apartments or the potential 2,000 to 2,500 units envisaged for the Laganside. This housing will almost certainly be private and geared toward higher income earners.

Two major strands exist in terms of inner city housing as far as planning is concerned. First is the redevelopment of working class family areas such as Divis, Unity and Laganside communities. Second is the drive to provide housing for the young single households in the inner city. Local working-class communities have been given a very low priority in the planning of their areas. This is particularly evident in the Northside and Laganside proposals, where the mix of public and private housing and thus the eventual social mix of the area is weighted heavily in favour of the more affluent and independent. This will help undermine the cohesion and vitality of existing communities.

While it appears that there will be sufficient land available locally to house the remaining

Proposal

The Plan should establish exactly how many of these young professionals, etc. there are in the BUA. They should also consider whether or not this group in society should be allowed to have such a great amount of the scarce land resources available.

The Plan should pay greater attention to the needs of the indigenous populations when allocating land and when conflict arises the needs of the indigenous community should be given priority.

Land should be identified to allow the development of the local community without

174

population of the Divis Complex after the remaining blocks have been removed, there is a danger that provision of local residential amenities will be minimal. The provision of social and recreational amenities will be played off against the strength of the desire of the local community to stay together. This is an unsatisfactory situation that leads to the perpetuation of substandard provision in the area.

To rehouse the growing population of the Unity Flats area in low-rise accommodation at acceptable standards cannot be achieved with the current space limits. To attempt such an exercise would produce an overspill of about 40% of the present population. Local amenity provision would again be threatened and standards kept at their existing low level.

Attention needs to be given to the particular housing problems in the University area of South Belfast. This area is very important to often vulnerable minority groups such as students, nurses and short-stay tenants. Market mechanisms can operate in such a way that these groups are open to exploitation and hardship.

sacrificing standards of amenity and open space provision.

Additional land must be identified to accommodate the overspill population from this area. Every effort should be made to ensure that the overspill population is not lost and absorbed into other areas scattered throughout the city if that is their desire.

The Plan must face up to this problem and seek a means of remedying the situation by encouraging appropriate housing association and NIHE involvement.

VI. Infill Sites

Problem

The Plan only considers infill housing sites of potential for 10 units or more within the Stopline. This land is termed "Housing Land within the existing urban area". The Plan identifies 8,750 currently approved or potential sites for 'private housebuilding':
32% in Greater North Belfast
27% in Greater East and South Belfast
25% in Lisburn
16% in Greater West Belfast.
The Plan also identifies 8,350 sites for public housing in the existing urban area, i.e. infill, that would result in a net increase in public housing in the BUA of 5,500:
  824 in East Belfast
  489 in South Belfast
  442 in West Belfast
1,880 in North Belfast
  60 in Holywood BUA
  313 in Castlereagh BUA
1,385 in Lisburn BUA
(Table H/27 Housing Supplement).

Proposal

Infill sites of less than 10 units capacity should be included in the equation designed to assess the need for rezoning for housing in the BUA. Failure to do so means that the estimates of need for rezoning for housing in peripheral locations is founded on a false view of the current situation. The cut-off point of 10 is arbitrary and misleading. The Preliminary Proposals Housing supplement contains 10 sites that could accommodate 10 units but absolutely no sites that could accommodate 9,8 or 6 units. This is unsatisfactory and should be rectified. Much unidentified space capacity already exists within the urban area. Figures obtained by the N.Belfast Steering Committee show that in that area there are 1,119 long-term vacant residential properties, (4,690) for the city as a whole and 754 long-term vacant non-residential properties (3,778) for the city as a whole.
The Plan's failure to confront this issue would seem to undermine its dual policies of limiting the sprawl of suburban Belfast and tackling the problems of inner city decline.

Policy H6 relating to infill housing in suburban residential areas should also be applied to inner city residential areas.

This policy and the criteria on which applications are judged should also be applied to inner city infill sites and such issues as affect neighbourhood layout, landscape, etc.

176

VII. Locational Impacts

General

Housing development on greenfield sites may have an impact on adjoining areas, with possible conflicts resulting.

Problem

Proposal

Conflict may arise with adjoining farming uses through tresspass, vandalism, destruction of fences, crop or stock damage around Old Holywood Rd., Dundonald, Cairnshill, Lagmore or Hightown.

All applications for housing development on greenfield sites for which a definite need has been proven, must take note through strict development control of any possible conflict.

Conflict with neighbouring industrial land through traffic conflict such as goods vs. private vehicles, tresspass, security, amenity, noise and air pollution, for example at Hightown.

Conflict with neighbouring residential areas through increased traffic, loss of amenity, visual intrusion at Dundonald, Cairnshill, Lagmore, Hightown, Jordanstown/Monkstown.

General

Housing development on greenfield sites will have serious environmental and amenity consequences.

The greenfields and hills surrounding Belfast provide an 'individuality and magnificent setting' that 'needs to be protected from pressures of urban development' (BUAP 2001, p. 45). They provide a natural

Greenfield sites that threaten the natural setting of Belfast should be removed from the Plan, for example, Hightown, Ligoniel, Hannahstown Rd., Cairnshill/Beechhill, Dundonald, Old Holywood Rd. and a strict greenbelt break between town and country and hold a prominent position in the landscape. They should not be encroached on by greenfield housing developments.

According to the UTNC, several waterways are under threat in the Ballyoran, Dunlady, Millmount, Glen Rd./ Hannahstown Hill, Ligionel and Monkstown sites.

While the Antrim Hills are of such agricultural quality as to be limited to grazing, the Co. Down hills have good quality land intensively farmed.

The hills and valleys surrounding the BUA display a wide variety of natural habitats that are now under threat.

enforced.

If a need for those developments is proven, a buffer zone should be inserted between the proposed development and the waterway.

Good quality agricultural land should not be developed for suburban housing as in the Old Holywood Rd., Dundonald and Cairnshill/Beechill areas and other uses (recreational, cultural) be put forward. Habitats of particular interest (as mentioned above) should be protected from housing development.

VIII. Access

General

The development of housing on greenfield sites may create problems of access, particularly to and from the city centre. This often results in roads being proposed through existing housing or scenic areas to facilitate the new population.

Problem

In the BUAP there would appear to be a clear link between greenfield housing sites (existing, rezoned or proposed) and new roads or improvements to existing roads to facilitate movement between these areas and the rest of the BUA, for example:

i. N3 Shore Rd.improvements: Greenisland site

ii. N10 Lynda Rd. proposal: Jordanstown site; Monkstown site

iii. N5,N11,N13 Carnmoney Hill road proposals: Glebe Rd./ Ballyduff Rd. Doagh Rd.sites

iv. N6 road improvement: Ballyhenry site

v. N21 Hightown Rd. improvement: Hightown site and extension

vi. W19 Wolfhill route proposal: Ligoniel site

vii. S18, B11, S16 Southern Approaches Strategy: Beechill site; Cairnshill/Knockbracken site

viii.A16 Ballygowan Rd./ Castlereagh Rd. flyover: Rosemount site

ix. E12, E13, E14(1)(2) Eastern Approaches Strategy: Comber Rd./New Line site; Millmount site; Ballyoran site; Dunlady site; Ballyregan site.

Proposal

Greenfield sites should only be developed when all sites in the BUA are utilized and demand for housing land still exists to prevent destruction of the environment on site and on route.

Limit greenfield sites/densities to the level that existing roads can support without requiring major improvements or new routes.

General

The Plan identifies land release on greenfield sites to meet housing demand 1986-1993. A reappraisal in 1993 will determine whether land between the Limit to Development Line and the Inner Edge of the Greenbelt will be released (see map).

Problem

Proposal

Certain areas where greenfield housing exists and to which access has been improved and land is available, will be under threat:
Greenisland
Jordanstown/Monkstown
Hightown
Ligoniel
West Belfast
Poleglass
Beechill
Cairnshill
Dundonald.

Greenfield sites should only be developed when all feasible sites within the BUA are utilized and a demand for housing land still exists.

The Inner Edge of the Greenbeld should be drawn in to at least meet the Limit to Development Line 1993 in all areas, but preferably the existing limit of the BUA except in the Lagmore area of West Belfast.

IX. Specific Areas

General

No greenfield sites on the fringe of the urban area should be zoned for housing development until a definite need has been established and other sites within the BUA exhausted.

Area	Proposal
Greenisland: The definite break between Newtownabbey and Carrick is under threat from the zoning of land for housing, a threat that could be even more significant following the 1993 reappraisal when land between the Limit to Development and the Inner Edge of the Greenbelt could be zoned for housing.	A definite greenbelt should be established to prevent coalescence, possibly along the line of the Silverstream River. If there is a definite need to develop this site and land west of this at Jordanstown/ Monkstown, a circular route could be developed through the Greenisland site, serving it and the proposed recreation scheme, then running northwest to meet and follow the disused railway line, then running south along the Monkstown Rd. through the industrial estate and along the GlenvillE Rd. to meet the Shore Rd. This would serve all sites mentioned and preserve the amenity of Jordanstown village and the proposed greenbelt.
Jordanstown/Monkstown: Extensive greenfield housing development beyond the former Matthew Stopline (amounting to 740 dwellings) and at a higher density than that nearby, threatens the character and amenity of Jordanstown Village and presents access problems resulting in the need to build a new road, Lynda Rd., to service additional traffic.	If a need is proven for the development of these sites, densities should be similar to those already in existence nearby. The proposed circular route outlined above could resolve access problems and protect the amenity of Jordanstown village.

Carnmoney Hill:
Rezoning has resulted in land of high scenic amenity becoming available for up to 400 (probably private) dwellings on the North and West faces of Carnmoney Hill in juxtaposition with land reserved for landscape, recreation and amenity potential. Such development would be visually instrusive over a city-wide area and extends beyond a Stopline recommended in the unimplemented Carnmoney Local Plan 1977 which ran along the Ballyduff Rd., West of Doagh Rd., the Old Irish Highway, Glebe Rd. and Carnmoney relief road.
This zoning also contradicts the BUAP's aim of conserving the natural beauty of the hills surrounding the city. Also the route of the N11 road proposal isolates a triangle of land that in the future would probably go to housing development.

This area should be dezoned to protect the scenic amenity of the Hill in the natural setting of Belfast.

Hightown:
A proposal, again outside the former Matthew Stopline, to zone land for 430 dwellings (8/acre) on the lower slope of the Antrim Hills. Development would be visually intrusive and result in the loss of scenic amenity in an area previously undisrupted. Also, potentially serious problems exist of building at this height (150-180m) with regard to water provision.
This contradicts the landscape policy of the BUAP which aims to protect the natural setting of the BUA.

This site should not be developed as it would be visually intrusive and would present problems of water provision.

Ligoniel:
A proposal to zone land for 145 dwellings (8/acre) at 140-180m on the lower slope of the Antrim Hills. This will prove visually intrusive over a wide area and may conflict with land reserved for landscape amenity and recreation.

The site, outside the former Stopline, would be more accessible following the construction of a new road between Wolfhill and the Crumlin Rd. However, this will disturb the area of Wolfhill, described in "Natural Belfast" (RSPB, UNC, CV) as an "area of particular interest" with regard to natural habitats (i.e. wooded glen with hazel, ash trees, beech and gorse).

West Belfast:
Further lands zoned for housing at Lyndhurst, Whiterock, Glen Rd./ Hannahstown or the lower edge of the Antrim Hills would also prove visually intrusive city-wide and should not be developed until a definite need has been established.

While greenfield sites in other areas of W. Belfast have been opposed, land zoned in the Lagmore area should be developed to cater for local housing needs. However, this should take the form of public rather than private housing and should form the limit to housing development in this area.

This site should not be developed as it would prove visually intrusive, present problems of water provision and disrupt important natural habitats.

Brooke Park Area:
White land formerly recreation (football pitch) and open space (woodland and stream) proposed and in some cases already being used for housing and not shown on the plans or development strategy map.

Land should be used for amenity/recreation purposes or at least should have been identified on the development strategy map so that people have the chance to realize what is happening in the area.

Arema Estate:
Not shown in the Plan.
This NIHE programme of 30 units was not designated on the strategy map or identified in the technical supplement because the land was already in residential use. It was part of the NIHE programme covered by Policy H2 of the BUAP. The DoE said the site is primarily of local rather than strategic importance.

The NIHE should have identified this area and others like it that appear to be slipping through without the public's attention being brought to them. As the Plan identifies sites with a capacity for 10 units, it should identify those being used to accommodate 30 sites such as this one.

North Parade:
Concern at the lack of control over change of residential use of building to other uses - in particular, several houses have become psychiatric patient homes. These 'homes' should not be concentrated in one area.

Development Control Policies must be strictly enforced and monitored.

Cairnshill/Beechill:
Both sites (for 1,000 and 750 dwellings respectively) represent major extensions of the BUA southward. Outside the former Stopline, they are also highly related to the proposed Southern Approach Road Strategy. Their zoning, coupled with proposed road improvements, would encourage further expansion southward following 1993.

A definite need to develop these sites must be proven.

184

Laganside:
Concern that the housing needs of the local population living in the area will not be adequately catered for.

Local housing needs must be taken into account and have priority over all others.

East Belfast:
Residents of East Belfast (as in North) believe better use should be made of existing and potential sites within the urban area rather than looking to suburban greenfield sites. Too many vacant sites in the area have already been developed for profit only at the expense of the local community.

Zoning of land in suburban greenfield locations should be removed and sites within the urban area identified and developed to cater for local housing requirements, public and private sector.

Dundonald:
A series of proposed zonings and rezoning of greenfield land around Dundonald at Comber Rd./New Line, Millmount, Ballyoran, Dunlady and Ballyregan presents a serious threat to the amenity of Dundonald and the Dundonald Village. These sites are on rising meadowland, often with mature trees and natural habitats for wildlife. Some are highlighted as areas of particular interest in the "Natural Belfast" Report (e.g. glens in the Dunlady and Ballyregan sites).

For amenity, environmental and agricultural reasons land on the outskirts of Dundonald should not be zoned for housing.

These zonings disrupt the natural setting of Dundonald and coupled with road improvements would encourage further expansion eastward following 1993.

This land is also of high agricultural quality.

185

Old Holywood Rd:
A proposal remains in the Plan to zone this greenfield site on the lower slopes of the Holywood Hills for 65 dwellings at 45/acre.

This site, however, is in itself visually prominent city-wide and forms a natural break between the city and hills and a countryside break between Belfast and Holywood.

Development would promote ribbon development giving the impression that Holywood is part of Belfast, and would be difficult to access, screen and landscape. The site is also a natural part of Glenmachan which the DoE felt should be dropped from the Plan.

This is a quality agricultural and wildlife area and as elsewhere the proposed zoning contradicts Plan policy to control urban development into the surrounding countryside and the protection of scenic assets that fringe the city.

Glenmachan, Gothic Wood, Hydebank:
The dropping of these proposals is to be commended but further confirmation that these areas would not be under threat in the future is required.

The site should be dezoned and preserved as a regional amenity or natural parkland extending the County Park at Redburn through to Stormont.

Appendix 5

The DoE's pre inquiry response to CTA's objections to the draft BUAP (reproduced with the permission of the Department)

BELFAST URBAN AREA PLAN 2001
PUBLIC INQUIRY
STATEMENT OF EVIDENCE: OBJECTION NUMBER: 0452
OBJECTOR: COMMUNITY TECHNICAL AID

1.0   NATURE OF THE OBJECTION

1.1   The main points of the objection may be summarised as follows:-

Conservation

1.2   (i)   Recycling of waste should be introduced.
      (ii)   The Belfast Lough and the Harbour Area should be designated as a nature reserve.
      (iii)   There should be improved access to forests and woodlands which are important in terms of conservation.
      (iv)   Concern is felt over traffic pollution.
      (v)   Cave Hill should not be commercialised.
      (vi)   The Green Belt should be broken only in exceptional circumstances.
      (vii)   Every effort should be made to keep buildings of character intact.

Public Health

1.3   (i)   The Plan deals inadequately with the matter of Public Health.
     (ii)   The reduction of numbers in institutional care is not dealt with adequately.
     (iii)   Concern over traffic pollution.
     (iv)   The detrimental effect of poor housing must be taken into account.

Housing

1.4   (i)   Local people should have a greater say in housing types, etc.
     (ii)   Private housing has been favoured at the expense of public housing.
     (iii)   Local amenities should be provided in residential areas.
     (iv)   In some areas over-concentration of land has left a shortage of land for other uses.
     (v)   The Plan ignores the housing needs of minority groups.
     (vi)   The local communities needs should be taken into account in the Laganside development.
     (vii)   There is a need for greater assessment of land needs. In many parts of the urban area there are opportunities for infill development.

Industry and Commerce

1.5   (i)   The Plan policies are based on attraction of multi-national investment.
     (ii)   The policy statement on industry does not properly take into account local need, failing to address the problem of severe local unemployment.
     (iii)   Industry should be located nearer the Inner City where it is more accessible.
     (iv)   Too much emphasis has been placed on private sector investment.

Laganside

1.6   (i)   The total zoning of residential land along the Lagan for private sector development.
     (ii)   The Plan ignores the community requirements of the indigenous population.

Recreation

1.7   (i)   The Plan does not provide sufficient or appropriate recreation facilities for the needs of the population of the Belfast Urban Area.

     (ii)   The Plan does not provide a recreation policy which would meet the needs of local areas.

Retailing

1.8   (i)   The total inadequacy of the retailing strategy - focusing on retailing in the City Centre and ignoring local shopping.

Transportation

1.9   (i)   Orientation towards private transport is out-of-balance, inappropriate and out-of-date.

     (ii)   Roads orientated consultants brief means the Plan takes the form of a road building strategy rather than a transportation strategy.

     (iii)   Existing public transport systems are inadequate, have an inappropriate route network, insufficient frequency and suffer from lack of integration between bus and rail.

     (iv)   The Plan fails to address the transport requirements of the disabled, elderly and needs of women and children.

     (v)   There is an overwhelming need for an increase in availability, accessibility (physical and financial) and efficiency of public transport. It should be recognised as a consumer orientated public service and not be profit based.

     (vi)   Alternative methods of transportation are not given sufficient, if any, considerations. Role of 'black taxis', smaller buses, dial a ride, park and ride, light rail transport, cycle lanes are ignored. A wider brief should have been issued.

     (vii)   Two comments which amount to advocacy of vehicle restraint.

     (viii)   There is a need for a Transport Review Authority to ensure the transport needs of the whole population of the BUA are met.

Women's Issues

1.10 (i)   Housing and recreation provision should take greater account of the needs of women.

189

	(ii)	Facilities for nursing mothers should be provided in retail outlets.

Education

1.11	(i)	No mention is made of particular educational needs such as adult education, Irish language or integrated schools.

Local Plans

1.12	(i)	There is a need to prepare local plans and community plans so that a comprehensive, integrated and sensitive approach can be taken in the planning of local areas.

General

1.13	(i)	The consultation process has been inadequate and there was a lack of time for consultation.
	(ii)	The Plan neglects working class communities.
	(iii)	The Plan ought to address social issues not merely land use.
	(iv)	During the period made available for consideration of the Plan by the public, the Government announced that major components will definitely proceed - Castle Court, Laganside and the Cross Harbour Link.

2.0 OBSERVATIONS OF THE DEPARTMENT

Non-Planning Issues

2.1 The observations of the Department can only properly address the land use planning issues raised. It does not attempt to deal in detail with the non-planning issues which should be raised directly with the appropriate agencies with legislative responsibility for these matters. These non-planning issues include, for example, the actual provision and creation of jobs, the provision of shops, housing finance, health and education. However, in order to be helpful the Department has provided, <u>for information purposes</u>, additional material on some non-planning issues such as the promotion of community enterprises.

2.2 The observations of the Department are for convenience set out below topic by topic:

3.0   CONSERVATION

Waste Disposal

3.1   Re-cycling of waste is regularly cited as an alternative
       method of disposing of refuse. There is no doubt that the
       reclamation of salvaged materials does reduce the volume of
       waste for disposal and the re-use of certain materials instead
       of using virgin material is a prudent way to conserve scarce
       natural resources. However, it is important to bear in mind
       that re-cycling can only play a minor part in the disposal of
       solid waste.

3.2   The Government's Green Paper of September 1974 reflected
       the growing concern at the waste of potentially useable
       resources and heralded a new national drive to promote
       reclamation with improved understanding and information,
       expanded research, Government co-operation with industry
       to stabilise the market and the consideration of legislative
       measures. In response, the Department sought to stimulate
       interest by approaching councils individually and arranging
       seminars. In 1978 the Pollution Control and Local
       Government (Northern Ireland) Order empowered local
       authorities to take such steps as they considered appropriate
       for the reclamation of waste (Art 23) and to use waste to
       produce heat and electricity (Art 24).

3.3   In its 11th Report "Managing Wastes: the duty of care", the
       Royal Commission on Environmental Pollution set down a
       detailed exposition on recycling in which the Commission
       asserts that opportunities for recycling and resource
       recovery from waste materials are not exploited as vigorously
       as they might.

3.4   The Report, however, does also recognise a number of
       difficulties in re-cycling. The difficulties cited apply in
       Northern Ireland and indeed those of matching outlets to
       particular re-cycled streams of material are even greater
       here. For example, glass re-cycling through the use of
       bottle banks is severly restricted because the only user of
       such material is in Dublin and apart from transportation costs
       there have been problems with excise duty to be paid.

3.5   It is clear that re-cycling is a worthy venture - the Royal
       Commission concluded that such measures are valuable
       because they help to demonstrate to the public that every
       effort is being made by those in positions of responsibility to
       reduce the size of the waste stream, but it must not be
       forgotten that councils are charged with the task of collecting

and disposing of rubbish at the least cost without detriment to the environment.

3.6   However, the Department has indicated in Policy SER3 that it will assist in formulating long-term policy for refuse and waste disposal for the BUA. The long-term waste disposal strategy will therefore be a matter of further study when the full range of disposal options, including the latest technological possibilites, can be explored.

3.7   So far as the North Foreshore is concerned the Department has already forbidden the practice of tipping refuse into sea water in the interest of preventing pollution and protecting amenity. Policy SER2 also indicates that the area for refuse and waste disposal on the foreshore will be restricted.

Wildlife in the Harbour Area

3.8   The Department agrees that the Harbour Estate and foreshore of Belfast Lough are of special importance for nature conservation and wildlife attracting a variety of wading birds in numbers of national and international importance. Designation of the Area of Special Scientific Interest (ASSI) on the shore of Belfast Lough will help to protect these important bird habitats. The present situation is that the Department has designated the Inner Belfast Lough Area of Special Scientific Interest under the Nature Conservation and Amenity Lands (Northern Ireland) Order 1985.

3.9   Declaration as an ASSI requires landowners and occupiers to consult the Department on proposals to undertake certain notifiable operations within the ASSI, unless planning permission for that operation has already been obtained. Declaration of an ASSI also enables the Department to enter into a management agreement with the landowners and occupiers relating to the conservation of the scientific interest of the site. In the case of the Inner Belfast Lough ASSI, the Department is negotiating with the Belfast Harbour Commissioners over the welfare of the over-wintering wildfowl and waders, and in the improvement of breeding habitats for those species which will have been displaced by the infilling of the Lagoon at the north-eastern end of the runway on the Belfast Harbour Airport.

Establishment of a Nature Reserve inside the ASSI

3.10   Designation as an ASSI under the Nature Conservation and Amenity Lands (Northern Ireland) Order 1985 provides for full protection of the scientific interest within the ASSI; the requirement for a landowner or occupier to consult on proposals to undertake a list of notifiable operations provides the Department with the opportunity to control land use in the ASSI. Nature Reserves may be established because of the scientific interest of the site and/or because the site provides special opportunities for study or research. Where the Department does not own the land in a nature reserve, arrangements for access and practical management have to be agreed with the landowners and occupiers. In the case of the Kinnegar Lagoons inside the Inner Belfast Lough ASSI, the landowners feel that the desire to facilitate public access is outweighed by the requirement to maintain security in that general area; the Department concurs with their view.

3.11 Elsewhere in the Belfast Urban Area Plan it is stated that the Department is considering developing facilities for public enjoyment of the wildlife on the North Foreshore.

Other Natural Habitats

3.12 CTAs comments on the importance of significant natural habitats are noted.

3.13 The Department has noted your comment in relation to small green areas and pockets of woodland. This is a sub-strategic matter which would be dealt with outside the scope of the Belfast Urban Area Plan. However, the Department is currently examining the scope for urban forestry projects within the Belfast Urban Area which could include "greening up" small pieces of land in a natural way in the interest of local ecology and amenity. Small areas suitable for such treatment could be pursued in this separate study and the Department would welcome suggestions of sites which might be suitable for more detailed investigation.

Cave Hill

3.14 The proposal outlined in Policy R6 is to develop the Cave Hill as a major recreational and amenity attraction with the clear emphasis on the enjoyment of the natural features. Large scale building development would of course be totally inappropriate. Any building activity would be limited to the sort of unobtrusive facilities which are provided for the benefit of the public in, for example, country parks or forest parks. The proposed scheme will be expected to respect and enhance the natural beauty and historic interest of the Cave Hill. However, the form and nature of the development will be the subject of further study by the implementing agency, Belfast City Council, and the public will have the usual opportunity to comment at the planning application stage.

Green Belt

3.15   The Department agrees that in principle it is essential to ensure the maintenance of a distinctive Green Belt around the Belfast Urban Area. The boundaries of the Green Belt have been drawn as part of the long-term strategy for the Belfast Urban Area to contain and direct urban growth. Only in exceptional circumstances will the Department consider an alteration to the boundaries during the period of the Plan's lifespan. Any alteration will be subject to statutory amendment procedures enabling public consultation and comment.

Conservation of Buildings

3.16   The Department welcomes the support for the protection and enhancement of important buildings and areas. The policy of the Department is only to give consent to demolish Listed Buildings as a last resort. Consent to demolish or radically alter a listed building will only be considered by the Department where it can be demonstrated that a building is structurally unsound or that concerted efforts to find alternative uses for the building have failed and it is no longer capable of re-use in its present form. The Department accepts the need to consider access to buildings for the disabled and this can be dealt with when planning applications are being processed.

4.0   PUBLIC HEALTH

4.1   The statutory responsibility for health provision lies with the Health Authorities. The Department has consulted with the Health Authorities to ensure that land use implications are covered by the Belfast Urban Area Plan. It should be noted in regard to detailed health matters that the Health Boards produce five-year strategic plans and current annual operational plans which are subject to wide public consultation and these provide the opportunity to raise issues such as those mentioned. Strategic health plans envisage some concentration of development in the major hospitals, a reduction in the numbers of people in institutional care and a build up of services in the community.

Lead in Petrol

4.2   The Motor Fuel (Lead Content in Petrol) (Amendment)
       Regulations 1985, which apply throughout the UK, reduced
       the permitted level of lead in petrol by 60% from 0.4 grammes
       to 0.15 grammes per litre, from December 1985.   Petrol
       conforming with these regulations may be used in engines
       currently in production, without any modifications being
       necessary.   This action reduced the levels of lead in the
       atmosphere by 50% between December 1985 and October 1986.

4.3   In June 1986, additional measures were announced to
       encourage the introduction of lead-free petrol in advance of
       October 1989, the date specified in the European Community
       Directive 85/210/EEC (which was adopted at the instigation
       of the UK) for the requirement of widespread availability of
       unleaded petrol throughout the European Community. These
       measures included the creation of a tax differential to offset
       the higher production costs of unleaded petrol, an
       undertaking to implement the earliest dates possible, under
       the draft European Community Directive on vehicle emissions,
       if adopted, for requiring new cars to be capable of running
       on unleaded petrol, and the provision of a minimal network
       of stations selling unleaded petrol.

       Poor Housing

4.4   Substantial progress has been made in the renewal of the
       housing stock in Belfast over the last 10 years. The Housing
       Strategy of the Plan emphasises that further renewal of a
       poor housing stock is a development priority.   The NIHE
       House Condition Survey indicated almost 13,000 unfit
       dwellings in Belfast in 1984.   Of these NIHE has identified
       two-thirds for improvement and 4,800 for small-scale
       redevelopment.

5.0   HOUSING

       Laganside

5.1   Laganside is dealt with in Section 7.0.

       Housing Type

5.2   The Department agrees that it is desirable to encourage a mix
       of housing types throughout the Belfast Urban Area to widen
       choice and meet the wide range of housing needs.

Travelling People

5.3   The Department recognises that there is a need for suitable
        sites for the Travelling People. The finding of sites is not
        appropriate to a Plan of a strategic nature. However, after
        due consideration, the Department concluded that the lengthy
        Area Plan process was not the best way to produce speedy
        results on the ground and this is what is really required.
        Instead, the Department has adopted the quicker and more
        direct approach of liaison with Belfast City Council as the
        responsible public authority. This has been done through
        the Community Services and Town Planning Committees and
        their respective officials with a view to examining the extent
        of the Travellers needs, seeking suitable sites of the
        necessary size and moving straight to the planning
        application stage. In this way the process is foreshortened
        and more applicable to the special nature of the task.

        In specific terms this has involved all the relevant bodies
        either by direct action or through consultation (including
        representatives of the Travellers themselves) and the general
        public. The Department have produced a draft Development
        Scheme for Glen Road seeking to find a comprehensively
        planned solution to alleviate the hardship existing on the
        overcrowded and unplanned Travellers Site. The City Council
        have recommended that an integrated approach is required
        whereby all of the present families on Glen Road should be
        accommodated on properly planned sites elsewhere in the
        City. The Department has accepted this recommendation and
        sought in conjunction with City Council Officials to identify
        other sites. A number of sites have now been identified,
        planning applications have been submitted and these are
        being progressed through the normal development control
        process involving public consultation.

        The Department is therefore taking positive action designed
        to meet the particular needs of all the Travellers in the
        Belfast Council area and approached by a process in which
        the views of the public at large and their representatives are
        fully taken into account. It is hoped that the outcome will be
        a number of properly serviced sites suited to the needs of
        the Travellers.

Public Housing

5.4   In relation to public housing, the prime responsibility of a
        strategic land use plan is to ensure sufficient land is
        available to meet the anticipated public housing programme.
        The Plan indicates enough land to meet the Northern Ireland

Housing Executive target and to enable it to complete its comprehensive housing strategy for housing redevelopment areas and housing action areas. The concerns expressed by the objectors about finance for public housing have been noted. However, overall housing policy and public finance are matters which are determined separately by government outside the Belfast Urban Area Plan. Indeed, all the proposals in the Belfast Urban Area Plan are subject to the availability of finance as indicated in the section headed "The Development Programme" on Page 19 of the Plan. The strategic land use plan is primarily concerned with facilitating, co-ordinating and controlling housing and other developments on the ground. The town planning role largely relates to the shaping of the built environment including the location, arrangement, form and design of physical development proposals.

5.5   The selling off of Housing Executive property is a matter of government housing policy outside the scope of a strategic land use plan.

Infill Development

5.6   The Department agrees that priority should continue to be given to housing sites within the urban area in particular to the Inner City housing drive and that is why the housing release at the periphery of the urban area has been strictly controlled. In fact, 75% of housing land indicated in the Belfast Urban Area Plan lies within the existing built-up area. However, the Department recognises that while there is land available within the Belfast Urban Area which could be developed for housing, there is not enough to meet the likely land demand throughout the Plan period or to meet every choice with regard to housing location.

5.7   On past experience of housing patterns the development of small sites within the urban area is unlikely to make a significant contribution numerically to meeting housing needs, particularly at the strategic level where it is estimated that 24,500 sites are needed in the first half of the Plan period alone. Following standard planning practice in Great Britain, only sites with a potential capacity for 10 or more dwellings were identified as making up the main housing land supply. The contribution to total housing production of small sites for less than 10 dwellings is unpredictable. However, the Department acknowledges that the development of small sites can assist housing renewal at local level and is a bonus to total housing provision. It would not be good planning to use every site for housing, and it is important to ensure that small sites are used for other important community purposes such as open space, shopping and social facilities.

5.8   However, the Belfast Urban Area Plan does not impede in any way the development of these smaller sites for housing. The most appropriate way for these to be handled, within the planning process, is by bringing forward development proposals in the form of planning applications. By this means, planning approval can be obtained quickly, often within two months, without the necessity of the lengthy procedures involved in land use zoning within area plans. For small sites, the Department considers the normal development control process to be a most effective means of speeding up progress on the ground so far as these sites are concerned. Much of the vacant land and property in Belfast is in Inner City areas where redevelopment and improvement are in progress and proposals to use these lands are contained in the Public Sector Housing Programme. Some of the sites are already identified in the land use plans prepared by the Housing Executive for Housing Redevelopment Areas and Housing Action Areas. For the remaining sites the first step would be to identify a willing developer, public or private, and submit a planning application for approval.

5.9   The Department also acknowledges that the land situation is always changing over time. The Department is satisfied that its survey gave a comprehensive picture of the main sites likely to be available for housing at the base date of 1986. Minor changes in the form of a few new potential housing sites are unlikely to make a significant difference to the overall estimates of housing land required.

5.10   To sum up this point, the Department shares the concern of the objector about getting the right balance between Inner City renewal and suburban expansion. Accordingly, the Development Strategy at the beginning of the Plan lays emphasis on the importance of balancing the re-use of land within the urban area with a modest expansion at the edge. The Department is satisfied that there is not sufficient land within the Inner City to meet all of the likely housing demand or to meet every choice.

Development of Vacant Sites

5.11   Housing development has concentrated into certain areas of Belfast. This leads to greater pressure to take up undeveloped or underused portions of ground. Where the circumstances are appropriate private and public authority

198

housing have been approved to help meet the high demand. It is agreed that a balance must be struck between land for housing and open spaces in the community interest. The Plan sets out a strategy to protect and develop recreational and amenity uses in the urban area.

5.12 Similarly, the Department agrees that it is important to set aside land for business development similarly in the interest of job creation. A balance must be struck between housing and industrial/commercial lands. For this reason, the Department has indicated in Policy IND2 that it considers it vital to reserve former industrial areas for business development. However, it accepts that in some cases it may be possible to set aside a small part of a site for housing.

Consultation

5.13 Consultation arrangements for public sector estates are a matter within the functional responsibility of the Northern Ireland Housing Executive and these matters would be best taken up directly with the Executive.

6.0 INDUSTRY AND COMMERCE

6.1 The purpose of the Plan is to establish <u>physical development policies</u> for the Belfast Urban Area up to 2001. Within this overall aim, a key strategic objective is to create a physical environment which will assist the strengthening of the economic base of the Belfast Urban Area. Planning cannot of itself create employment but it can help to promote and encourage job creation by a framework which is sympathetic to industry and commerce and sensitive to the economic goals of the community as a whole. Furthermore, planning can ensure that there are no unnecessary obstacles of a land use nature which would inhibit job creation. The strategy identifies a range of sites within the urban area for new business creation. Simplification of planning control will be introduced to industrial areas as a means of reversing environmental decline and to retain flexibility at a time when the nature of employment activities and their demands for accommodation are rapidly changing. Other elements of the strategy will improve the advantages which the urban area already has as a business location.

6.2 The Department takes the view that the Belfast Enterprise Zone has checked and, to some extent, reversed the drift of jobs and investment from the Inner City and has accelerated the development of the reclaimed land at the North Foreshore. The Enterprise Zone contained 5,700 jobs in 1986 of which 2,300 were new jobs arising from new businesses or the expansion of existing businesses. The value and necessity of these job gains, produced by the Enterprise Zone is even more important when viewed against the background of declining traditional industries which have been operating in the Enterprise Zone area for many years. Declines in long established engineering and textile firms resulted in a net overall job loss of 3%. Clearly, the job losses have been substantially larger but for the succes of Enterprise Zone in attracting businesses to this area. Indeed, it should be noted that the base of jobs has been extended and strengthened significantly with an overall increase in establishments from 165 to 291.

6.3   The Department is also satisfied that, from a planning point of view, the Belfast Enterprise Zone has made an important contribution to urban renewal in the north and west of the City bringing new development and jobs to an area previously marked by dereliction and decay. The figures indicate that the Enterprise Zone has provided new jobs and assisted the sustaining of existing jobs. Many of the Enterprise Zone firms are local and the Department agrees that much of the future industrial level in the Belfast Urban Area will come from an indigenous background rather than from multi-national investment.

6.4   The Department also acknowledges that it is desirable to take a flexible approach towards the development of small business units in or near residential areas. The Department accepts that it is desirable to promote job creation and new business development integrated into local communities. Areas of mixed use on main roads could be suitable locations for such development. Proposals for small business or community workshops of a light industrial nature may therefore be permitted in some situations where they would not give rise to an unacceptable risk of public nuisance, pollution or loss of amenity. Full account will be taken of general traffic considerations and the likely environmental effects on housing of any noise, smell or emissions likely to be produced.

6.5   In addition there are commercial opportunities within the existing built-up areas as part of the continuing thrust towards Inner City renewal the Department will seek to encourage new business by identifying suitable sites and premises in local plans and feasibility studies. Where necessary the Department will facilitate the modernisation of existing industrial areas by using its powers of comprehensive development and urban renewal. Sites which have provided large numbers of jobs in the past in the Inner City are identified as Business Development Areas to be reserved primarily for industrial and commercial purposes. The renewal of these areas could accommodate small businesses and community workshops. The Plan identifies such a Business Development Area at Springfield Road.

6.6 The Department recognises the value of training programmes to prepare people for work, but this is not a matter for a strategic land use plan.

6.7 Financial matters such as rent or rate reductions are beyond the scope of a strategic land use plan which is primarily concerned with securing the orderly and consistent development of land in accordance with the Planning (NI) Order 1972.

6.8 The Department welcomes the support of Community Technical Aid for its strategy of encouraging industrial development in central locations. The emphasis on providing land in central locations will contribute to the overall objective of renewal and re-invigoration of the Inner City and will help to ensure that new employment opportunities are accessible to all sections of the urban population.

6.9 The actual development of the allocated industrial and commercial lands is the responsibility of other public and private agencies, that is, entrepreneurs encouraged by the government agencies given the task of promoting industrial and commercial development. It is widely recognised that small businesses and local enterprises will play a key role in future industrial and commercial development in the Belfast Urban Area. The thrust of the Industrial and Commercial Strategy, in line with Government policy, is to assist the creation of an enterprise culture which will be the 'seedbed' for the formation of new small businesses, some of which would expand to become substantial employers.

6.10 The development of workshop space and nursery/incubator units for new small business is a prominent part of current Government policy throughout the Province. LEDU, under the Local Enterprise Programme, is assisting towards the establishment of a network of enterprise centres offering managed workspace in most areas of Northern Ireland. Along side this Programme, LEDU also encourages private developers by way of grant assistance to provide accommodation suitable for small business needs.

6.11 Ways in which community and business enterprise activity might be stimulated and encouraged is an important part of the government's Pathfinder strategy for enterprise and International Fund Ireland support may be available towards viable projects.

6.12 Community enterprise must of course emerge from the community. LEDU in particular is keen to encourage community enterprise development to release the skills and talents that are available within local communities and interested groups might wish to contact LEDU to explore what might be possible in their area of interest.

6.13 So far as retailing and services are concerned, the Department takes the view that such development can stimulate urban regeneration as well as making an important contribution to the creation and maintenance of jobs.

7.0 LAGANSIDE

7.1 The department acknowledges the interest in and concern about the detailed nature of the Langanside proposals and particularly the Gas Works site. The proposals in the Belfast Urban Area Plan only represent the first step in the planning process. So far as the Gas Works is concerned the BUA Plan indicates that it is a major site available for development and should, in principle, be redeveloped. The case for redevelopment is generally accepted in that the closure of gas production on the site will create a large derelict industrial site near the heart of the city and adjoined on three sides by residential communities. Redevelopment for a useful purpose is clearly in the public interest.

7.2 However, it would be premature to be definite about any land use proposals for the Gas Works in advance of detailed proposals for the site except in relation to open space. The BUA Plan states in Policy LS2 that part of the site near the Lagan will be used for recreational open space. A landscaped 'face' toward the river is desirable mirroring the green setting of the Ormeau Park on the opposite bank. The precise shape, extent and nature of this space will be a matter of further detailed study and it will be included in the local development plan to be prepared in due course.

7.3 The BUA Plan makes it clear in Policy LS1 that the final mix of uses and form of develoment on key sites will be the subject of planning schemes. All the normal planning processes will apply to the riverside lands and the public will have the usual rights, including a Public Inquiry if required, in relation to detailed proposals. The Department considers that the development of this site could be a benefit both to the city as a whole and to the local community. Since the site is in public ownership, the Department will have the opportunity to oversee and influence its development in order to ensure that the end result is in the widest public interest. The Department recognises it is vital that such a valuable site within the City Centre and prominently situated on the riverside must be put to the very best advantage for the city as a whole.

7.4   While there has been speculation about prestige London Dockland type of development, this is not proposed and we feel the reality in Belfast will be of an appropriate local scale and type because the economic and geographical circumstances are so different. The Department sees scope for a mix of public and private housing development along the riverside.

8.0   RECREATION

8.1   The Belfast Urban Area has 1202 hectares of open space to which the public has access for informal recreation. Policy R1 is intended to protect existing open spaces and to help maintain the overall level of recreation provision. In addition the Plan zones 850 hectares of land for new recreational open space. The Department will seek to protect from building development the major sites (one acre plus), listed in Appendix 6 of the Plan within the urban area and which have been included in the programmes of the Department, District Councils or voluntary bodies for new open space developments. Additional facilities will be provided by the recreation developments proposed in Policies R3, 4, 5, 6, 7 and 8, that is, Linear Parks, the Lagan Valley Regional Park, Recreation and Amenity Development in the Belfast Hills and Cave Hill, Carnmoney Country Park and Dundonald Leisure Park. Schemes for Laganside will also provide new recreation opportunities, particularly of a water-based nature (Policy No Ls2).

8.2   The Plan acknowledges that there are areas, particularly in the Inner City, which are deficient in small open spaces. The Department accepts that in addition to providing the proposed new open spaces and protecting existing open spaces, it is desirable to have smaller open spaces and play areas to meet local needs. Such spaces should continue to be provided as land availability and development opportunities permit.

8.3   The sites covered by Policy R2 range from large sites of over 10 acres down to sites as small as one acre. Smaller open spaces below one acre are not identified in the strategic Belfast Urban Area Plan but some are included in the recreation programmes of the District Councils. These proposals will be brought forward as individual planning objections by the respective Councils.

Additional small open spaces or playgrounds can be brought forward through the development control process as opportunities arise. As sites become vacant or derelict in the ongoing cycle of urban change, it may be possible to have some of these lands used as small open spaces or playgrounds. The actual implementation of such spaces will depend very much on the commitment of the District Councils. When such "opportunity" sites are identified, the first step necessary to achieve a result on the ground, is to raise the matter with the respective District Council. The council may wish to submit a planning application not only to obtain Departmental approval but also to test public support for the proposal. Open space proposals can be controversial and past experience indicates that in some cases adjoining residents who are directly affected may wish to oppose the use. Assuming planning permission is granted, the power to vest the land lies with the District Council as implementing authority.

8.4   The Belfast City Council has identified Areas of Open Space Deficiency in the Environment Technical Supplement (Appendix B). The densely built-up nature of many of these areas with new and rehabilitated housing precludes provision of new large areas of open space because of the extreme scarcity of suitable land. However, in the event of land in the deficiency areas becoming available, suitable sites could be raised directly with the Belfast City Council for appropriate open space uses.

8.5   Leisure is recognised as an essential social provision. As stated in the Plan a main element of the Development Strategy is to "raise the quality of the urban environment" including amongst other things environmental policies for landscape and recreation (BUAP Page 17).

8.6   The open space/recreational proposals and zonings indicate the main strategic aspects to be pursued and facilitate their implementation. However, they do not preclude new forms of recreational leisure use or innovative methods of implementing or managing the resulting facilities. The relevant public, private and voluntary implementation agencies are the appropriate bodies to pursue these matters.

9.0 SHOPPING

9.1 The Department recognises that it is important to sustain the vitality and viability of existing shopping centres which serve the community and provide local employment. The Shopping Strategy emphasises the need for a range of retail provision to cater for the varying needs of the urban population. The City Centre provides specialised shopping for the entire population of the Belfast Urban Area. However local shopping centres have a special role in serving their local communities which is complementary to that of the City Centre. The Department's policy is to encourage the retention and strengthening of existing local centres, and to seek to ensure that new retail developments are located where they will support the continued viability of established shopping centres. The Department recognises the role of traditional local and linear shopping centres on the main radial roads in providing an essential service to local communities, particularly for those without a car. Compared with the City Centre, shoppers in these centres have a distinctive pattern of characteristics. They shop more frequently, travel extensively by foot, spend less per trip and have grocery shopping as their main motivation to shop.

9.2 In addition the Department envisages the preparation of local plans or policies to enhance linear and local shopping centres. The Department would welcome development proposals in appropriate locations which would strengthen the provision of local shopping throughout the City.

10.0 TRANSPORTATION

Balance Between Roads and Public Transport

10.1 The Consultant's remit was to review the existing transportation strategy as defined in the 1978 report. Future proposals had to recognise first, what funds were likely to be available for expenditure on transportation in Belfast over the 15-year period (1986-2001) and, secondly, what expenditure commitments had already been made.

10.2 The first figure was termed the Financial Planning Assumption (FPA) and was given as a range from £200m to £280m. The second was termed the cost of the Do-Minimum Strategy and was broken down as follows:

	£m
Highways	20.89
Car Parks	12.90
Private Transport	33.79
Bus: Capital Grant	14.90
Rail: Capital Grant	9.10
Service Grant	13.10
Concessionary Fares	40.05
Public Transport	77.60

Committed expenditure is therefore heavily biased towards expenditure on public transport, and over half the lower amount in the FPA range was already allocated.

10.3 A second fundamental area of study in the Belfast Transportation Strategy Review (BSTR) was the need to establish the worth of the cross harbour structures, both highway and rail, and recognising that the rail link could not be built unless the highway bridge was also constructed

10.4 BTSR evaluations demonstrated that both these projects were viable, would give value-for-money and would play key roles in Belfast's future transport system and development initiatives. With the inclusion of the Cross Harbour Road and Rail Links in the Basic Highway Strategy the expenditure allocation then becomes as follows:

	Private Transport	Public Transport
Committed Expenditure	33.79	77.60
Basic Strategy	44.94	14.05
	£78.73m	£91.65m

Public Transport expenditure still dominates, but much less so because the Cross Harbour Road Bridge project will involve considerable expense. However, it must be emphasised that the rail link can only be justified if a road bridge is also provided and hence public transport is gaining from road investment.

10.5 A large number of road schemes and bus/rail options were investigated and their socio-economic worth assessed. This resulted in some road schemes being abandoned or postponed until further finance becomes available. The retained schemes tended to support and enhance the large investment made in the Basic Strategy. The resultant allocations were as follows:

	Private Transport	Public Transport
Committed Expenditure	33.79	77.60
Basic Strategy	44.94	14.05
Remaining Strategy	49.38	4.20
Total	128.11m(57%)	95.85m(43%)

Grand Total   £223.96m

This allocation is not unduly biased towards private transport, bearing in mind that 80% of all daily trips in the Belfast Urban Area are made by private transport.

10.6   The Preferred Transportation Strategy includes recommendations for investment in buses, and a major investment which should cut the costs of operating Northern Ireland Railways, as well as further investment in roads. It should also be appreciated that investment in roads also gives benefits to the bus passengers and operators through reducing road congestion.

Development of Public Transport

10.7   The Belfast Urban Area Plan policy statements TR1 and TR6 all demonstrate a commitment to public transport in the urban area.

TR1 - Public transport services will be maintained at a level to ensure reasonable access to jobs, shops, schools and recreation.

TR2 - Bus services will continue to be developed as an integral part of the transportation system.

TR3 - The provision of better bus station accommodation will be considered with the bus companies.

TR4 - The provision of new railway stations and halts will be kept under consideration.

TR5 - Developments in alternative public transport technologies will be kept under review.

TR6 - It is envisaged that concessionary fare facilities will continue to be available in respect of bus and rail transport.

10.8   The Cross Harbour Rail Link, which will make possible significant savings in rail operating costs and ease travel by

207

rail, is confirmed as part of Belfast's transportation strategy.

10.9   In addition, a large number of proposals which were investigated are designed to contribute to the further development of bus transport. These covered, inter alia:

- bus routing   :   eg, more cross-town and non-radial services;
- bus frequency   :   eg, limited stop services from outer suburbs;
- areas of operators :   eg, to rationalise Ulsterbus/Citybus operating areas;
- fares   :   eg, changes in ticketing systems and structure to make use of new technology to give benefits to passengers by ease of use and flexibility (eg, easier transfer arrangements) and benefits to operators by giving better control (eg, to provide better information and counter fare evasion);
- bus types   :   eg, use of minibuses to give more flexible and higher frequency services;
- bus design   :   eg, change in bus design to make the service more attractive and easier to use for groups such as the disabled; and
- bus stops   :   eg, more shelters and better information.

More positive marketing of bus travel was also suggested to encourage greater use, as were means of counteracting vandalism.   The implications of these and other recommendations will be the subject of discussion between the bus companies and the Department.

Needs of Disabled and Elderly

10.10   The special needs of groups such as the elderly, disabled, mothers and young children could not be addressed in detail in a strategic review. However, suggestions have been made where changes in bus design could help such groups. Such matters will be the subject of discussion between the bus operators and the Department.

10.11 Policy TR6 states that concessionary fares will continue to be available in respect of bus and rail transport. Moreover, the Department is committed to the continued support by subsidy of unremunerative rail services.

10.12 Future demand for public transport was predicted in the Review and a system proposed to meet this situation. The need to market bus travel to try to encourage its greater use was recognised and a number of initiatives recommended to this end, eg, minibus services.

10.13 The interest of the travelling public is of prime concern to the transport companies. They are, however, obliged to operate as commercially as possible in order to minimise the need for public financial support.

Alternative Forms of Transport

10.14 A pre-feasibility study was undertaken to assess whether it was likely that a case could be made for an alternative form of transport in Belfast in the context of the planning period, expenditure constraints and potential demands. Several alternatives were considered viz, busways, trolley buses, light rail (LRT) and it was decided that an assessment of the practicability of introducing LRT in one of the main movement corridors of Belfast would best illustrate its potential. Thus the case was examined where demand could be high and future road traffic congestion excessive, both pre-conditions for establishing a good economic case for LRT.

10.15 Costs were based on building a new system rather than incorporating LRT running into Northern Ireland Railway's operation, or on-street, at-grade running both of which would cause operating difficulties for trains or road traffic. The model was robust enough to show that a case could not be made, nor was it realistic to envisage diverting scarce financial resources into a system with limited scope in terms of route coverage and high levels of accessibility within the populated areas of the BUA.

Park and Ride

10.16 Park-and-ride has not proved to be a successful system in Belfast up to now except during the pre-Christmas period. Such systems elsewhere have only worked in situations where parking demand in a city centre has far out-stripped supply and this is not the case in Belfast nor is it expected to be in the future when existing commitments (Castle Court, Mongomery Street, Chichester St. multi-storey car parks) should ensure that forecast demand is satisfied.

Dial-a-ride

10.17 Dial-a-ride systems are essentially non-strategic in nature and therefore were not considered within the scope of the Belfast Transportation Strategy Review studies. However the bus company is at present considering the feasibility of such a service.

10.18 'Black Taxi' operations in West and North Belfast are still receiving consideration by the Department and because of the complexities of the situation they are not included in the Plan.

10.19 Restraining travel by car borne commuters to the city centre was considered inappropriate within the 15-year time frame of the Plan since it would also run counter to a prime goal of making the city centre as attractive as possible by encouraging investment in its development for commerce and retailing.

10.20 The 1978 Report on the Review of Transportation Strategy recommended that a Transport Review Authority should be set up to enable consultation and participation by the travelling public in the implementation of the tansportation strategy for Belfast.

10.21 This recommendation was rejected by the Department on the grounds that there already existed in Northern Ireland a number of bodies with a statutory role or an accepted interest in transport, eg the former Northern Ireland Transport Users' committee (since superseded by the General Consumer Council), the District Councils and the Northern Ireland Economic Council. It was the Department's view at the time that it was preferable to conduct the consultation process through the bodies already in being rather than by the establishment of another consultative body.

10.22 The Department would still hold to this view. For example, the General Consumer Council maintains a very active interest in transport matters as indeed do the District Councils and the Northern Ireland Economic Council. Indeed these bodies have all made significant contributions to the consultation process of the BUA Plan 2001.

Effect of Transportation Proposals on Local Area

10.23 Transportation proposals involving the provision of new roads and railways or major improvements of the existing networks can affect wide areas of the city.

The Department has provided the opportunity for the lodging of formal objections to the proposals contained in the Draft Plan so that the views of all interested parties and those directly or indirectly affected can be considered at the public inquiry.

Any decision by the Department regarding the implementation of a major transportation proposal is taken in the light of the Report on the public inquiry having regard to all the relevant considerations including the adverse effects of the scheme on particular areas and the benefits to the community as a whole.

Landscaping of Railway Lands

10.24 The former Comber railway lands are in the ownership of the Department. When the railway line was closed the lands were acquired by the then road authorities Belfast County Borough Council and Down County Council with the intention of constructing a motorway (M7) to Newtownards. The motorway proposal which formed part of the 1969 Belfast Transportation Plan was abandoned following a public inquiry in 1977 into the Review of Transportation Strategy for the Belfast Area, but the Department decided to retain protection lines for the construction of a strategic highway scheme, the Comber route.

Because the road was unlikely to be built for a number of years and the railway lands were difficult to maintain the Department decided that the cost of undertaking planting and landscaping along sections of the line would be justified by the environmental benefits which would be obtained pending the implementation of the scheme. The Department gave approval and financial assistance to the carrying out of the work on the clear understanding that the land would be required in due course for the construction of the Comber Route scheme.

Traffic-Related Environmental Pollution

10.25 The Department accepts that there are concerns about the environmental pollution consequences of increased traffic flows. The Department does not consider however that the proposals contained in the Plan will result in a significant level of traffic-related pollution.

Depreciation in Value of Property

10.26 Where the value of a property is depreciated by physical factors caused by the use of a new or improved road, eg noise, vibration, fumes, artificial lighting, the owner may be entitled to claim compensation for that depreciation from the Department under the provisions of the Land Acquisition and Compensation (Northern Ireland) Order 1973, copies of which can be obtained from HM Stationery Office.

Road Safety

10.27 The Department recognises that there are concerns about the safety aspects of roads provision and will ensure that the necessary measures to allow for the safe operation of proposed roads are incorporated in their design.

Pedestrian facilities will be provided at traffic signal controlled junctions, guard railing erected and kerbs lowered to facilitate the elderly, disabled and people with prams. Pedestrian crossings will also be provided at other locations where necessary.

Local Effects of Proposed Road Schemes

10.28 The road proposals contained in the Plan are strategic in nature and have not been designed in detail. The Department acknowledges that many people are concerned about the effects of proposed schemes and is always willing to meet local groups and householders, and to advise them of the likely effects of proposed schemes on particular areas and individual properties.

Provision for Cyclists

10.29 There is a very low use of bicycles in Belfast and hence the Department considers that it would not be practical or economic to provide special facilities for cyclists on a wide scale. However the Department is prepared to consider if local provision for cyclists might be justified in particular circumstances.

212

Provision of Pedestrians

10.30 The movement of pedestrians is non-strategic in transportation terms and therefore was not considered within the scope of the transportation study.

The needs of pedestrians are taken into account at the detailed design stage of transportation proposals such as roads, bus stations, railway stations, car parks, etc. since passengers travelling by whatever mode normally walk at the beginning and end of their journeys.

Provision for pedestrians is also made where required in the design of minor road improvement schemes, in the implementation of traffic management measures such as the installation of traffic signal control pedestrian crossings and guard railing and by lowering kerbs at the junctions of side streets when footways are reconstructed.

It is the Department's policy to improve the environment for pedestrians in the main shopping areas by restricting the movement of vehicles and extending pedestrianisation where appropriate, planting street trees and providing landscaped areas, seating and amenity lighting.

Transportation Consultants' Terms of Reference

10.31 The Department's Transportation Consultants, Halcrow Fox and Associates, were asked to make a comprehensive and independent assessment of the transportation requirements of the Belfast area and to make recommendations to the Department on the need for new roads and the balance between private and public transport which would be appropriate during the Plan period.

Albertbridge Road Widening

10.32 The Department considers that Albertbridge Road will have to be widened to 4 lanes in order to cater for the estimated growth in traffic demand during the Plan period and increase the capacity of the traffic signal controlled junction with Templemore Avenue.

Widening the carriageway to provide 4 traffic lanes would avoid vehicles having to park partly on the footways, increase road safety and reduce delays caused by parked vehicles and vehicles waiting to turn right off Albertbridge Road.

213

Loss of Trade due to Road Widening

10.33 The prime function of a main road is to cater for the movement of vehicles. Where widening of a main road is proposed in order to increase its capacity considerable lengths of the kerbside lanes are normally available for parking at off-peak times.

If the footways along a main road are of sufficient width the Department may consider the feasibility of constructing lay-bys to provide off-street parking adjacent to existing shops, provided the cost of doing so is not excessive.

S12 Ormeau Road Widening -Cromac Street to Ormeau Bridge

10.34 The Department has received a large number of objections to the widening of the lower Ormeau Road including submissions from various residents groups and business interests. The Department acknowledges that the prime concern of objectors relates to environmental considerations. These include concerns about the loss of properties, impact on local shopping, severance of residential areas, increased noise, difficulties for pedestrians and safety/convenience in relation to heavy traffic flows.

10.35 However, the Department has a responsibility to consider how it can best handle the growing traffic flows between the south side of the city and the City Centre/northern side of the city in the widest public interest. The transportation consultants have shown that there is a case on traffic grounds for improvement of the lower Ormeau Road. The lower Ormeau Road is a busy radial traffic route which at present carries about 30,000 vehicles per day. Traffic queues for much of its length during peak periods and throughout the day there are large numbers of conflicting traffic movements due to vehicles turning in and out of side streets and pedestrians crossing the road.

10.36 The Department considers that the existing road would not be capable of coping with the anticipated growth in traffic demand which it is estimated would exceed 35,000 vehicles per day by the end of the Plan period. The proposed widening of the Ormeau Road would assist the movement of the extra traffic flows. However, the Department recognises, as the Consultants have demonstrated, that improvements to the Ormeau Road corridor north of the River Lagan would have the effect of drawing through traffic off the Cross Harbour Bridge and Short Strand routes to the east and on the City Centre roads via Oxford Street, Cromac

Street, Ormeau Road and Ormeau Embankment.

The traffic gains of widening the Ormeau Road must of course be weighed against the environmental considerations.

10.37 A number of submissions to the Department have made the case that the Ormeau Embankment Extension could provide an alternative route for traffic in the southern corridor moving to and from the City Centre and areas to the north. It is contended that it would in effect provide an eastern by-pass of the City Centre connecting eventually to the new Cross Harbour Road Bridge and taking through traffic off the lower Ormeau Road.

10.38 The Department has investigated the possibility of identifying other routes for traffic in the Southern Approaches corridor which would reduce the traffic demand on the lower Ormeau Road. In particular, the Department has re-examined the respective merits of the Ormeau Road widening and the Ormeau Embankment Extension to test the argument made in submissions to the Department. It is satisfied that the extension of the Ormeau Embankment to the Albert Bridge and Short Strand would relieve the lower Ormeau Road of traffic which wishes to by-pass the City Centre on its eastern side. The resultant reduction in projected traffic flow might obviate the need for the proposed major widening of the section of the lower Ormeau Road between Donegall Pass and Artana Street within the Plan Period.

Conclusion

10.39 The Department's road scheme to deal with traffic growth in the southern corridor is the lower Ormeau Road widening scheme known as the S12 in the Belfast Urban Area Plan and the Department is confident that this would make adequate provision for the projected flows. However, the Department acknowledges that there is considerable merit in the alternative scheme involving the Ormeau Embankment Extension, proposed for abandoment in the Plan, and this deserves further examination. Initial study suggests that the alternative could relieve traffic flows on the lower Ormeau Road and produce environmental gains for both the lower Ormeau and Ravenhill residential neighbourhoods. It would, however, affect commercial properties along the riverside at Ravenhill and this would have to be taken into account along with any other consequences there may be in relation to traffic flows in the lower Ravenhill area.

10.40 A scheme involving a route along the Ormeau Embankment may, in the final analysis, be preferable to the lower Ormeau Road widening.

10.41 In the light of all the objections received, the Department would therefore welcome the views of the Planning Appeals Commission on the respective merits of the two schemes

- the Plan proposal for widening lower Ormeau Road
- the Plan proposal to abandon the Ormeau Embankment extension

taking account of any other views that may be placed before the Public Inquiry.

D2 Cross Harbour Road Link

10.42 The Cross Harbour Road and Rail Links formed part of the transportation strategy which was approved in 1978 following a public inquiry into the Review of Transportation Strategy for the Belfast area. The Report of the Department's Transportation Consultants, Halcrow Fox Associates, confirmed that the road and rail links are still warranted as a central feature of the Plan and the Department therefore decided that the schemes should proceed subject to the availability of finance.

The Cross Harbour Road Link has therefore been listed in the draft BUA Plan as a Strategic Highway Measure which has already been confirmed

11.0 WOMENS' ISSUES

11.1 The Department notes the issues of concern expressed in relation to the needs of women in the environment. It is noted that in England and Wales, specific policies are sometimes included within structure plans and local plans to deal with these issues, where the local authority has direct responsibility for relevant land use and public expenditure policies. In Northern Ireland, the areas of responsibility of the various government and local government bodies are very different. The strategic land use plan, which is the policy of the Department of the Environment, is primarily concerned with facilitating, co-ordinating and controlling development on the ground. Many aspects such as the provision of day-care facilities, playgrounds, employment, etc. are the responsibility of the other bodies. Other aspects of the design of the environment, such as to make residential environments pleasant and safe, are the concern of the

216

Department but are related to the local planning level rather than the strategic level which deals with broad land use matters.

11.2   Generally, the Department will require the submission of an overall layout for major suburban sites to enable a comprehensive assessment of the design to be made. A comprehensive landscape assessment and analysis may be necessary to assist the Department in ensuring that layouts, roads and open spaces respond sympathetically to existing topography and vegetation. Similarly, a mix of house types and densities will be required to ensure there is a variety of style in order to avoid unattractive monotonous schemes. The layout will also be expected to pay regard to the character of existing housing in the locality.

11.3   The Department has also made it clear in the Housing Technical Supplement that it may require parts of the suburban housing sites to be set aside, if so required, for necessary ancillary uses to serve the new housing community. This point is set out in Paragraph 9.12 of the Technical Supplement which states:

The term 'housing' applied to the zoning of new housing lands is interpreted by the Department to mean 'predominant residential use'. It is normal practice, in the interest of good planning, to reserve the new housing community. The Department therefore reserves the right to allocate parts of a new housing area for other uses such

12.0   EDUCATION

12.1   The responsibility for education lies with the Department of Education and the Education Authorities and is outside the scope of the Plan. The Department of the Environment has consulted with the Education Authorities which have indicated that at present there is no requirement for land for new education developments.

12.2   The Plan is intended to show strategic land uses and to facilitate the orderly development of the city and it will certainly not be an obstacle to the meeting of educational needs. Education and School Authorities will be free to apply for planning permission to develop a school on any site or building either now or at any time during the Plan period. Indeed, if the building chosen was formerly in use as a school, planning permission may not even by necessary. If the school sponsors wish to explore informally the acceptability in Planning terms of establishing educational facilities in any specific building or site they should contact the Belfast Divisional Planning Office. Planning permission may be sought on buildings not yet in the ownership of the applicant.

13.0 LOCAL PLANS

13.1 The first step in the planning process of guiding and controlling development in the Belfast Urban Area over the years to 2001 is the preparation of the current strategic land use plan. This will provide the policy framework within which more detailed development proposals can be determined within the Plan period. After the completion and adoption of the BUA Plan, the Department envisages that local plans will be prepared, if required, to deal with more localised land use issues which will arise from time to time in the changing urban scene. Types of local plan can include comprehensive development schemes, local development plans, local planning studies to guide, for example, development control, redevelopment plans, housing action area plans and plans for conservation areas.

13.2 Local plans may be required, for example, to deal with a concentration of local land use issues which would justify a more detailed plan to provide a basis for the co-ordination of development or the protection of the environment. The Gas Works area is an example of the former and the Lagan Valley Regional Park is a good example of the latter. In both cases, the Department recognises the need for a more detailed local development plan and accordingly it proposes to prepare a comprehensive development scheme for the Gas works and a local plan for the Lagan Valley Regional Park. The Belfast Harbour area is another example of a local area where the Department has confirmed that it will prepare a local plan.

13.3 In the case of the built-up area of Belfast, much of the Inner City is already covered by detailed land use plans which have been prepared for Housing Redevelopment Areas, Housing Action Areas or local comprehensive development areas. In addition, the Department has commenced preparing local planning studies to assist the upgrading of arterial routes. This range of local plans will be extended by the preparation of development schemes for the key sites indicated in the Laganside Strategy and by the formulation of detailed development policies for the proposed new Conservation Areas.

13.4 Local plans are not, however, necessary in all areas. For example, they may not be needed in areas where there is little pressure for development and no need to encourage development or to stimulate growth. In such cases the BUA Plan should provide an adequate guide for developers and basis for the consideration of planning applications.

13.5 The Department will consider the case for a local plan in an area on its merits taking into account such factors as likely land use change in an area, conflicting land demands, identified land use issues and their nature, the relationships between different land uses, scale and timing of potential development and available resources. The Department will wish to be satisfied that a local plan is necessary and that it will assist the bringing forward of more appropriate development solutions. In many localised situations where there are concerns about a scatter of unrelated pieces of land, the most appropriate way of dealing with the problem will continue to be through the normal development control process, in the form of a planning application, after the identification of an implementing agency or developer. The planning application process provides opportunities for public consultation and scope for a local public inquiry under Article 22 of the Planning Order where a development affects the whole of a neighbourhood.

14.0 GENERAL

Consultation Arrangements

14.1 The Belfast Urban Area Plan, like all development plans in Northern Ireland, must follow the procedures laid down in Part III of the Planning (NI) Order 1972, which sets out the arrangements for public consultation. The Department published its intention to prepare the BUA Plan in the Press during June/July 1985 and the public was invited to put forward suggestions for the future development of the area. There was further consultation with Councils and the general public at Article 5 stage, the stage which was reached with the publication of the Department's Preliminary Proposals in May 1987. The publication of the Preliminary Proposals was announced in the Press and a public display was held in eleven venues widely distributed throughout the urban area. Similar publicity was given to the publication of the Draft Plan in November 1987. The consultation arrangements during the preparation of the Plan provided Councils and the public with a year from the publication of the Preliminary Proposals in May 1987 to the convening of a Public Inquiry in May 1988 to comment on the Department's proposals and - if they wish - to develop their case against the proposals.

14.2   The Plan provides land for a wide range of developments across all parts of the BUA, taking in various types of community. The Department considers that the provision of a stategic land use framework is an important step in creating an appropriate environment and climate for the encouragement of investment and development within the Belfast Urban Area generally. Within this overall strategic framework the Plan repeatedly stresses the importance of continuing and endeavouring to complete the Inner City renewal process which embraces many of the deprived areas. A principal aim of the Plan is to improve the quality of life of the citizens of Belfast. The improvement of the built environment of the City will be a major element in the strategy to achieve this aim and to assist economic and social regeneration.

Social Issues

14.3   The strategic land use plan is designed to provide a basic framework for social and economic activity and has sufficient flexibility to accommodate a comprehensive and changing development programme involving the public and private sectors in partnership and the people of the city. However, land use plans cannot provide an all-purpose remedy for every social, economic and community issue in the city. The problems and complexities of 20th Century life in a major city extend far beyond the built environment. The Plan can facilitate, co-ordinate, guide and control development and it provides the land use framework within which economic and social activity is free to operate.

Laganside

14.4   So far as the Department's Laganside Company is concerned, the Department wishes to confirm that there is no conflict whatsoever with the planning procedures. This Company's role is primarily in the field of promotion and marketing. All development proposals must go through the normal planning procedures. The Department will continue at all times to be the planning authority in relation to the development of the riverside. The BUA Plan only deals with the first step - indicating a number of key sites which should be subject to major redevelopment. The second step will be the preparation of comprehensive development schemes for the major sites with the usual rights of public consultation. At this stage the main land uses within the site will be indicated. The third step is the submission of individual planning applications with detailed designs of buildings and their surroundings. In other words the process is rather akin to the housing redevelopment procedures:-

Stages: 1.   Strategic plan (the old 1969 Plan) showed areas of change.
         2.   Preparation of overall development scheme.
         3.   Submission of planning applications for plots of land within the redevelopment area.

Castlecourt

14.5   The Comprehensive Development Scheme for Royal Avenue/Millfield including Castlecourt has been presented at Public Inquiry and adopted upon the report of the independent Planning Appeals Commission.

Cross Harbour Bridges

14.6   The Cross Harbour Bridges have been processed through Public Inquiry on a previous occasion. These are now confirmed schemes following government decision to proceed to implement long established proposals.

Bibliography

Albrow, M. (1970), 'The role of the sociologist as a professional: the case of planning' in Sociological Review Monograph No. 16, *The Sociology of Sociology*, University of Keele.

Alty, R. and Darke, R. (1987), 'A City Centre for People: involving the community in planning for Sheffield's central area', *Planning Practice and Research*, no. 3.

Ambrose, P. (1976), *The Land Market and the Housing System*, Urban and Regional Studies Working Paper No. 3, University of Sussex, Brighton.

Ambrose, P. (1986), *Whatever Happened to Planning?* Methuen, London.

Armstrong, J. (1985), *Sizewell Report: a new approach for major public inquiries*, Town and Country Planning Association, London.

Arnstein, S. R. (1969), 'A ladder of Citizen Participation', *Journal of American Institute of Planners*, vol. 35, no. 4, July.

Ash, J. (1979), 'Public participation: time to bury Skeffington?', *The Planner*, September.

Bains Report (1972), *The New Authorities*, HMSO, London.

Ball, M. (1983), *Housing Policy and Economic Power*, Methuen, London.

Bauman, Z. (1987), *Legislators and Interpretors: On Modernity, Post-modernity and Intellectuals*, Polity Press, Cambridge.

BDP (Building Design Partnership) and Travers Morgan & Partners (1976), *Belfast Urban Area Plan: Review of Transportation Strategy - Main Report*, BDP and R. Travers Morgan & Partners.

Beckenbach, F. (1989), 'Social Costs in Modern Capitalism', *Capitalism, Nature, Socialism*, no. 3, November.

222

Bew, P. Gibbon, P. and Patterson, H. (1979), *The State in Northern Ireland, 1921-1972*, Manchester University Press.
Birrell, D. and Murie, A. (1980), *Policy and Government in Northern Ireland: Lessons of Devolution*, Gill & Macmillan, Dublin.
Blackman, T. (1984), 'Planning in Northern Ireland: the shape of things to come?', *The Planner*, vol. 70, no. 1.
Blackman, T. (1987), *Housing Policy and Community Action in County Durham and County Armagh: A Comparative Study*, Unpublished Ph.D Thesis, University of Durham.
Blackman, T. (1988), 'Community Technical Aid (Northern Ireland) Limited', *Town Planning Review*, vol. 59, no.4.
Boys, J. (1989), 'Right Up Your Street', *Marxism Today*, vol. 33, no. 9, September.
Brown, S. (1987), 'Belfast Retailing Report has "Shortcomings"', *Scope*, May.
Building Design Partnership (1981), *Belfast Urban Area Plan*, vols. 1 and 2, BDP, Belfast.
Bulletin of Northern Ireland Law (1983), 'Planning Appeals Commission Ref. A119/1983, 2 November 1983', no. 9.
Bulletin of Northern Ireland Law (1985), 'Planning Appeals Commission Ref. A173/1985, 13 December 1985', no. 10.
Bulletin of Northern Ireland Law (1986), 'Re: Blair's Application, QBD (Lord Lowry LCJ), 15 February 1985', no. 7.
Bulletin of Northern Ireland Law (1988), 'Planning Appeals Commission Ref. A260/1987', 9 March 1988, no. 5.
Byrne, D. (1989), *Beyond the Inner City*, Open University Press, Milton Keynes.
Castells, M. (1978), *City, Class and Power*, Macmillan, London.
Cockburn, C. (1977), 'The local state: management of cities and people', *Race & Class*, no. 18.
Cockburn, C. (1978), *The Local State*, Pluto Press, London.
Cullingworth, J. B. (1982), *Town and Country Planning in Britain*, Unwin Hyman, London.
Cullingworth, J. B. (1988), *Town and Country Planning in Britain*, Unwin Hyman, London.
Davies, J. G. (1972), *The Evangelistic Bureaucrat*, Tavistock, London.
Dennis, N. (1970), *People and Planning*, Faber & Faber, London.
Dennis, N. (1972), *Public Participation and Planners' Blight*, Faber & Faber, London.
Department of Local Government, Housing and Planning (Northern Ireland) (1975), *Northern Ireland Discussion Paper: Regional Physical Development Strategy 1975-95*, HMSO, Belfast.
Department of the Environment (1981a), 'Compulsory Purchase Orders made under Housing Powers', Circular 13/81, 5 May.
Department of the Environment (1981b), 'Housing Act 1957 Part III Derwentside District (Railway Street, Langley Park) Compulsory Purchase Order 1980: Report of the Department of the Environment Inspector on Public Local Inquiry held 3 February 1981', Ref.

NH/5196/8/9.

Department of the Environment (Northern Ireland) (1981), *Belfast Integrated Operations Document*, HMSO, Belfast.

Department of the Environment (Northern Ireland) (1985), *Integrated Operations: Belfast Urban Area*, HMSO, Belfast.

Department of the Environment (Northern Ireland) (1976), *Regional Physical Development Strategy, 1975-95*, HMSO, Belfast.

Department of the Environment (Northern Ireland) (1987), *Belfast Urban Area Plan 2001*, HMSO, Belfast.

Department of the Environment (Northern Ireland) (1989), *Belfast Urban Area Plan 2001: Adoption Statement*, HMSO, Belfast.

Devine, P. (1988), *Democracy and Economic Planning*, Polity Press, Cambridge.

Dickens, P., Duncan, S., Goodwin, M. and Gray, F. (1985), *Housing, States and Localities*, Methuen, London.

Doyal, L. and Gough, I. (1984), 'A Theory of Human Needs', *Critical Social Policy*, issue 10, summer.

Duncan, S. S. and Goodwin, M. (1982), 'The local state and restructuring social relations: theory and practice', *International Journal of Urban and Regional Research*, vol. 6, no. 2.

Duncan, S. S. and Goodwin, M. (1988), *The Local State and Uneven Development*, Blackwell, Oxford.

Dunleavy, P. and O'Leary, B. (1987), *Theories of the State: The Politics of Liberal Democracy*, Macmillan Education, Basingstoke.

Flynn, R. (1981), 'Managing consensus: strategies and rationales in policymaking' in Harloe, M. (ed.), *New Strategies in Urban Change and Conflict*, Heinemann, London.

Frankel, B. (1987), *The Post Industrial Utopians*, Polity Press, Cambridge.

Franks Report (1957), *Report of the Committee on Administrative Tribunals and Enquiries*, Cmnd. 218, HMSO, London.

Gaffikin, F. and Morrissey, M. (1990), *Northern Ireland: the Thatcher Years*, Zed Press, London.

Gamble, A. (1988), *The Free Economy and the Strong State: The Politics of Thatcherism*, Macmillan Education, London.

Gillespie, N. (1983), *The Vital Statistics: Shankill Employment Report*, Shankill Community Council, Belfast.

Gottdiener, M. (1986), *The Social Production of Urban Space*, University of Texas Press, Austin.

Gramsci, A. (1971), *Prison Notebooks*, Lawrence and Wishart, London.

Gwilliam, M. (1989), 'The future of regional and strategic planning' *Town & Country Planning*, vol. 58, pp. 274-275.

Ham, C. and Hill, M. (1984), *The Policy Process in the Modern Capitalist State*, Wheatsheaf Books, Brighton.

Hansard (1989a), *Parliamentary Debates*, vol. 155, no. 1490, col. 579-586, June.

Hansard (1989b), *Parliamentary Debates*, vol. 155, no. 1492, col. 579-586, July.

Harrison, M. L. (1987), 'Property Rights, Philosophies, and the Justification of Planning Control' in Harrison, M. L. and Mordey, R. (eds), *Planning Control: Philosophies, Prospects and Practice*, Croom Helm, London.

Harvey, D. (1973), *Social Justice and the City*, Edward Arnold, London.

Harvey, D. (1981), 'The urban process under capitalism: a framework for analysis' in Dear, M. and Scott, A. J. (eds.), *Urbanization and urban planning in capitalist society*, Methuen, London.

Harvey, D. (1989), *The Urban Experience*, Basil Blackwell, Oxford.

Hayek, F. A. (1944), *The Road to Serfdom*, George Routledge and Sons, London.

Hayek, F. A. (1960), *The Constitution of Liberty*, Routledge and Kegan Paul, London.

Herington, J. (1990), *Beyond Green Belts: Managing Urban Growth in the 21st Century*, Jessica Kingsley Publishers, London.

Home, R. K. (1985), 'British planning law and the politics of inner city renewal: the case of Coin Street', *Urban Law and Policy*, vol. 7, pp. 75-87.

House of Commons (1986), *Fifth report from the Environment Committee, session 1985-86*, HMSO, London.

House of Commons Employment Committee (1988), *The Employment Effects of Urban Development Corporations*, Third Report, Session 1987-88, HMSO, London.

Howard, M. (1989), 'Planning applications, appeals and development plans' in Journal of Planning and Environment Law, *New Orders, new rules, new assessments - in practice*, Occasional Paper 16, Sweet & Maxwell, London.

Howes, C. K. (1988), 'Urban regeneration initiatives in England', *Land Development Studies*, vol. 5, pp. 57-65.

Hutton, N. (1986), *Lay Participation in a Public Inquiry: a Sociological Case Study*, Gower, Aldershot.

Institution of Environmental Health Officers (1981), *Area Improvement: the report of the area improvement working party*, Institution of Environmental Health Officer, London.

Jessop, B. (1982), *The Capitalist State: Marxist Theories and Methods*, Martin Robertson, Oxford.

Jessop, B. Bonnett, K., Bromley, S. and Ling, T. (1985), 'Thatcherism and the Politics of Hegemony: a Reply to Stuart Hall', *New Left Review*, no. 153.

John, P. (1990), *Recent Trends in Central-Local Government Relations*, Policy Studies Institute/Joseph Rowntree Foundation, London.

Kilbrandon Report, (1973), *Report of the Royal Commission on the Constitution*, Cmd 5460, HMSO, London.

Kraushaar, B. (1981), 'Policy without protest: the dilemma of organising for change in Britain' in Harloe, M. (ed.), *New Perspectives in Urban Change and Conflict*, Heinemann, London.

Labour Party 87 (1988), *Regional Government and a Bill of Rights for Northern Ireland*, LP 87, 41 Donegall Street, Belfast, BT1 2FG.

Lash, S. and Urry, J. (1987), *The End of Organized Capitalism*, Polity Press, Cambridge.

Lavery Report (1978), *Belfast Urban Area Plan Review of Transportation Strategy*, HMSO, Belfast.

Lefebvre, H. (1968), *Le droit à la ville*, Anthropos, Paris.

Lefebvre, H. (1977), Reflections on the politics of space' in Peet, R. (ed.), *Radical Geography*, Maaroufa Press, Chicago.

Le-Las, W. (1987), *Playing the Public Inquiry Game: an objector's guide*, Osmosis Publishing Services, Mirfield.

Leopold, E. (1989), 'The impact of proposals to develop the King's Cross Railway Lands', *Local Economy*, vol. 4, pp. 17-28.

Ley, D. (1983), *A Social Geography of the City*, Harper & Row, New York.

Loughlin, M. (1980), 'The scope and importance of "material considerations"', *Urban Low and Policy*, vol. 7, pp. 171-192.

Matthew Report (1963), *Belfast Regional Survey and Plan: Recommendations and Conclusions*, Cmnd. 451, HMSO, Belfast.

Mellor, R. (1989), 'Urban sociology: a trend report', *Sociology*, vol. 23, no. 2.

McAuslan, P. (1980), *The Ideologies of Planning Law*, Pergamon Press, Oxford.

Milne, R. (1989), 'A visit to the government inspector', *New Scientist*, no. 232, pp. 241-260.

Ministry of Housing, Physical Planning and Environment of the Government of the Netherlands (1989), *To Choose or to Loose: National Environment Plan*, Government of the Netherlands, The Hague.

Mohan, J. (1984), 'Hospital Planning and New Town Development: Examples from North East England' in Clark, M. (ed.), *Planning and Analysis in Health Care Systems*, Pion, London.

Mooney, S. and Gaffikin, F. (1987), *Belfast Urban Area Plan 1987: Reshaping Space and Society*, Belfast Centre for the Unemployed.

Moore, R. (1987), 'The development and role of standards for the older housing stock', *Unhealthy Housing: prevention and remedies*, Conference proceedings, Institution of Environmental Health Officers, London.

Mukherjee, R. (1989), *The Quality of Life: valuation in social research*, Sage Publications, London.

Munt, I. (1989), 'Development tail wagging the Docklands dog', *Town and Country Planning*, vol. 58, pp. 341-343.

Neill, W. J. V. and Singleton, D. (1990), 'Private housebuilding in Greater Belfast: the not so anomalous region', *Housing Review*, vol. 39, no. 1.

Northern Ireland Assembly (1983), *Report of the Environment Committee into the Housing Executive Belfast Housing Renewal Strategy*, HMSO, Belfast.

Northern Ireland Assembly (1985), *Environment Committee Minutes*

of Evidence on Belfast Urban Area Plan Review, 3 December 1985.
Northern Ireland Housing Executive (1983), Belfast Housing Renewal Strategy, Housing Executive, Belfast.
Northern Ireland Planning Appeals Commission (1989), The Planning (Northern Ireland) Order 1972: Article 6 Report to the Planning Appeals Commission on a Public Inquiry on Belfast Urban Area Plan 2001, Planning Appeals Commission, Belfast.
Nozick, R. (1974), Anarchy, State and Utopia, Basil Blackwell, Oxford.
Oliver, J. (1978), Working at Stormont, Institute of Public Administration, Dublin.
Pahl, R. (1975), Whose City?, Penguin, Harmondsworth.
Parson, D. (1981), 'Urban renewal and housing action areas in Belfast: legitimation and the incorporation of protest', International Journal of Urban and Regional Research, vol. 15, no. 2.
Paterson Report (1972), The New Scottish Local Authorities: Organisation and Management Structures, HMSO.
Phillips, D. R., Vincent, J. and Blacksell, S. (1987), 'Spatial concentration of residential homes for the elderly: planning responses and dilemmas', Transactions of the Institute of British Geographers, vol. 12, pp. 73-83.
Planning Appeals Commission (Northern Ireland) (1989), The Planning (Northern Ireland) Order 1972: Article 6 Report to the Planning Appeals Commission on a Public Inquiry on Belfast Urban Area Plan 2001, Planning Appeals Commission, Belfast.
Planning Appeals Commission (Northern Ireland) (1989a), Report on a reference to the Commission under Article 22 (2) of The Planning (Northern Ireland) Order 1972 in respect of an application at Nos. 6-10 The Hill, Portstewart, Ref. C12/1988.
Political Vetting of Community Work Working Group (1990), The Political Vetting of Community Work in Northern Ireland, Northern Ireland Council for Voluntary Action, Belfast.
Project Team (1976), Belfast Areas of Special Social Need Report, HMSO, Belfast.
Purdue, M., Young, E. and Rowan-Robinson, J. (1989), Planning Law and Procedure, Butterworths, London.
Reade, E. (1987), British Town and Country Planning, Open University Press, Milton Keynes.
Rees, J. (1988), 'Social Polarisation in Shopping Patterns: An Example from Swansea', Planning Practice & Research, no. 6, Winter.
Rodger, J. J. (1985), 'Natural justice and the big public inquiry', Sociological Review, vol. 33, no. 3, August.
Rutherford Report (1973), Belfast Urban Area Plan: Public Inquiry, HMSO, Belfast.
Ryan, A. (1987), Property, Open University Press, Milton Keynes.
Rydin, Y. and Myerson, G. (1989), 'Explaining and interpreting ideological effects: a rhetorical approach to green belts' Society and Space, vol. 7, pp. 463-479.

Saunders, P. (1981), *Social Theory and the Urban Question*, Hutchinson, London.

Saunders, P. (1986), *Social Theory and the Urban Question*, Century Hutchinson, London.

Secretary of State for the Environment (1989), *The Future of Development Plans*, Cmnd. 569, HMSO, London.

Singleton, D. (1983), 'Goodbye to the green belt?', *Fortnight*, April, pp 15-15.

Skeffington Report (1969), *People and Planning: Report of the Committee on Public Participation in Planning*, HMSO, London.

Stocks, N. (1989), 'The Greater Manchester Shopping Inquiry: a case study of strategic retail planning', *Land Development Studies*, vol. 6, pp. 57-83.

Transecon International (1986), *Transport in Belfast: a discussion paper*, General Consumer Council, Belfast.

Tyne Wear 2000 (undated), *A Regional Government for the North of England*, Tyne Wear 2000, 1, Carlton Terrace, Low Fell, Gateshead, Tyne & Wear.

Urry, J. (1985), 'Deindustrialisation, households and politics' in Murgatroyd, M. *et al* (eds.), *Localities, class and gender*, Pion Press, London.

Weber, M. (1946), *From Max Weber: Essays in Sociology*, translated and edited by Gerth, H. and Mills, C. W., Oxford University Press, New York.

Weber, M. (1949), *The Methodology of the Social Sciences*, translated and edited by Schils, E. and Finch, F., Free Press, New York.

Weiss, E. B. (1989), *In Fairness to Future Generations: International Law, Common Patrimony, and Intergenerational Equity*, The United Nations University, Tokyo.

White, S. K. (1989), *The Recent work of Jürgen Habermas: Reason, justice and modernity*, Cambridge University Press.

Whitelegg, J. (1984), 'Transport policy, fiscal discrimination and the role of the state', *Political Geography Quarterly*, vol. 3, no.4, October.

Wiener, R. (1980), *The Rape and Plunder of the Shankill*, Farset Cooperative Press, Belfast.

Williams, R. (1983), *Towards 2000*, Chatto & Windus, London.

Williams, R. (1988), *The Fight for Manod*, Chatto & Windus, London.

Williams, R. (undated), 'Socialism and the Environment', *Reclaiming the Earth: Development and the Environment*, Links 19, A Magazine from Third World First.

Wilson, R. (1988), 'Putting the Gloss on Belfast', *New Society*, 13 May.

Woods, R. (1989), 'The State and Community Work in Northern Ireland, 1968-1982', Unpublished D.Phil Thesis, University of Ulster.

Wraith, R. E. and Lamb, G. G. (1971), *Public Inquiries as an Instrument of Government*, Allen & Unwin, London.

Index

abstract space 110-111,
116-117
Albrow, M. 30
Alty, R. 40
Ambrose, P. 10-11, 24-25,
42
amenity 9, 105
Armstrong, J. 27, 33
Arnstein, S. R. 18-19, 89-90
Ash, J. 89, 100

Bains report 99
Ball, M. 24
Bauman, Z. 14-15
Beckenbach, F. 8
Belfast
  Alliance Party 109
  Areas of Special Social
    Need report 49
  Ballyhackamore traders 109
  Ballynafeigh Community
    Association 109
  Belfast Lough Nature
    Conservation Committee 112

Belfast Urban Wildlife
  Group 112
Carrick Hill Residents
  Association 112
Castlereagh Roundabout
  Action Group 111
Castle Court complex 61
city council 17, 44-48,
  59, 71-72, 86
Civic Trust 109
community action 20-23
Dundonald Green Belt
  Association 104, 107
Falls Womens Centre 95
Hightown Residents
  Association 104
Hilltop Environmental
  Committee 104
housing 102-107
Housing Renewal Strategy
  21-22
integrated operations
  58-59

Jordanstown Residents
 Association 104
Laganside 60-61, 73-74,
 100-102
Lower Lenadoon Housing
 Action Committee 95
Lower Ormeau Residents
 Action Group 95, 97,
 109
Making Belfast Work 18, 59
North Belfast Steering
 Group 96, 109, 112
North Queen Street
 Recreation Centre 112
Old Holywood Road,
 Glenmachan and Belmont
 Green Belt Assoc. 104
population change 102-103
public transport 107-109
Queen's University Popular
 Planning Unit 70-71
roads 109-112
Save the Shankill campaign
 70-71
Sinn Fein 112
Springfalls Redevelopment
 Association 77-78
Stop the Bypass Campaign
 109
transportation inquiry
 1977 48-56, 124
Urban Area Plan 1969
 45-47, 59, 68
Urban Area Plan 2001
 52, 55-92, 124
urban motorway 45-56, 124
West Belfast 81, 96, 97,
 100
West Belfast Steering
 Group 96-97
Bew, P. 14
Birrell, D. 100
Blackman, T. 5, 35, 45,
 47, 58, 64
Boys, J. 17
Building Design Partnership
 44-46
Byrne, D. 7, 12, 43

Carroll, P. 64
Carter, R. 57-58
Castells, M. 25
civil society 4
Cockburn, C. 17, 99
Coin Street inquiry 43
Community Groups Action
 Committee on Transport
 48-56, 124
Community Technical Aid
 21-22, 53, 63-115, 116
 121-125
Cullingworth, J. B. 2, 9,
 12, 17

Darke, R. 40
Davies, J. G. 25
democracy 119-120
Dennis, N. 25
Devine, P. 7, 119
Dickens, P. 5
Direct rule 14-17, 45,
 123-124
Doyal, L. 3
Duncan, S. 5, 16
Dunleavy, P. 3-4, 24

emotions 122-123
experts 126
extended interests 7-8
externalities 7

Faulkner, B. 56
Federation of Building
 and Engineering
 Contractors 104
Flynn, R. 25, 43
Frankel, B. 25
Franks report 31

Gaffikin, F. 15, 18, 61-63,
 69, 95
General Consumer Council
 52
Gibbon, P. 14
Gillespie, N. 64
Goodwin, M. 5, 16
Gottdiener, M. 1, 110-111

Gramsci, A. 116
Gray, F. 5
green belt 2, 39
  103-107
Gwilliam, M. 347

Habermas, J. 125-127
Ham, C. 3
Harrison, M. L. 7, 9, 10
Harvey, D. 1, 7, 24, 68
Hayek, F. A. 7
healthy cities 97, 98
Herington, J. 2
Hill, M. 3
Home, R. K. 37, 42
House of Commons
  Employment
  Committee 101
  Environment
  Committee 5, 36
Howard, M. 42
Howes, C. K. 101
Hutton, N. 19

inner city policy 18
Institution of
  Environmental Health
  Officers 37
Irish language 96, 98

Jessop, B. 4, 16, 118
John, P. 99
juridification 126

Keenan, F. 50
Kennedy, I. 64
Kilbrandon report 128
Kraushaar, B. 20, 22

Labour Party 87 129
Lamb, G. G. 38
Lash, S. 124
Lavery, C. M. 49-54, 78
  108
Lefebvre, H. 25
Le-Las, W. 18, 26
Leopold, E. 41
Ley, D. 119

local government 99-100 local
  plans 75, 113
localism 129
Loughlin, M. 41

Marx, K. 16
Matthew plan 48-49, 56
McAuslan, P. 13, 23, 31-32,
  126
McDonald, F. 22
Mellor, R. 36
Milne, R. 33
modernisation 126
Mogridge, M. 108
Mohan, J. 5, 6
Mooney, S. 15, 61-63, 69
Moore, R. 38
Morrissey, M. 18
Mukherjee, R. 118
Munt, I. 32
Murie, A. 100
Myerson, G. 39, 106

nature conservation
  112-113
need 126-128
Needham, R. 56
negotiated coordination
  119-120
Neill, W. J. V. 106
Netherlands' National
  Environmental Policy
  Plan 3
new towns 5
Northern Ireland
  Assembly 21, 60, 69
  Regional Physical
  Development Strategy
  56-58, 103
  Royal Society of Ulster
    Architects 109
  Ulster Trust for
    Nature Conservation
    104, 112
Nozick, R. 7

O'Boyle, U. 64
O'Leary, B. 3-4, 24

232

O'Neill, T. 14

Pahl, R. 18
Parson, D. 21
Paterson report 99
Patterson, H. 14
Phillips, D. R. 42
Planning Appeals
  Commission 35-36, 38-39
  41, 42, 78-79, 85-86,
  93-115
planning aid 90-91, 116, 128
planning gain 41
planning system
  goals 40-44, 94-100, 113,
  122-123
  ideology 14-15, 56, 59,
  62-63
  paradigms 68-69, 116-117,
  122
  regulations 94-95
Political Vetting of
  Community Work Working
  Group 20
postmodernism 124
prisoners' dilemma 3
private bills 30-33
professional judgement 120,
122
property rights 6, 9-10,
  117, 120, 127
public goods 6
public inquiries
  advocacy 26-30, 78-79,
  85, 88
  compulsory purchase
  orders 37-38
  officialdom 88-89
  pre inquiry meetings
  85
  procedures 19, 25-30,
  125-127
  public participation
  30-35, 121-123
public interest 34-39, 122
public participation
  community action 89, 121
  democracy 3-5

inadequacies 12-14, 88-91,
  114
planning goals 39-41
reform 129
public sphere 127
Purdue, M. 26

quality of life 2, 118-119

Reade, E. 6, 10, 40, 90
recreation 96-97
Rees, J. 11
regional government 128-129
Reid McHugh Partnership
  79-83
retailing 11, 99
Rodger, J. J. 30
Rowan-Robinson, J. 26
Royal Society for the
  Protection of Birds 112
Rutherford report 46
Ryan, A. 118
Rydin, Y. 39, 106

Saunders, P. 18, 25
Sheffield City Centre
  Plan 39-40, 89
Singleton, D. 39, 106
Sizewell B inquiry 28
Skeffington report 17, 40,
  98
Smyth, M. 76
social geography 128
social interest 127-128
social policy and
  planning 11, 24-25, 61-63
South Yorkshire County
  Council 72
state, theories of 3, 4,
  17-18, 118
Stocks, N. 30
sustainability 8

taxation 128, 129
Thatcherism 14, 16, 34
Transecon International
  52

transport planning 48-56,
  107-112
Tyme, J. 49
Tyne Wear 2000 128

urban development
  corporations 5, 12
    14-15, 101-102
urban managerialism 18
urban sociology and
  planning 25
Urry, J. 4, 124

Weber, M. 31
Weiss, E. B. 2, 8
welfare 118
White, S. K. 125-128
Whitelegg, J. 4
Wiener, R. 44, 45, 64
Williams, R. 5-6, 17,
  118-119, 123
Wilson, R. 95
Woods, R. 20
Wraith, R. E. 38

Young, E. 26